The Vogue
Book of Menus
and Recipes

FOR ENTERTAINING AT HOME

The Vogue
Book of Menus
and Recipes

FOR ENTERTAINING AT HOME

BY

JESSICA DAVES

WITH TATIANA McKENNA

AND THE EDITORS OF *VOGUE*

Harper & Row, Publishers   New York, Evanston, and London

LIBRARY OF CONGRESS CATALOG CARD NUMBER: 64-18050

CONTENTS

ACKNOWLEDGMENTS   vii

INTRODUCTION   ix

PART ONE   **BUFFET PARTIES**   1

1   VERY INFORMAL—MORE FOOD THAN SERVICE
DINNERS FOR THIRTY   5

2   BUFFET WITH PLACE CARDS
DINNERS FOR TEN TO FOURTEEN   28

3   CHOOSE ANY TABLE—SERVE YOURSELF
DINNERS FOR SIXTEEN TO TWENTY   45

4   ELEGANT LITTLE TABLES—BUFFET SERVICE
DINNERS FOR TWENTY-FOUR   61

5   SIXTEEN BUFFET LUNCHEONS
FOR TEN TO TWENTY-FOUR   78

6   BUFFET PARTIES ON THE GRAND SCALE   102

PART TWO   **THE SEATED DINNER PARTIES**   115

1   THE LITTLE DINNERS
FOR EIGHT TO TEN   118

2   THE "CIRCUMSTANTIAL" DINNER
FOR TWELVE TO TWENTY-FOUR   145

3   HOLIDAY DINNERS   182

v

PART THREE   LUNCHEONS, COCKTAILS,
              ELEVEN-THIRTY SUPPERS   199

        1   "SHE SPECIALIZES IN SUNDAY LUNCHEONS"
             FOR EIGHT TO FOURTEEN   202

        2   COMMITTEE FOOD: LUNCHEONS AND TEAS   238

        3   COCKTAILS: SMALL AND COZY, OR FOR
             FIFTY PLUS   246

        4   SUPPERS AT ELEVEN-THIRTY
             FOR TWELVE TO TWENTY   267

PART FOUR   FRIDAY-TO-SUNDAY GUESTS   283

             A WEEKEND WITH SIX GUESTS
             AND A HOSTESS-COOK

             CONCLUSION   324

             INDEX   325

ACKNOWLEDGMENTS

The recipes in this book have all been verified and, when necessary, edited by Tatiana McKenna, *Vogue*'s food consultant, a Paris Cordon Bleu student and one of the contemporary recognized cooking experts.

Through the years many accomplished hosts and hostesses have been generous in sharing their ideas about menus and food with *Vogue*. Their experience, imagination, and knowledge of food add a special quality to this book. The list is too long to publish in full; we are grateful to all of them, in particular: Madame Hervé Alphand, Mrs. Stewart Alsop, Mrs. Vincent Astor, Mrs. Bertrand F. Bell, Mrs. Louis Benoist, Lady Pamela Berry, Mrs. Thompson Biddle, Mrs. Barry Bingham, Mrs. Charles Blythe, Mrs. Louis Bromfield, Mrs. Harold W. Brooks, Mrs. Thomas D. Church, Jean Dessès, Christian Dior, Mrs. Frederick Eberstadt, Mrs. Emlen Etting, Mrs. William Ewing, Mrs. Philip Geyelin, Mrs. Dougherty Grace, Mrs. Lauriston Hardin, Madame Paul-Marc Henry, Mrs. T. Charlton Henry, Sheila Hibben, Mrs. Charles Hornburg, Madame Henrik de Kauffmann, Horace K. Kelland, Mrs. Benjamin R. Kittredge, Mrs. Alexander Knox, Mrs. Arthur Krock, Mrs. Albert D. Lasker, Mrs. Edmunds Lyman, Mrs. Guthrie McClintic, Henry P. McIlhenny, Lady Mendl, Mrs. Gilbert Miller, Mrs. Roland Penrose, Mrs. Arthur Pew, Mrs. Neil Phillips, June Platt, Mrs. William B. Priestley, Mrs. Warren Delano Robbins, Mrs. Artur Rubinstein, Madame Elsa Schiaparelli, Mrs. George M. Schlee, Frederick Louis Stagg, Mrs. Harold E. Talbott, Mrs. James Van Alen, Mrs. George Henry Warren, The Duchess of Westminster, The Duchess of Windsor.

Matters of protocol are based on *Vogue's Book of Etiquette*.

We are indebted to Mr. Michael Aaron for his help and approval in the choice of wines.

—*The Editors of* VOGUE

INTRODUCTION

One mark of a good party is that the guests go away feeling more attractive than when they came. And the guest is more important than the menu, the flowers, the wine, or the service. To plan the guests well is the first move; it it fairly improbable that there will not be some people invited because of "obligations"; but if all the guests are there for reasons of social debts, that fact hangs like a pall over the gathering. For a successful party there must be some free, attractive spirits who are invited simply because they are attractive, and who lift the amusement quotient by their presence. Also: variety in ages is becoming more and more a facet of good parties; and guests with differing interests are likely to make a more entertaining evening than, say, a whole company of stockbrokers or of dress designers or of college dons. But it is the hosts who set the tone; and thoughtful hosts have a way of making even dull guests glitter. All of us have felt it occasionally—the warm pleasure of having our special qualities appreciated and subtly presented to the company. The mere inviting of a guest is not enough for a memorable evening; he must be made to know that he is an asset to the party.

After the guests—the perfect guests—have accepted, entertaining well is dependent on logistics—a military term which has crept into the vernacular, perhaps because of the increasing need to use this science of "moving and quartering" in our daily lives. Logistics implies a plan to be carried out; and a plan for a successful party cannot be tossed off between children's ballet lessons and a visit to the hairdresser. Someone must take the planning seriously, must consider it a firm assignment; the accomplished plan *is* an accomplishment and a rewarding one. It is the hope that some of the plans can be found in this book. When this preplanning has been well done and all the preparations have come to fruition, there is a special satisfaction in creating an evening, an ambience, a mood that may remain with the guests as a visual and psychic delight. A felicitous composition of attractive people, superb food, unobtrusive service, and a charming background—all this is a triumph worth effort.

THE FOOD

Brillat-Savarin said, "Anyone who receives his friends and does not give his personal care to the meal prepared for them is not worthy of having friends." For an important dinner it is folly not to order the food well in advance; even the finest markets cannot be depended on for the best in quality, the exact foods you wish, unless they are ordered ahead. Go to market yourself, if you can, with your menu plan. Make a production of it; take your butcher, your fruit man, your grocer into your confidence. Stress the importance of your party to you, and also the importance of their help; and be flexible enough to change your menu if you find something unexpected and wonderful on the market—wild turkey or venison, for instance, where you had been planning capon or lamb.

Menus constructed by rule of thumb run the risk of seeming so. Even one variation from the usual is a pleasant menu addition—curry in the green turtle soup; braised lamb instead of a roast; veal *en croûte*; clam-stuffed mushrooms for an entrée; hominy squares instead of bread; a green rice salad; a robust hot dessert instead of a bland ice cream. These and other details can imply that the food has been thought about, not simply ordered.

It is not necessary to vary your plans too much from party to party. A menu made up of *spécialités de la maison* can be repeated without boring the guests. In any case, there will hardly be more than one or two guests who will have had that exact dinner before, that season. One privileged guest of one hostess we know asks pointedly whenever she dines there, "Aren't you going to have the fish soufflé tonight?" It has imprinted itself on her taste buds and, as far as she is concerned, it could be served to her over and over.

Nor is it necessary to vary the arrangements of flowers in the rooms. If you have discovered which flowers are most becoming to the rooms in which you entertain, settle on those flowers, or at least the colours, as accents. You don't particularly want your house to look decorated in any case—simply a little festive.

One cardinal rule in the matter of food might well have sprung from Mr. Samuel Pepys's remark, "My dinner was noble and enough." The fact that his dinner consisted of oysters, rabbits, lamb, beef, roasted fowl, a tart, fruit and cheese need not discourage. Enough need not mean all that, but rather that the dishes themselves seem ample and not calculated too precisely for the number of guests. A few noble dishes and enough of each is a good ground rule; the menus in this book are based on that principle, as you will see.

THE WINES

Similarly with wine; almost never, in any dinner except the really formal, is it necessary to serve more than one wine. Pleasant, yes, to serve a little Sherry with the soup, a nice Chablis with the fish, and a good claret with the rest of the dinner. Champagne can be added for the dessert, but these are not all really necessary for the perfection of the dinner. A famous and hospitable duchess serves these four wines almost invariably. But some good hostesses serve Champagne only, using it as an apéritif, and serving it throughout the dinner. Certainly one wine plus Champagne is a good plan; but again, here, we might, to paraphrase Pepys, make sure that the wines are not only "noble, but enough." Nothing seems more inhospitable than a scanty serving of wines, or wines of poor quality, at a real dinner party. Save inexpensive young red wines for young people's parties, or for your own country buffet luncheons. But, while "good wine needs no bush," good food does profit by a good wine. The impression of amplitude is a delightful impression for a guest to receive; it is far more agreeable than great variety with meagre quantity in wines.

The question of wines with dinners can be as complicated or

as simple as one wishes to make it. There are two wines that can be correctly served with any dinner menu. They are *vin rosé* and any Champagne that is not sweet—two choices for the hostesses who are not sure of their wine knowledge, or even for those who are.

In general, the sweet white wines are drunk only with desserts. The dry white wines (and this includes the light as well as the more full-bodied white wines) are good with all sorts of fish, with egg dishes, with poultry, and with veal.

The full-bodied red wines are classically served with red meat and with game of all sorts; they are also excellent with cheeses. But it is certainly not incorrect or unpalatable to serve a lighter red wine with fowl or lamb or veal. The red "country wines" (the *vins du pays*), both Italian and French, are suitable with characteristic country dishes, such as beef bourguignon, ragout of lamb, et cetera.

The study of wines—their sources, their years, the degree of dryness or sweetness—is for some people a life work. But for those who simply like wine and who would like to make correct and agreeable choices, suggestions are given with most of the menus in this book. They are *suggestions only*, and do not represent the only possible choice for each menu.

If there is a good wine merchant with whom you deal, it is a sound idea to take him into your confidence and ask for his suggestions. Many wine merchants are extremely knowledgeable and are glad to put their knowledge at your service.

THE SERVICE

At some parties, service is almost as important as food; before you decide on the kind of party you mean to have, it is good logistics to know exactly what you can count on in the way of household help. Better by far a well-planned buffet party, where a guest expects little or no service, than a seated dinner inadequately or incompetently served. If the family is co-operative, there are many kinds of parties that need not suffer from the lack of outside service. Little late suppers, small buffet dinners, country luncheons, afternoon teas or small cocktail parties, a seated dinner for six, can all be planned, comfortably, without a waitress.

Here are suggestions for estimating the service needed for conventionally correct procedures; but as planned informality increases, exceptions to this conventional pattern can be, indeed are, perpetually made. (Examples are cited throughout the menus in this book.)

One waitress can serve, correctly, a seated dinner for six to eight people, if the menu is fairly simple.

Two waitresses (or waiters) are needed for twelve to sixteen guests at a seated, correctly served dinner; four waiters, for sixteen to twenty-four guests.

For a well-planned buffet, where the guests really do most of the serving themselves and where the waitresses' only duties are to remove used plates and to bring in additional food for the service table, one agile maid can serve up to twelve or fourteen people; two can serve up to twenty-four.

For larger parties, the number of waiters or waitresses depends somewhat on the menu, the distance from the kitchen, et cetera. For forty or fifty guests at a dance and simple buffet supper at home, four waiters should be adequate. But for a big party, where you wish to seat a hundred guests at small tables for an after-dance supper or for a wedding breakfast, you will need at least ten waiters. Buffet service is convenient, but when there are as many as a hundred guests it is impossible for them to serve themselves and be seated at tables. Therefore, if you are planning a big party and cannot arrange for enough waiters, it is better to have the kind of food that guests can eat without necessarily being seated. Otherwise, mild pandemonium.

ENOUGH? TOO MUCH?

Every hostess knows the hint of a ghost at the dinner table, the ghost that sometimes lessens general pleasure. It is the stalking fear of eating too much (almost, of eating) that is a neurotic symptom of our day. The cult of slimness, for the reasons of fashion, and the very real danger of overweight create a curious sort of fixation in many people's minds that it is somehow un-ethical or at least unattractive to *enjoy* food. This is an asceti-cism (or Puritanism) that robs many people of an incompara-ble pleasure—a pleasure which is also, according to serious medical opinion, a physical benefit; that is, the real enjoyment of food. The sight of a succulent dish, the beauty of fresh straw-berries, the odour of bouillabaisse (or freshly baked bread, for that matter) can stir certain juices that not only encourage diges-tion but add to the appeasement of hunger another kind of satis-faction. Granted that very elaborate dinners hardly exist at smart tables, that sixteen- or even eight-course meals belong to another era, there is a new kind of aesthetics in a beautiful dinner, all the more important because the gross pleasure of enormous eating is no longer indulged in—at least, not in the presence of guests.

This book of menus is not a dietary volume; we do not prom-ise that these are menus that will prevent weight gain, or reduce weight; but they are menus compiled in the modern way, which is to say, with regard for the pleasures of quality rather than of quantity in eating. The attitude represented by "I don't care what I eat," which is occasionally a partner of the reducing syn-drome, is not only out of fashion but fairly unfriendly as well. A good appetite is a good companion, and to eat with selected pleasure can imply the niceties of choice that are one of the marks of civilization.

PART ONE

Buffet

Parties

The buffet meal has an ancient and royal lineage. Under Louis XIV, meals were not served in a designated salle à manger, *but from tables set up at will in one or another room of the royal apartments. Philippe Jullian, writing in* Maison & Jardin, *describes the procedure: on long trestle tables were placed various dishes—pots of soup, all sorts of great and small entrées—ready and in place before the diners came to the tables. Big silver cloches and other devices for keeping the food warm made this type of service practicable even in the chilly palace rooms. Each of the guests served himself without difficulty since the placing and the shape of the dishes indicated what was in them. The lackeys' duties were simply to change the used plates from time to time, and to bring trays of wineglasses which the* sommelier, *who presided at the buffet, filled and refilled. It was only when the time came for the roast, cut by the official carver, that the diners were presented with plates already served.*

"The buffets at the fêtes de Versailles," *Monsieur Jullian goes on, "were arranged with as much care and beauty as if Le Nôtre himself had designed them—pyramids of fruit, fortresses of pâté, pavements of shrimp. There were sometimes 100* entremets, *and almost as many entrées. But naturally the diners no more felt obliged to taste all of these than would a present day diner at a restaurant feel obliged to taste all the dishes on the restaurant card." (Each of the king's guests chose his own menu and served himself.)*

Under Louis XV, the buffet took on an even greater importance in a society which, fleeing its responsibilities, was tired of being surrounded by servants. At the end of Louis XV's reign, the famous cabinetmakers had invented devices for removing the dishes, and special coolers, which allowed the monarch to dispense with lackeys entirely during the course of the dinner.

In our times, although an absence of lackeys rather than a plethora first impelled hospitable people to plan the buffet dinner, now it is a preferred plan from coast to coast on its own merits. The idea of a buffet dinner immediately implies a feasible way to feed a great many guests; and indeed it is. But beyond this scheme for coping with an uncopable situation, the buffet dinner or luncheon has also become a pleasant way to entertain a smaller number of guests where seating can be arranged, but service is at a minimum. With a knowledgeable hostess who has a practical sense of the limitations of buffet service, added to a sense of good food, the buffet party can be delightful and, even more important, can be accomplished without the effort showing.

In this section are menus for buffet dinners for thirty guests, more or less; and also a series of menus for dinner and luncheon parties of ten to twenty-four seated at large or small tables.

1

Very Informal—
More Food Than Service

DINNERS FOR THIRTY

THE buffet dinner at which no special seating arrangements are indicated is at once the most informal for the guests, and the most demanding of the hostess. The menu must be carefully planned for people who will be "eating all over the house"—standing, leaning, sitting on the floor, on the stairs—and eating under those circumstances should be made as simple as possible. Nothing that requires cutting with a knife is possible; and ease of service is almost as important as convenience in eating.

These big, amorphous buffet parties can be among the gayest parties you give; but even when it is understood that no seating is planned, it is a sound idea to have a collection of small, low tables near sofas and chairs, or conveniently stacked so that guests may fetch them for themselves if they feel the need. There are many new attractive designs in this sort of little folding table; the best of them, for buffet purposes, are so light that they can be moved around at will, and removed when the meal is over. The table with folding legs and a removable top like a big tray has been the classic butler's table for generations, but there are inexpensive new low versions of this, too useful to overlook. Six of the big, light removable trays with their supporting legs folded take very little room to store; they do add comfort to the buffet parties.

5

Two workable buffet plans are given here. One plan centers around one big dish, made in quantity for thirty, supplemented by salad, and one or two minor dishes. The other plan is for several main dishes from which guests can choose; both involve putting the buffet food on a long table or a sideboard, with plates, silver, and napkins at one end. The guests serve themselves and, after they have finished eating, return the plates to the table, or the plates are taken from them before the dessert is eaten. The desserts, or dessert plates, are usually put on the long serving table when it appears that the guests have almost finished the first course. And the self-service starts again.

THE À LA CARTE BUFFET

One plan is to have several *pièces de résistance*, which amounts, actually, to an *à la carte* menu. It is not expected that any guests will want some of each dish.

In constructing such an *à la carte* menu, a useful pattern is: one substantial dish with meat of some kind; one vegetable; perhaps one seafood dish; one starchy dish such as spoon bread, or spaghetti, noodles, lasagne (any one of the Italian pastas prepared in any one of a hundred ways). Add to these main dishes a salad, bread-and-butter finger sandwiches or tiny rolls, and perhaps two kinds of dessert. It is naturally rather chancy to know which of the dishes will be most popular with the guests, and hence impossible to prepare exactly the correct amount of food. But, roughly speaking, if one expects thirty guests and if there are, say, five different main dishes, it would seem sensible to make each of the dishes in a quantity for eight to ten people. This implies, of course, some leftover food; but that is inevitable and certainly more to be desired than a series of dishes entirely emptied.

Here are four *à la carte* menus for thirty people. In each instance the choice of menu is predicated on dishes that will not suffer from delay in serving. Variety, quantity, ease in serving, ease in eating are the considerations here. Recipes in measurements to serve ten or twelve or more are given for the starred dishes.

MENU 1 *(for thirty)*

*Terrine of Country Pâté**
with
Crusty French Bread
Sweet Butter

*Shrimp Curry**
in
Buttered Rice Rings
with
Crumbled Bacon
Chutney, Peanuts
Shredded Coconut

Veal and Water Chestnut
*Casserole**

Three-Layer Aspic Salad

Assorted Pots de Crème*

Lace Cookies

The Wine:

Champagne or a full-bodied Rhone such as Châteauneuf-du-Pape. Beer would also be correct.

* Recipes on pages 12-14.

MENU 2 *(for thirty)*

*Tendrons of Veal**

*Corn Pudding**

Lump Crab in
Russian Dressing
with
Crumbled Bacon

*Ham Mousse**

Cold Vegetable Bouquets

Scandinavian Breads
Tubs of Sweet Butter

Bowl of Cut Fruit
with
Champagne and Walnuts

Apple Tarts with
Whipped Cream Laced
with Calvados

The Wine:

A Rhine wine such as Schloss Johannisberger or a vin rosé.

* Recipes on pages 15-16.

MENU 3 (for thirty)

MENU 4 (for thirty)

*Cold Poached Salmon
Green Mayonnaise*

*Tomato Aspic Ring
with
Cucumber and Avocado*

*Chicken and Ham
with Noodles**

*Chafing Dish
of Chicken Livers
in Madeira Sauce**

*Buttered Rice
with Chopped Parsley*

Mixed Green Salad

*Cheese Tray
Crackers, Hot Rolls*

*Chocolate Mousse Cake**

*Hot Blueberry Pudding
with Hard Sauce*

*Szekely Goulash**

*Cous-Cous**

*Cannelloni Leonardo
da Vinci**

*Peeled Whole Tomatoes
with
Cottage Cheese and Chives*

*Smoked Turkey
in
Finger Sandwiches
of
Thin Brown Bread*

*Baba Ring
Filled with Strawberries
and
Whipped Cream
with Rum**

*Stewed Pears
with
Vanilla Sauce*

The Wine:

A white wine—Italian Verdic-chic, or a white Burgundy such as Meursault.

The Wine:

Carafes of red Italian table wine, at room temperature.

* Recipes on pages 16-18.

* Recipes on pages 18-21.

THE ONE-BIG-DISH BUFFET

The second plan for the buffet dinner for thirty concentrates on one hearty dish with perhaps one or two accompanying minor dishes, plus a salad and a dessert. These must all be in quantities for thirty except, perhaps, the dessert; you may plan to have two or three desserts from which the guests may choose, and these would naturally be made in smaller quantities. It is also a good idea to have these desserts in varying degrees of richness. For instance, for cheese lovers you might offer one or two cheeses with water biscuits or melba toast, and with one or two kinds of jam or preserves. Then there should be another real dessert for people (and there are many) who still consider cheese an accompaniment for salad and not in the real dessert class.

This plan, the one big dish for thirty guests, is in one way less complicated than the *à la carte* menus in the preceding pages. It is much easier to serve, and naturally much easier to estimate the quantity. But there are some *pièces de résistance* which do not "multiply" very well, and of course it is only sensible to choose as the one big dish something reasonably sure to have a general appeal. A dinner like this is not the time or place for dishes unfamiliar to the majority, or so original that it may leave the more unadventurous hungry.

In addition to the menus listed here, the whole field of gumbos and fish stews offers a wide-ranging choice; and there is also Brunswick stew, a famous picnic dish in the South for generations. Or, if you are sure of your guests, you might have curry as the one main dish and supplement it with several appetizers and condiments. The exotic and not always understood Bombay duck is one; more familiar pleasures include several kinds of crumbled nuts; grated coconut; baked bananas; chutney, of course (you might try peach chutney); chilled sliced cucumber; riced hard-boiled eggs; crumbled bacon and poppadums (to be bought in cans). After the curry, a big salad of mixed greens —lettuce, romaine, endive and watercress, perhaps. And since you have offered only one main dish, you might have two or three kinds of desserts—such as lemon sherbet with cut-up oranges; moist, delicious layer cake; a baked custard with caramel sauce; a deep-dish fruit pie served with hard sauce.

MENU 5 (for thirty)

*Beef Paprika**

Hot Buttered Noodles with Poppy Seeds

*Spinach Rings with Slivered Parsleyed Carrots**

Hearts of Palm Salad

Thin-Sliced Breads Pumpernickel and Rye Spread with Sweet Butter

Miniature Peach Turnovers

*Raspberry Charlotte**

The Wine:

A St. Émilion or Pomerol from Bordeaux, or a Pinot Noir or Cabernet Sauvignon from California.

* Recipes on pages 22-23.

MENU 6 (for thirty)

*Chicken Czarina on a Bed of Kasha with Sour Cream and Mushrooms**

Salad of Endive, Beets, and Celery

Rye Melba Toast

Hot Deep-Dish Apple Pie

Brie Cheese Water Biscuits Bar-le-Duc Jam

The Wine:

A light, white Burgundy from Mâcon or Pouilly-Fuissé, or vin rosé.

* Recipe on page 24.

MENU 7 (for thirty)

Fish Mélange
Sole, Scallops, and Shrimp
with
Wild Rice*

Cucumber and Dill Salad
Sour Cream

Corn Bread Sticks

Filled Pancakes
with
Strawberry Preserves*

The Wine:

A light Moselle, such as Scharz-hofberger, or a California Riesling.

* Recipes on pages 25-26.

MENU 8 (for thirty)

Navarin of Lamb*

Salad of
Lettuce, Watercress, Fennel

French Bread

Cheese Tray
Water Biscuits

Peach Cobbler

Lemon Mousse Pie

The Wine:

A château-bottled claret, such as Château Lascombes from the township of Margaux.

* Recipe on page 27.

MENU 1   Terrine of Country Pâté (for 20)

2 large onions, chopped
2 tablespoons butter
½ pound cooked ham
1 pound fresh pork, ground fine
1 pound veal, ground fine
1 pound chicken livers, cut fine with scissors
1 pound fresh pork fat, ground
3 garlic cloves, minced
4 teaspoons salt
2 teaspoons black pepper

½ teaspoon each of allspice, mace, rosemary, and thyme
⅛ teaspoon powdered cloves
3 eggs, slightly beaten
½ cup pistachios (optional)
½ cup Cognac
1 cup heavy cream
Several dashes cayenne pepper
1 large bay leaf, cut in two
Chopped parsley

Preheat the oven to medium (350°). Brown the onions in the butter. Dice ham and combine all ingredients except the bay leaf, mixing until well blended. Fill an oval 16-cup terrine with the mixture. Insert half a bay leaf at each end of the dish. Cover the terrine and set it in a pan of water. Bake in the oven for 2½ hours. Remove the cover and bake for another 20 minutes. Cool under a weight, perhaps a smaller bowl filled with something heavy. Remove weight and refrigerate for several hours before using. This pâté will keep very well for many days, if uncut and left covered. When serving, sprinkle with lots of chopped parsley. Serve the pâté in the terrine.

MENU 1   Shrimp Curry (for 12)

½ cup butter
½ cup minced onion
5 pounds raw shrimp, cleaned
1½ teaspoons salt
Cayenne pepper

3 tablespoons Indian curry powder
3 cups hot chicken broth
Curry sauce (see below)
Juice of 1 lime

Melt half the butter in a heavy saucepan large enough to hold the shrimp. Simmer the onion in this butter until transparent, without browning. Add remaining butter and, when it is hot, add the shrimp. Cook for 2 minutes on each side, turning them to cook evenly, until they are all bright pink. Add salt, quite a few dashes of cayenne pepper, and the curry powder. Cook, stirring, for about 1 minute, and add the chicken broth, which has been heated almost to boiling; simmer for about 5 minutes. Combine the prepared curry sauce with the shrimp mixture and add the juice of 1 lime, or more to taste. Correct seasoning and reheat. Serve in a moulded ring of buttered cooked rice, with coconut meat and other condiments in little bowls around the ring. Other suitable condiments are chutney, mixed nuts, preserved kumquats, Bombay duck.

CURRY SAUCE

3 cups shredded coconut	2 large garlic cloves, minced
3 cups boiling milk	4 tablespoons curry powder
¾ cup butter	4 teaspoons ginger
½ cup minced onion	½ cup flour

In a large bowl steep the shredded coconut in the boiling milk for 30 minutes. Cut the butter in pieces and melt in a 16- or 20-cup saucepan. Simmer the minced onion and garlic in the butter without browning. Add curry powder and ginger and cook slowly, stirring, for 3 minutes. Sprinkle in flour and continue to cook, stirring for another 2 to 3 minutes. Strain the milk from the steeped coconut, pressing out all the juice, and add this liquid to the sauce. Set aside the coconut to serve as one of the condiments. Stir until the mixture is thick and smooth and finish the sauce by simmering for 15 minutes.

MENU 1 Veal and Water Chestnut Casserole *(for 12)*

1 cup butter	2 cups beef bouillon
4 pounds boneless veal, cut in 1-inch cubes	¼ teaspoon nutmeg
2 onions, minced	1½ bay leaves
2 garlic cloves, crushed	Four 5-ounce cans of water chestnuts, drained and sliced
2 teaspoons salt	4 cups heavy cream
½ teaspoon black pepper	½ cup Cognac
3 dashes cayenne pepper	¼ cup chopped parsley
2 pounds fresh mushrooms, quartered	

Preheat the oven to medium (375°). Melt half the butter in a heavy frying pan. Brown the veal in batches on all sides, adding the onions and garlic with the last batch to brown along with the meat. Season with the salt, black pepper, and cayenne pepper. When the meat is brown, place in a 16-cup oven casserole with a cover. Melt the remaining butter in the same frying pan used for the meat and sauté the quartered mushrooms quickly, stirring to cook evenly. Add the mushrooms to the meat. Deglaze the frying pan with a little of the bouillon. Add to the casserole with the remaining bouillon. Add the nutmeg, bay leaves, and the sliced water chestnuts. Add more bouillon or water if needed to cover two thirds of the meat. Stir, cover the casserole, and place in the oven. Cook until meat is tender—about 1½ hours. Add the cream, stir, and cook uncovered for 15 minutes. Add the Cognac, stir, and reheat. Sprinkle with parsley and serve.

MENU 1   Assorted Pots de Crème
(each recipe serves 12)

VANILLA POTS DE CRÈME

4 cups milk or cream	8 egg yolks
Pinch of salt	4 whole eggs
2-inch piece of vanilla bean	1 cup plus 2 tablespoons sugar

Scald the milk with the pinch of salt and the vanilla bean. Beat the yolks and the whole eggs with sugar. Add the hot milk, stirring fast. Open the vanilla bean and scrape the seeds into the custard. Strain into 12 individual custard cups. Place in a large pan containing 1 inch of boiling water, and bake for 35 to 40 minutes in a medium oven (350°), or until a knife inserted into the custard comes out clean.

COFFEE POTS DE CRÈME

Omit the vanilla bean. Add 6 tablespoons instant coffee to the milk before scalding it.

CHOCOLATE POTS DE CRÈME

Omit the vanilla bean. Add 4 squares unsweetened chocolate, melted in 2 tablespoons water or coffee, to the scalded milk before mixing with beaten egg yolks.

STRAWBERRY POTS DE CRÈME

Omit the vanilla bean and the sugar. Use only 3 cups milk or cream. Add 1 cup strawberry syrup to the scalded milk just before mixing with well-beaten egg yolks.

MENU 2   Tendrons of Veal *(for 10)*

4 pounds boneless veal, cut in 1-
   inch cubes
½ cup butter
⅓ cup flour
3½ cups hot beef bouillon
2 teaspoons dried tarragon

2 teaspoons salt
2 medium onions
4 tablespoons tarragon vinegar
4 egg yolks
1½ cups heavy cream
¼ cup chopped parsley

When purchasing the veal, ask for the horseshoe cut, the part just above the knuckle, known also as the heel of the round.

Melt the butter in a large heavy iron frying pan. When sizzling hot, add the veal and brown lightly, turning pieces over with a pancake turner. If too much juice forms, preventing browning, drain off some but save it.

When meat has browned very lightly, sprinkle with flour, stirring with a wooden spoon, and gradually add the bouillon. When the sauce is well mixed, smooth, and has thickened, pour back into the sauce any juice you may have drained off. Sprinkle the sauce with the tarragon and salt and add the onions, peeled and quartered. Transfer to a large earthenware casserole or porcelain-lined Dutch oven, cover tightly, and simmer gently on top of the stove until meat is tender, or for at least two hours. Stir occasionally to prevent sticking. When tender, stir in the tarragon vinegar, and remove casserole from the heat. Beat the egg yolks into the cream and add some of the hot sauce to them, stirring briskly. Add the egg-yolk and cream mixture to the casserole and stir the sauce until heated through and slightly thickened. Do not let it boil. Serve the veal sprinkled with parsley.

MENU 2   Corn Pudding *(for 12)*

2 dozen ears of corn, or 5 packages
   frozen corn
6 egg yolks
2 cups light cream
1 tablespoon sugar

1½ teaspoons salt
   Freshly ground black pepper
¼ cup butter
4 egg whites, beaten stiff

Cut the kernels from the corn, scraping off the pulp with the dull side of the knife. Or, defrost frozen corn. Butter a large oven dish and put in the corn.

Beat the egg yolks and cream until just well mixed and add the sugar and the salt. Mix well with the corn. Add some freshly ground pepper. Add the melted and cooled butter. Fold in the beaten egg whites. Place in a preheated medium oven (350°) and bake for about 45 minutes. Serve immediately.

MENU 2   Ham Mousse *(for 8 to 10)*

¼ cup butter	4½ cups ground cooked ham
3 tablespoons flour	Cayenne pepper
2 cups chicken broth	Salt
3 egg yolks, beaten	3 egg whites, beaten stiff
2½ tablespoons gelatine	1½ cups heavy cream, whipped
¾ cup cold water	1 bunch watercress
5 tablespoons medium-dry Sherry	1 cup mayonnaise
	1 cup sour cream

Melt the butter in a large saucepan. Add the flour and cook slowly for 2 minutes. Gradually pour in the chicken broth and stir over low heat until thick and smooth. Mix a little sauce with the egg yolks, then stir into sauce briskly to prevent curdling. Soften the gelatine in the cold water and dissolve in the hot sauce, then add the Sherry and the ham. Season with cayenne pepper and salt if needed. Cool to lukewarm, then fold in the stiffly beaten egg whites and the whipped cream. Wash a 12-cup ring mould in cold water and fill with the ham mousse; chill for several hours until firm. At serving time unmould onto a platter. Fill the ring with well-washed whole watercress and serve with a sauceboat of the mayonnaise and sour cream, mixed.

MENU 3   *Chicken and Ham with Noodles (for 10)*

1 pound thin egg noodles	2 cups sour cream
1 pound mushrooms, sliced	1 teaspoon dry mustard
3 shallots, chopped	¼ cup grated Parmesan cheese
½ cup butter	Salt and freshly ground black pepper
2 cups diced cooked chicken	
2 cups diced cooked ham	3 tablespoons bread crumbs
1 cup chopped green pepper	1 tablespoon chopped parsley
3 cups white sauce (see page 20)	½ teaspoon dried orégano

Cook the noodles moderately firm (*al dente*) and drain. Sauté the mushrooms and the shallots in 3 tablespoons of the butter until tender but not browned and add them to the diced meats. Sauté the chopped green pepper in 3 tablespoons of the butter and add. Bring the white sauce barely to a simmer and stir in the sour cream. If the sauce seems too thick, add a little milk or cream. Sprinkle the mustard and the grated cheese into the sauce and stir in until the sauce is well blended and the cheese is beginning to melt. Remove from the heat and add salt and freshly ground pepper to taste; do not add too much salt as the ham will be a little salty.

Butter a large oven-to-table baking dish, a shallow one rather than a deep one. Mix the noodles with 2 cups of the sauce and fill the bottom of the baking dish, leaving a well in the centre. Mix 2 more cups of the sauce with the meats and sautéed vegetables and spoon the mixture into the well in the centre of the dish. Pour the remaining sauce over all. Mix the bread crumbs with the chopped herbs, sprinkle them over the surface, and dot with the remaining 2 tablespoons butter. Bake in a hot oven (400°) for 15 to 20 minutes, until bubbly and golden.

MENU 3   Chafing Dish of Chicken Livers in Madeira Sauce *(for 12)*

2 cups prepared brown sauce	4 pounds chicken livers
1 cup beef bouillon	Salt and black pepper
3 tablespoons tomato paste	½ cup Madeira wine
1 bunch scallions	½ cup chopped parsley
½ cup butter	

In a saucepan combine the brown sauce, bouillon, and tomato paste, and simmer for 15 minutes. Meanwhile, chop the white part of scallions and a little of the green stalks. Melt the butter in a large frying pan and sauté the scallions. After 3 minutes add the chicken livers and sauté gently, tossing them to cook evenly, for 8 minutes, or until the juices start to run. Season with salt and pepper; pour in the sauce. Simmer for a few minutes to blend the flavours, then add the Madeira and half the parsley. Correct the seasoning and serve from a chafing dish with remaining parsley sprinkled over the top of the livers.

MENU 3   Chocolate Mousse Cake *(for 12)*

6 squares unsweetened chocolate
¼ cup strong coffee
¾ cup butter
1⅔ cups granulated sugar
10 eggs, separated

1½ cups sifted cake flour (not self-rising)
2 teaspoons vanilla extract
Vanilla sugar (see page 27)

Butter and flour a large springform cake pan. Preheat oven to very hot (450°). Melt the chocolate in the coffee in a large saucepan, over very low heat, or in a double boiler. The coffee should not boil and the chocolate should be just very soft. Separately melt the butter, cut into pieces, then add the sugar and just melt. Add sugar and butter to the chocolate and mix well. Remove from the heat and add egg yolks, one at a time, beating well with a wooden spoon each time. (By the time the 8th yolk is added the mixture will begin to stiffen.) Then add the flour in four portions, beating well each time. Add vanilla extract. Beat the egg whites very stiff, until they do not slide out of the bowl when it is inverted. Add one fourth of the whites to the chocolate mixture and mix well. Then pour the mixture over the rest of the whites and continue mixing, gently but thoroughly. Pour into the springform pan and cover with a lid. Bake for 15 minutes. Remove lid and cover the cake with a large piece of buttered foil. Fold it down on the sides, but don't secure it tightly, as the cake rises. Turn the heat to medium (350°) and bake for 45 minutes. Turn heat to low (300°) and bake for about 15 minutes more. Take from the oven and cool for 10 minutes before removing foil. Cake should be close textured and moist. After 10 to 15 minutes more, remove the sides of the springform pan. Slide the cake onto a cake platter and sprinkle heavily with vanilla sugar. Serve with a bowl of coffee-flavoured foaming sauce, or with whipped cream sweetened and flavoured with vanilla.

MENU 4   Szekely Goulash *(for 12)*

4 pounds small butterfly pork chops, about ½ inch thick
5 tablespoons bacon fat
2 large onions, minced
4 tablespoons paprika

Salt and black pepper
3½ pounds sauerkraut
1 teaspoon caraway seeds
½ teaspoon dried tarragon
4 cups sour cream

Bone the pork chops and cut them in half, or have the butcher do it.

Sauté the pork chops in the bacon fat in a large frying pan, turn them, add the onions and finish browning them, along with the paprika and a little salt and pepper. Add a very little water, cover, and simmer over very low heat for 1 hour, adding more water in small amounts if necessary. At the same time simmer the sauerkraut, caraway seeds, and tarragon, with the juice from the sauerkraut plus water to cover, for 1½ to 2 hours over very low heat. The sauerkraut should be very tender. Drain the sauerkraut and combine with the meat in a serving casserole. Mix in the sour cream and heat thoroughly on top of stove but do not allow to boil. Serve the goulash from the casserole.

MENU 4   Cous-Cous *(for 10)*

1 cup olive oil
1 pound stew lamb, cut into 1-inch cubes
1 pound bottom round of beef, cut into 1-inch cubes
3½-to 4-pound chicken, disjointed as for fricassee
10 medium onions, chopped
2 cans chick peas
6 carrots, cut up
6 cups beef bouillon

1 teaspoon each of saffron, salt, and black pepper
Cayenne pepper to taste
Semolina (see below)
3 tomatoes, skinned, seeded, and cut up
1 pound yellow squash, cut up
4 parsley sprigs
1 teaspoon dried chervil
½ cup raisins

Heat half the olive oil in a large pot or in the lower part of a steam cooker (a double boiler with a perforated top), and brown the meat and chicken, adding oil as needed. Add the onions and brown. Depending on the size of the cooking vessel, this may have to be done in separate batches. Return everything to the large pot and add the drained and rinsed chick peas, the carrots, beef bouillon, saffron, salt, black pepper, and several dashes of cayenne pepper. Cous-cous should be peppery. Meantime, prepare the semolina (see below) and place in a colander over the stew. Cover and simmer for 1 hour; then add the tomatoes, squash, parsley, and chervil to the meat and vegetable mixture. Simmer for 45 minutes longer, then add raisins and simmer long enough for them to plump up. Remove meat and vegetables to a serving platter and keep warm. Reduce sauce and remove fat. Pour some sauce over the meat and serve the rest separately.

Serve the steamed and well-buttered semolina along with the meat. If you like, serve some red peppers in a separate dish.

SEMOLINA

2 pounds semolina   ½ cup butter
6 cups boiling water

Pour 2 cups boiling water over 2 pounds semolina and let it stand for 20 minutes. The water will be absorbed by the semolina and the grains will swell. Repeat this procedure twice, then put the grain into the top part of the steam cooker, or in a colander on top of a large saucepan, over the stew. Let it steam over the meat and vegetables for the whole time the stew is simmering. Add the butter and mix well.

MENU 4   Cannelloni Leonardo da Vinci (for 10)

1 box lasagne   ½ teaspoon dried sweet marjoram
2 pounds spinach, blanched and   ¾ cup grated Parmesan cheese
   chopped   Salt and black pepper
¼ cup butter   4 eggs
1 pound ricotta cheese   White sauce (see below)
¼ teaspoon nutmeg

Cook the lasagne according to the directions on the box, then plunge into cold water, drain well, and cut each strip in half, crosswise. Sauté the finely chopped spinach, which has had the moisture well pressed out, in 2 tablespoons butter. Take off heat. Mix in the ricotta, nutmeg, marjoram, 4 tablespoons Parmesan cheese, and salt and pepper to taste. Add the eggs one at a time, beating well each time. Butter a large casserole dish. Place the squares of pasta on a flat surface and put a spoonful of the spinach mixture on one side the length of each square. Roll up and put in the casserole with fold facing down. Add the remaining Parmesan cheese and butter to the white sauce, stirring to melt the butter and blend in the cheese. Pour the sauce over the *cannelloni* and brown in a very hot oven (450°) for 10 to 15 minutes.

WHITE SAUCE

½ cup butter   5 cups milk
6 tablespoons flour   Salt and cayenne pepper

Melt the butter, add the flour, and simmer, stirring, without browning for 2 minutes. Add the milk and cook, stirring, until thickened and smooth. Season to taste with salt and cayenne pepper.

MENU 4   Baba Ring *(for 12)*

1 cup scalded milk
2-inch piece of vanilla bean
1½ packages dry yeast
1 cup sugar
⅛ teaspoon salt
2 whole eggs
4 egg yolks
⅔ cup butter, melted

3½ cups sifted flour, approximately
Liqueur syrup (see below)
¼ cup rum or Kirsch, or more to taste
6 cups fresh raspberries, or fresh or frozen whole strawberries
3 cups heavy cream, whipped and sweetened

Scald the milk with the vanilla bean, and cool to lukewarm. Remove and reserve the vanilla bean, and pour the milk into a heated bowl. Add the yeast, 2 tablespoons sugar, and the salt. Stir to dissolve. In another bowl beat the eggs, egg yolks, and the remaining sugar until very light in colour. Add the cooled melted butter and combine with the milk mixture. Open the vanilla bean and scrape the seeds into the milk. Beat with a wooden spoon while adding flour until you have a thick, very heavy batter. Set in a warm place and let rise, covered with a towel, for about 1½ hours, or until it is doubled in volume. Beat down with a few punches of the fist. Butter a ring mould about 11 inches in diameter and pour in the batter until the ring is just under half full or less. Cover and let rise until double in volume and bake for 35 minutes in a preheated medium oven (350°). Remove to a cake rack to cool.

Make liqueur syrup (see below). Pour a little cooled syrup in the bottom of the ring mould. Replace the cake. Make holes in the cake with a skewer and pour the remainder of the syrup over it. Let marinate for several hours or overnight.

Unmould the cake on a platter, pour rum or Kirsch over it, and fill the centre with the raspberries or strawberries mixed into the sweetened whipped cream. Add a little more liqueur, if desired. Heap the rest of the fruit mixture around the cake.

LIQUEUR SYRUP

1½ cups sugar

2 cups water

⅓ cup rum or Kirsch, or more to taste

Simmer sugar and water for 10 minutes. Cool and add rum or Kirsch.

MENU 5   Beef Paprika *(for 30)*

15 pounds lean beef, bottom round or rump

4 tablespoons sweet paprika

Salt and black pepper

1 cup butter, or more

3 cups chopped onions

4 cups red wine

4 garlic cloves, minced

One 6-ounce can tomato paste

One 1-pound, 13-ounce can whole tomatoes, drained

4 cups strong beef bouillon

2 tablespoons caraway seeds, or more to taste

Chopped parsley

This dish is best made a day ahead, as it improves with reheating. Remove skin and fat from the meat, or have the butcher do it, and have the meat cut into 1-inch cubes. Roll the meat well in paprika, salt, and pepper. Be sure to use sweet paprika. Sauté the meat in batches in very hot melted butter in a heavy frying pan to sear well all over. With the last batch add the onions and brown them too. Transfer the meat and onions to three heavy 16-cup heatproof casseroles. Deglaze the frying pan with a little wine and add to the meat. Combine garlic, tomato paste, tomatoes, and bouillon and cover meat with this mixture; simmer on top of stove over very low heat for about 3 hours, or longer if meat has not become tender. Reheat slowly at serving time, stir in the caraway seeds, and simmer again for 30 minutes, the last 10 minutes uncovered. Serve with a little chopped parsley sprinkled over the meat.

MENU 5   Spinach Rings with Slivered Parsleyed Carrots *(for 30)*

12 pounds raw spinach

Salt and black pepper

¾ teaspoon nutmeg

1 cup butter

4 bunches carrots

½ cup chopped parsley

Cook the spinach in the least possible water, drain and chop. Press all the moisture from the spinach before measuring. There should be 12 cups. Season with salt, pepper, and nutmeg. Melt half the butter and stir into the spinach. Pack into well-buttered ring moulds. Keep hot until serving time.

Scrape and trim the carrots and cut them into the thinnest possible lengthwise strips about 2 inches long. Cook them in salted water to cover until tender, about 6 to 8 minutes. Drain them, add the remaining butter and the parsley, and toss to mix well. Unmould the spinach rings and fill the centres with the buttered carrots.

MENU 5   Raspberry Charlotte *(for 10)*

3 packages frozen raspberries	1½ cups milk, scalded
2 cups light brown sugar	1½ cups heavy cream
8 egg yolks	3 tablespoons sugar
Pinch of salt	2 tablespoons Kirsch
3 tablespoons unflavoured gelatine	Fresh raspberries
½ cup water	Sweetened whipped cream

Defrost the raspberries and force them through a sieve to make a purée. Put the brown sugar and egg yolks in the top of a double boiler over barely simmering water, add the pinch of salt, and stir with a wooden spoon until the mixture becomes light in colour and thick. Soften the gelatine in the cold water and reserve. Pour the scalded, slightly cooled milk into the egg mixture and cook over hot water, stirring all the time, until the mixture coats a wooden spoon, about 8 to 10 minutes. Remove from the heat, add the softened gelatine, and stir until it is dissolved. Add the raspberry purée and stir until smooth. Cool, stirring occasionally. Whip the cream, adding the 3 tablespoons sugar, and fold it into the purée with the Kirsch. Pour into a mould rinsed in cold water; chill for several hours.

Unmould the raspberry charlotte onto a platter. Surround with fresh raspberries and serve more sweetened whipped cream, flavoured with Kirsch if desired.

MENU 6   Chicken Czarina *(for 30)*

3 pounds whole buckwheat, or kasha
3 cups butter
15 double chicken breasts
2 onions, minced
2½ cups fine soft white bread crumbs
¾ cup milk, approximately
3 teaspoons salt
¾ teaspoon black pepper
Few dashes of cayenne pepper
¾ teaspoon nutmeg
5 egg whites
5 cups sour cream
2½ pounds mushrooms, sliced
3 cups beef bouillon

Shake the buckwheat in a strainer until all fine dust is removed. Do not wash it. Melt ¾ cup butter and sauté the buckwheat over high heat, stirring all the time to prevent scorching, for about 10 minutes. Put into a heatproof dish, cover with boiling water to 1½ inches above the wheat, and stir once. Bake in a preheated medium oven (350°) for 2 hours, or until buckwheat is dry and each grain is separate.

Bone the chicken breasts and grind the meat several times until it is very fine. Sauté the onion in 4 tablespoons butter without browning, just until transparent. Soak the bread crumbs in enough milk to make a smooth thick batter. In a large bowl mix onion and ground chicken, add salt, black pepper, cayenne pepper, and nutmeg. Add the bread and milk; mix until very smooth. Add the unbeaten egg whites. Set the bowl in a container filled with cracked ice or ice cubes and work the mixture well with a wooden spoon. Add ¾ cup sour cream and work again until well mixed. Form into small flat round or oval cakes about ¾ inch thick.

Clarify 1½ cups butter by melting very slowly and straining the oil away from the milk and whey. Heat this oil as needed in a frying pan and fry the little cakes until golden on both sides. Sauté the sliced mushrooms in the remaining ½ cup butter or more and stir the butter and mushrooms into the buckwheat. Deglaze the frying pan with the beef bouillon, add the remaining sour cream, and warm the mixture. Pour the warmed sauce over the kasha, stirring it in gently. Divide the grain among several shallow ovenproof dishes and arrange the little chicken cakes over the kasha. Reheat in a low oven (300°) and serve in the baking dishes.

MENU 7   Fish Mélange *(for 30)*

6 cups raw wild rice	1 pound mushrooms, finely
2½ cups butter	minced
5 pounds bay scallops	1 cup sifted flour
4 cups dry white wine	5 egg yolks
5 pounds fillet of sole	2½ cups light cream
5 pounds fresh shrimp	3 large carrots, cut in very fine
Salt and black pepper	julienne
Court bouillon (see below)	6 big truffles, cut in very fine
¾ cup minced shallots	julienne

Boil the rice briskly in about 16 cups water for 20 to 25 minutes. Drain. While rice is hot, add about ½ cup butter, mixing well to melt butter and coat rice. Butter three or four large oven casseroles; shallow ones make a prettier appearance. Line the casseroles evenly with the buttered rice.

Poach the scallops in the white wine with a little salt and pepper for about 3 to 4 minutes. Set them aside. Pour enough court bouillon into a shallow cooking pan to poach the sole fillets. Poach the fillets for 5 to 8 minutes, depending on their thickness, or until they are just cooked. Remove carefully with a slotted spatula. Arrange the sole on the wild rice. Pour all the court bouillon, including that used to cook the sole, into a large pot and add the shrimp. Poach them for 7 minutes, until they are bright pink and shells are loose. Cool, shell, and devein.

Melt ½ cup butter in a large frying pan and sauté the shallots for 3 minutes. Add the mushrooms, with more butter if needed, and cook slowly until the mushrooms are tender but not browned. Melt 1 cup plus 3 tablespoons butter in a deep saucepan. When hot, add the flour, and cook over low heat without browning for a few minutes. Add the court bouillon and the scallop liquor, both strained through a fine sieve lined with a cloth. Cook, stirring, until smooth and thickened. Remove from the heat and add the egg yolks beaten into the cream, the mushrooms, the shrimp, and the scallops. Divide among the dishes, arranging on top of the sole.

Sauté the carrots in the remaining 5 tablespoons butter; when they brown a little and are nearly done, add the truffles and continue to cook for a minute or so. Remove from the heat and sprinkle the carrots and the truffles on top of the fish mélange. Reheat in a low oven (300°), watching that the sauce does not separate.

COURT BOUILLON

2 carrots, chopped	Parsley sprigs
4 celery stalks, diced	2 large bay leaves, crumbled
3 large onions, chopped	6 whole cloves
8 shallots, chopped	12 peppercorns
1 teaspoon dried thyme	7 cups water
2 cups white wine	Salt

Put everything together in a large kettle, bring to a boil, and simmer, uncovered, for 20 minutes. Strain before using.

MENU 7   Filled Pancakes with Strawberry Preserves *(for 30)*

4 cups twice-sifted flour	2 cups butter
¼ cup sugar	⅓ cup dark rum, or 2 teaspoons
Pinch of salt	vanilla extract
6 eggs	Strawberry preserves
4 egg yolks	Vanilla sugar (see below)
4 cups milk, scalded	

In a large bowl place the flour sifted with the sugar and salt. Make a well in it and put in the eggs and extra yolks. With a wire whisk work the eggs, slowly absorbing the flour. Add the milk when the mixture gets thick and continue to mix. The mixture should be shiny. Lightly brown ½ cup of the butter, cool and add to the dough, stirring briskly. Let stand for 1 hour before making pancakes. Add the rum or vanilla extract.

Clarify the remaining 1½ cups butter. Heat a 5-inch pancake pan or small frying pan, and pour in 1 teaspoon clarified butter. Pour in just enough batter, turning the pan to spread it, to cover the bottom of the pan. Cook until golden, turn over, and cook for about 30 seconds on the other side, adding butter if needed. Repeat until all pancakes are done, stacking them on a dish to keep warm.

At serving time put about a tablespoon, or more, of strawberry preserves on each pancake and roll up. Reheat in oven (turned very low) with a little butter. Sprinkle with vanilla sugar and serve.

Pancakes may be made well ahead of time and may even be frozen. Defrost when needed, fill with strawberry preserves, roll up, and heat in the oven in a little butter. Sprinkle with vanilla sugar and serve.

V ANILLA S UGAR

Place 2 cups extra-fine granulated sugar in a jar with a tight screw cap. Add a 3-inch piece of vanilla bean and let stand for several days.

MENU 8   Navarin of Lamb *(for 30)*

15 pounds leg or shoulder of lamb
1 cup flour
1 teaspoon salt
1 teaspoon black pepper
1 cup olive oil
1 cup butter, or more
3 cups chopped onions
8 cups light beef bouillon, approximately
Bouquet garni composed of 6 celery stalks with leaves, 6 garlic cloves, handful of parsley sprigs

One 6-ounce can of tomato paste
1 teaspoon dried thyme
60 tiny white onions
20 carrots, quartered lengthwise
12 turnips, cut into olive shapes
4 packages frozen whole string beans or peas, cooked
Chopped parsley

Leg of lamb provides the most solid meat, but the shoulder is very good and the bones add a great deal of flavour, although the shoulder does not have quite the amount of meat the leg does. Bone the lamb, reserving the bones, and cut the meat into 1½-inch cubes, or have the butcher do this.

Mix flour with salt and pepper. Roll the meat in the seasoned flour and shake off excess. Heat the oil and half the butter as needed to brown the meat. Browning will have to be done in batches. Brown the onions and bones with the last of the meat; wrap bones in cheesecloth and transfer with meat and onions to two or more large cooking pots. Deglaze the browning pan with some of the beef bouillon and add to the meat. Add the *bouquet garni* tied in little cheesecloth bags, one for each pot. Add the tomato paste, thyme, and enough bouillon to barely cover the meat. Simmer the meat for 1 hour. Meanwhile sauté the onions, carrots, and turnips in remaining butter until golden. Add to the meat and simmer about 45 minutes more, until the meat and vegetables are tender. Remove from heat and discard the bones and the *bouquet garni*. Correct the seasoning and arrange the meat and vegetables on heated platters.

Reduce the sauce a little and remove the fat; pour sauce over the meat. Arrange the peas or green beans or both around the meat and sprinkle with chopped parsley.

Buffet
with Place Cards

DINNERS FOR TEN TO FOURTEEN

EVEN though this plan is for a serve-yourself dinner, place cards are useful to avoid possible confusion when guests are asked to find their places. The first course is already on the table. All the rest of the food, except desserts, has been put on the serving table or sideboard. Sometimes it is a good idea to put extra plates on the buffet table in the event that guests prefer to eat salad or a fish dish separately.

Just before the main course is finished, the desserts are brought in and put on the serving table. The used plates are then taken away and the guests serve themselves the desserts. After dinner, coffee may be served at the table from an urn on the sideboard, or may be brought into the living room after the guests leave the table.

Here are eight menus planned for this sort of dinner.

MENU 9 (for ten)

Cold Cucumber Soup*

*Mousse of Salmon
with
Green Mayonnaise**

*Hot Casserole of Lasagne
with
Beef Sauce**

*Salad of Several Greens,
Mixed*

*Mould of Mocha Cream
filled with
Coffee Ice Cream*

The Wine:

Vin rosé *throughout the dinner.*

---

* Recipes on pages 33-34.

MENU 10 (for ten)

Coquilles St. Jacques*

Jellied Beef Tongue

Endive Salad

*Hot Beaten Biscuits
Buttered*

Sherry Macaroons*

The Wine:

A *good Rhine such as Marco-
brunner.*

---

* Recipes on pages 35-36.

MENU 11 (for ten)

---

*Francillon Salad**

*Watercress Sandwiches
with
Sprigs of Fresh Dill*

*Roast Fillet of Beef
in Aspic**

Vegetables in Casserole

*Eggs à la Neige**

The Wine:

*A red wine—a Burgundy, an
Italian Chianti, or perhaps a
California claret.*

* Recipes on pages 36-38.

MENU 12 (for twelve)

---

*Prosciutto
with
Melon or Figs*

*Beef Poivrade**

*Gratin of Potatoes**

Lettuce and Romaine Salad

*Bowl of Fresh Fruits
with
Scoops of Lemon Ice*

The Wine:

*On the table carafes of red and
white wine—a California Pinot
Blanc for the white; Pinot Noir
or Zinfandel the red.*

* Recipes on pages 38-39.

MENU 13 (for twelve)

*Low-Country Oysters
with
Mushrooms**

Hot Baked Ham

*Ring of Red Rice
Filled with Green Peas**

*Escarole Salad
Roquefort Dressing*

Hot Rolls

*Pears in Orange Juice
with
Orange Liqueur*

The Wine:

*Chablis has been called the
"oyster wine," and it is good with
the rest of this menu, too.*

* Recipes on page 40.

MENU 14 (for twelve)

Fish Stew*

Poulet Chasseur*

*Tiny Finger Rolls
Sweet Butter*

Fruit Pudding
with
Vanilla Sauce**

The Wine:

*A well-chilled dry white wine
—a Puligny-Montrachet would
be excellent.*

* Recipes on pages 41-42.

MENU 15 (for fourteen)

Hot Vegetable Gumbo*

Cold Meats in Thin Slices
Smoked Chicken
Rare Roast Beef
Roast Veal

Baked Brown Beans*

Thin Slices
of
Buttered Whole-Wheat
Bread

Tomato Aspic Ring

Apple Pie with Cheese

The Wine:

*A light red wine—a claret—is
the usual choice for this kind of
dinner.*

* Recipes on pages 42-43.

MENU 16 (for fourteen)

Jellied Borscht*
with
Caviar and Sour Cream

Cold Fried Chicken

Watercress and Raw
Mushroom Salad

Small Hot Popovers

Crème Brûlée*

The Wine:

Champagne sans année.

* Recipes on pages 43-44.

MENU 9   Cold Cucumber Soup *(for 10 to 12)*

8 young cucumbers, peeled and chopped
2 medium onions, minced
Top leaves from a heart of celery, chopped
¼ cup chopped parsley
2 teaspoons salt

8 cups chicken broth
⅓ cup flour
½ cup butter
Dash of cayenne pepper
2 cups light cream
¼ cup cut chives

Place the cucumbers, onions, celery leaves, parsley and 2 teaspoons salt in a saucepan with the chicken broth. Simmer slowly for about 30 minutes, keeping the pot covered, and stirring once or twice. Make a paste of the flour and butter and add, little by little, to the cucumbers, stirring until perfectly smooth. Cook again gently for about 5 minutes. Cool and purée the soup in a blender or put through a sieve. Add more salt if necessary, and cayenne pepper to taste, and combine with the cream. Chill well. Serve in chilled cups sprinkled with cut-up chives.

MENU 9   Mousse of Salmon with Green
Mayonnaise *(for 10)*

1 carrot, sliced
1 onion, chopped
Bouquet garni composed of 1 bay leaf, 2 parsley sprigs, 1 thyme sprig
½ cup dry white wine
2¼ cups cold water
2 pounds salmon
1 teaspoon salt

2 peppercorns
10 tablespoons sweet butter
Thick white sauce (see below)
3 tablespoons dry Sherry
1 tablespoon unflavoured gelatine
½ cup heavy cream, whipped
1 bunch watercress for garnish
Green mayonnaise (see page 93)

Place the carrot, onion, *bouquet garni,* white wine, and 2 cups of the water in a large saucepan; simmer for 15 minutes. Wrap the salmon in cheesecloth with long ends which can be used to lift the cooked fish out of the liquid. Put the salmon in the court bouillon and add enough cold water barely to cover the fish; add the salt and peppercorns. Bring the liquid slowly to a simmer and cook for about 15 minutes, or until the fish flakes easily. Let the salmon cool in the stock. Lift out the salmon and strain and reserve the stock. Skin and bone the salmon. In a mortar, pound the salmon with the butter. Fold in thoroughly the cooled thick white sauce and the Sherry. Correct the seasoning. Simmer the fish stock until only 1 cup remains. Soften the gelatine in the ¼ cup cold water and dissolve it in the hot stock. When the stock is cool, add it to the fish mixture. Fold in the whipped cream and pour the mousse into a 10-cup mould. Smooth the surface and put the mould in the refrigerator to set. At serving time turn the mousse out onto a platter, surround with watercress, and serve with green mayonnaise.

THICK WHITE SAUCE

6 tablespoons butter
5 tablespoons flour

1½ cups milk
Salt and white pepper

Melt the butter over low heat and add the flour slowly to make a smooth paste. Cook for 2 minutes, stirring constantly. Bring the milk almost to a boil and add it to the flour and butter. Cook, stirring, until the flour is cooked and the mixture has the consistency of very thick cream. Season with salt and pepper.

MENU 9   Hot Casserole of Lasagne with
Beef Sauce (for 10)

1 box lasagne
⅓ cup olive oil
2 onions, chopped fine
2 pounds lean beef, ground
1½ teaspoons salt
½ teaspoon pepper
2 garlic cloves, minced
One 1-pound, 13-ounce can of Italian tomatoes, drained

One 6-ounce can of tomato paste
1 teaspoon dried basil
2 tablespoons chopped parsley
½ teaspoon orégano
1 cup ricotta cheese
1 cup grated Parmesan cheese, or more

Cook the lasagne in 12 cups rapidly boiling salted water for 20 minutes, stirring often to prevent them from sticking. Rinse immediately in cold running water.

Drain well and cut in half. Heat the oil in a large saucepan. Sauté the onions until they are golden, add the ground beef, and continue to cook, stirring, until no red meat shows. Season with salt and pepper, add the garlic, tomatoes, tomato paste, and the herbs. Stir and cover. Simmer for 1½ hours, stirring often, and leaving the cover open just a little so that the steam escapes. Taste for seasoning; if the tomatoes are very acid, add 1 to 2 teaspoons sugar.

Butter a large shallow casserole, and arrange in it layers of lasagne, meat sauce, and ricotta and Parmesan cheeses, ending with sauce and Parmesan cheese. Heat in a hot oven (400°) until bubbly, about 20 minutes. Serve at once.

If served as a main dish at a family dinner, this casserole will serve 6 to 8.

MENU 10   Coquilles St. Jacques *(for 10)*

2 pounds scallops
1 cup dry white wine
   Salt and white pepper
1 pound mushrooms, sliced
½ lemon, juice only
6 tablespoons butter

4 shallots, or 1 medium onion, minced
¼ cup flour
2 egg yolks
1 cup heavy cream
10 large scallop shells
   Bread crumbs

If the scallops are large, slice them into bite-sized pieces. Poach the scallops in the white wine and enough water barely to cover with a little salt and pepper for about 5 minutes. Drain, reserving the liquid. Poach the sliced mushrooms in the lemon juice, 1 teaspoon butter, and a little water with a few grains of salt for about 8 minutes. Drain, reserving the liquid. Add the mixture to the scallops and cook together for a few minutes. Melt 4 tablespoons butter in a saucepan and cook the minced shallots or onion very gently without browning. Blend in the flour and cook for 2 minutes, again without browning. Add the liquid from the fish and mushrooms to make a smooth sauce, stirring until the mixture thickens. Beat the egg yolks into the cream and add to the sauce, stir, and heat without boiling. Add salt and pepper to taste. Pour a little of the sauce into the buttered scallop shells. Place some scallops and mushrooms in the sauce and cover with more sauce. Sprinkle with bread crumbs and dot with the remaining 5 teaspoons butter. Place under the broiler to brown a little and serve.

MENU 10   Sherry Macaroons *(for 10)*

2 pounds macaroons
2 cups sweet Sherry, approximately
2 cups heavy cream

2 tablespoons sugar
½ cup toasted slivered almonds

Crumble the macaroons in a bowl and add enough Sherry to make a moist paste. Mound on a round platter. Whip the cream until it holds its shape; add sugar and a little Sherry and whip again until firm. Cover the macaroons completely with the whipped cream, mounding into shape. Chill well before serving. Sprinkle with toasted almonds at the last moment.

MENU 11   Francillon Salad *(for 10)*

1 quart shucked mussels or clams, or 2 pounds scallops
4 large Idaho potatoes
8 cups beef bouillon
3 tablespoons white-wine tarragon vinegar
2½ cups white Bordeaux wine

½ cup olive oil
Salt and freshly ground black pepper
2 teaspoons chopped parsley
1 teaspoon chopped tarragon
1 teaspoon chopped chervil
2 shallots or 1 small onion, minced
2 large black truffles, sliced

About 7 to 8 pounds of mussels in their shells will give 1 quart shucked. For directions for cleaning and opening them, see the recipe for billi-bi soup on page 56. About 4 to 5 dozen clams will give 1 quart shucked. Ask your fish dealer to open them for you. If the scallops are very large, halve them.

Scrub the potatoes and boil them in their jackets in beef bouillon until tender but still firm. Strain the bouillon and reserve for some other use. Peel and slice or dice the potatoes. Combine with the vinegar, ½ cup wine, and the oil, and add salt and freshly ground black pepper to taste.

Meanwhile, marinate the mussels in the remaining wine. If using clams or scallops, which are not already steamed as the mussels are, simmer them in the white wine over low heat for 5 minutes and cool. Drain the shellfish and reserve the liquid for other uses. Combine the mussels, or other shellfish, with the potatoes. Add the chopped fresh herbs and shallots or onion. Season with additional salt and pepper if needed, arrange in a salad bowl, and cover with the sliced or chopped truffles. Serve chilled, but not cold enough for the oil to congeal.

MENU 11   Roast Fillet of Beef in Aspic *(for 10)*

½ cup butter
3 shallots or 1 medium onion, chopped
1 carrot, sliced thin
  5-pound fillet of beef, tied and larded
  Salt and black pepper

2 cups strong beef bouillon
1¼ tablespoons unflavoured gelatine
⅓ cup cold water
11 slices *pâté de fois gras*
1 cup Cognac
4 large truffles
  Watercress

Melt the butter in a roasting pan and sauté the shallots and carrot for a few minutes. Place the fillet on the vegetables and roast in a preheated hot oven (400°) for 20 minutes. Season with salt and pepper and roast for another 20 to 25 minutes, or until meat registers 140° on a meat thermometer, for rare beef. Cool the beef until very cold. Meanwhile remove all fat from the pan, and deglaze with bouillon. Strain the bouillon. Soften the gelatine in the cold water, dissolve it in the strained bouillon, and cool.

Slice the cold fillet into 12 slices and place a slice of *pâté* between each two meat slices, rebuilding the meat to look whole. Use skewers at ends to hold all the slices together in one piece. Place meat on a rack over a dish. Add the Cognac to the cooled aspic and spoon some aspic over the beef. Chill, and continue adding aspic and chilling until there is a good ¼ inch of aspic on the meat. Slice the truffles, dip the slices in aspic, and arrange on the beef. Add more aspic and chill. Continue until there is ½ inch or more of aspic coating the beef. When the aspic is firm, gently pull out the skewers, covering the hollows with more aspic to make a smooth coating. If aspic becomes too jelled to pour, melt it over hot water. Pour the remainder of the aspic into a flat pan, adding any that trickled into the dish under the meat. Chill until set. Arrange meat on a platter, rake the extra aspic with a fork, and arrange it around the meat. Place watercress at each end of the dish.

MENU 11   Eggs à la Neige *(for 10 to 12)*

4 cups milk	2-inch piece of vanilla bean
1 cup heavy cream	10 eggs, separated
½ cup sugar	1 cup very fine granulated sugar
	3 to 4 tablespoons Cognac

In a wide deep saucepan combine the milk, cream, 2 tablespoons sugar, and the vanilla bean and bring to a bare simmer. While this is warming, beat the egg whites until stiff, then gradually beat in the very fine sugar. When the meringue is smooth and thick, form egg shapes with a large cooking spoon. Poach the meringues very gently in the milk mixture, turning them to cook on all sides, for about 3 minutes. Remove them with a slotted spoon and pile them in a serving dish.

Make a custard sauce: Open the vanilla bean and scrape it into the milk. Add the beaten egg yolks to the milk and cook in a double boiler over simmering water, stirring constantly, until the mixture coats a spoon. Strain and cool. Add Cognac to the sauce and pour it around the meringues. Caramelize the remaining 6 tablespoons sugar in a small skillet and dribble over the meringues.

MENU 12   Beef Poivrade *(for 12)*

Two 4-pound fillets of beef	1 teaspoon dried thyme
Narrow strips of fat pork	3 bay leaves, crumbled
Salt	¼ teaspoon nutmeg
2 cups red Burgundy	⅛ teaspoon cloves
½ cup tarragon wine vinegar	2 onions, chopped
⅓ cup Calvados	Sauce poivrade (see below)
1 teaspoon dried tarragon	

Have the butcher trim and remove the connective tissue and skin from two whole fillets of beef and tie them. Lard them with narrow strips of fat pork. Put the larded roast in an earthenware dish and sprinkle with very little salt. Pour over the meat the red Burgundy, tarragon vinegar, Calvados, tarragon, thyme, bay leaves, nutmeg, cloves, and onion. Cover with a cloth and marinate in the refrigerator for three days, turning the meat three or four times a day. Drain and dry the fillets, reserving the marinade for use in making the sauce, and roast it for 16 minutes per pound in a medium oven (350°) for medium rare, basting frequently. When the beef is roasted, remove the strings, and slice and reshape the fillets. Arrange the fillets on a heated serving platter, or platters. Pour some sauce poivrade over the roast and serve the rest in a sauceboat.

POIVRADE SAUCE FOR BEEF

1 cup chopped carrots

1 cup chopped onions

Bouquet garni composed of
    4 parsley sprigs,
    2 celery stalks, and
    2 garlic cloves

⅓ cup olive oil

3 tablespoons butter

⅓ cup tarragon wine vinegar

2 cups strained marinade, approximately

2½ cups prepared brown sauce

12 peppercorns

Salt

Cook carrots, onions, and *bouquet garni* in olive oil and half the butter, until the vegetables begin to take on colour, stirring frequently. Add the tarragon vinegar and 2 cups strained marinade. Reduce the mixture over high heat to two thirds of its original volume, stirring constantly. Add brown sauce and simmer gently for 30 minutes. Crush the peppercorns, add them to the sauce, and simmer for 10 minutes longer. Pour off the fat and strain through a very fine sieve. Return to the heat, bring to a boil, and add salt to taste. When ready to serve, stir in remaining butter.

MENU 12   Gratin of Potatoes *(for 12)*

6 large Idaho baking potatoes

1 medium onion, grated

½ cup butter

1 cup freshly grated Parmesan cheese

Salt, freshly ground black pepper

2 cups heavy cream, or more, scalded

Preheat the oven to hot (400°). Scrub the potatoes and bake them until they are very tender when pierced with a fork. Open and let the steam escape for a few minutes. Peel and rice the potatoes, and mix with onion, butter, ⅔ cup cheese, and salt and pepper to taste. Add cream slowly until the mixture has the consistency of a heavy cream sauce. Pour into a shallow baking dish. At serving time, sprinkle with the remaining ⅓ cup cheese, dot with butter, and reheat in a hot oven until bubbly and slightly brown. Serve immediately.

MENU 13   Low-Country Oysters *(for 12)*

Two 5-ounce cans pimientos
1 pound mushrooms, sliced
½ cup butter
½ cup flour

4 cups heavy cream
Salt and black pepper
2 quarts shucked oysters
Sautéed bread triangles

Drain and slice the pimientos. Sauté the sliced mushrooms in the butter and add the pimientos. After mushrooms have cooked for a few minutes, sift the flour over them. Stir over low heat until the mixture begins to bubble. Add the cream and stir until smooth and thick. Season with salt and pepper to taste. In another saucepan let the oysters simmer in their own juices until the edges start to curl. Add the oysters and juices to the mushrooms. Add more cream if the mixture is too thick. Serve from a chafing dish or a heated platter, surrounded by sautéed bread triangles.

MENU 13   Ring of Red Rice filled with Green Peas *(for 12)*

¾ cup butter
1 large onion, chopped
3 cups raw long-grain white rice
3 cups chicken broth

4 cups tomato juice
Salt and black pepper
One 4-ounce can pimientos
5 cups young peas, fresh or frozen

Melt 5 tablespoons butter in a heavy 16-cup saucepan and brown the onions for a few minutes. Add the rice and stir over low heat until the rice looks transparent. Meanwhile, combine the broth and tomato juice and season with salt and pepper. Heat to the boiling point, pour over the rice, and stir well, once. Reduce the heat, cover, and simmer for 18 to 20 minutes, or until all moisture is gone. Drain and finely chop the pimientos. Add 5 more tablespoons butter and the pimientos to the rice. Pack in two well-buttered ring moulds and let stand at least 30 minutes; keep warm. Cook peas in just enough water to be absorbed in cooking—about 18 to 20 minutes if fresh, a shorter time if frozen. Add remaining 2 tablespoons butter to the peas. Turn each rice ring out onto a round platter and fill the centres with the peas.

MENU 14   Fish Stew *(for 12)*

¼ cup butter
4 shallots minced, or 1 medium onion, finely chopped
3 pounds sole, scrod, or halibut fillets
Three 8-ounce cans minced clams

3½ cups heavy cream
Salt and freshly ground black pepper
½ cup cracker crumbs

Melt the butter in a large ovenproof casserole and simmer the shallots without browning. Add the fish cut in chunks, then the clams and their liquid, and pour the cream over all. Season with salt and pepper and sprinkle with cracker crumbs. Cover and cook in a preheated medium oven (350°) for 30 minutes. If you wish to brown the top, put the casserole under the broiler for a few minutes at the end. If served as a main course without another major dish, this stew will serve 8.

MENU 14   Poulet Chasseur *(for 12)*

Three 3-pound chickens
3 teaspoons garlic dressing mix
3 tablespoons salad oil
3 tablespoons butter
⅓ cup sliced shallots or chopped onions

1 pound fresh mushrooms, sliced
2 tablespoons flour
1-pound can whole tomatoes
2 teaspoons dried tarragon
1¼ cups Sauterne

Cut each chicken into 8 pieces. Wash and dry the pieces, using a paper towel to pat dry. Sprinkle with 2 teaspoons of the garlic dressing mix. Heat the salad oil in a casserole and brown the chicken on all sides. Pour off the oil and add the butter, the shallots or onions, and the mushrooms, and cook until tender, about 5 minutes. Sprinkle with the flour, stir in the canned tomatoes, the tarragon, 1 cup of the Sauterne, and the remaining garlic dressing mix. Cover and simmer for 35 to 40 minutes, or until chicken is tender. Remove chicken to a hot platter and add remaining Sauterne to the sauce. Bring sauce to a boil and simmer uncovered for 10 minutes. Pour over the chicken.

MENU 14   Fruit Pudding with Vanilla Sauce *(for 12)*

1-pound jar preserved figs

6- or 8-ounce jar preserved ginger

1-pound can greengage plums

2 large bananas, sliced

1-pound can Bartlett pears

1-pound can apricots

Rind of 1 orange, cut in thin strips

1 cup brown sugar, approximately

Cinnamon

Vanilla sauce (see below)

Drain the fruit, reserving the syrup. Put the orange rind in a saucepan with enough syrup from the preserved fruit to cover, and simmer, uncovered, for 35 minutes. Combine all the fruit and arrange in a round, deep, buttered oven dish, sprinkling each layer with the orange rind and brown sugar, and a light sprinkling of cinnamon. Add a few spoons of syrup and bake in a medium oven (350°) for 35 to 40 minutes. Turn out on a round serving platter or serve from the dish, warm or cold, with vanilla sauce.

VANILLA SAUCE

3 cups milk

6 egg yolks

½ cup sugar

3 teaspoons vanilla extract

½ cup heavy cream, whipped

Scald the milk. Beat the egg yolks with the sugar and combine slowly with the hot milk, stirring briskly. Pour into the top of a double boiler and cook, stirring, over an inch of barely simmering water in the bottom part of the double boiler. Cook until the custard coats a spoon. Cool, stirring occasionally, add vanilla, and fold in the whipped cream.

MENU 15   Hot Vegetable Gumbo *(for 14)*

½ cup butter

4 large onions, chopped

3 garlic cloves, minced

2 cups diced celery

4 peppers, seeded and diced

1 pound young okra, sliced

14 cups strong beef bouillon

2 pounds spinach, well washed

3 teaspoons gumbo filé powder

Salt and black pepper

2 cups cooked white rice

Melt the butter in a large soup kettle and slowly cook the onions until they brown. Add the minced garlic and cook until soft. Add the celery and diced pepper and a little more butter if needed, so the vegetables don't burn. Meanwhile, pour boiling salted water to cover over the okra and boil for 5 minutes. Drain okra and add to the other vegetables. Add the bouillon and simmer the mixture, covered, for 30 minutes. Add the spinach and cook for 10 minutes longer. Add the gumbo filé powder, add salt and pepper to taste, and add the rice. Heat thoroughly and serve in heated covered bowls.

MENU 15   Baked Brown Beans *(for 14)*

3 pounds dried pea beans
½ pound salt pork, cut in small strips
2 onions, each stuck with a clove
1 cup molasses
1½ teaspoons dry mustard
2 teaspoons salt
1 cup chili sauce
½ cup strong coffee
½ cup Bourbon

Soak beans overnight in cold water. Drain and discard any imperfect beans. Cover with fresh water and simmer over low heat until beans are tender but still whole. Drain beans, reserving the cooking water, and put them into a bean pot or deep baking dish with a cover. Bury the pork and the onions in the beans. Mix bean water with molasses, mustard, salt, and chili sauce and pour over the beans. Stir a little to mix, cover, and bake in a low oven (300°) for about 6 hours, adding water as needed so beans do not dry out. Pour the coffee and Bourbon over the beans and cook them for 1 hour longer, uncovered. Serve in the baking dish.

MENU 16   Jellied Borscht *(for 14)*

12 cups beef bouillon
1 onion
3 bunches grated raw beets, or 2 cans chopped beets
6 tablespoons unflavoured gelatine
1 cup cold water
1 lemon, grated rind and juice
1 tablespoon sugar
Salt and black pepper
8 ounces black caviar
2 cups sour cream
¾ cup dill, cut up with scissors

Bring the bouillon and the onion to a boil and simmer until onion is soft. Remove and discard the onion and combine bouillon and beet juice, reserving chopped beets. Soften the gelatine in 1 cup water and dissolve it in the hot broth. Add lemon juice and sugar gradually until a slight sweet and sour taste is achieved. Season with salt and liberally with pepper. Add the chopped beets and pour into a large bowl to jell for several hours, or overnight if possible. Divide into 14 cups at serving time. Make a little hollow in the jelly and put in 1 teaspoon caviar. Add the grated lemon rind to the sour cream and serve it separately, along with a bowl of the cut-up dill.

MENU 16   Crème Brûlée (for 14)

6 cups heavy cream
3-inch piece of vanilla bean
12 egg yolks

Dash of salt
2 cups light brown sugar
Fresh raspberries or strawberries

Scald the cream with the vanilla bean in the top of a large double boiler. Meanwhile pour an inch of water into the bottom of the double boiler and bring it to the merest simmer. Beat the egg yolks with the dash of salt until thick and lemon-coloured. Pour a little of the scalded cream into the yolks, stirring briskly. Pour back into the top of the double boiler. Place the top into the lower part, over the barely moving hot water, over very low heat. Stir with a wooden spoon until the cream is thick and coats the spoon. Lift the top of the double boiler frequently to make sure the water does not boil up. The thickening of the custard takes a good 10 minutes. Strain into an ovenproof dish. The vanilla bean may be cut open and scraped into the cream after straining it. If vanilla bean is not available, 2 to 3 teaspoons vanilla extract may be added before straining the cream. Chill the cream overnight, or for at least 8 hours.

About 3 hours before serving the cream, cover it with the light brown sugar, so that no cream at all shows. Place the ovenproof dish into a large pan filled with cracked ice and slide the pan under the broiler to caramelize the sugar. This takes only about 2 minutes and must be watched with great care. It may be necessary to turn the dish to reach all parts of it. The sugar should be bubbly and darker all over. After heat is off, it will continue cooking and form a hard crust. Chill again thoroughly before serving. Fresh raspberries or strawberries may be served with the crème brûlée.

3

Choose Any Table—
Serve Yourself

DINNERS FOR SIXTEEN TO TWENTY

THESE little tables are not formally set, but have been arranged with tablecloths, flowers, or a candled centrepiece, nuts and candies. Silver, napkins, and china are on the buffet table or sideboard. The advantage: this plan requires a minimum of service, and the guests can eat comfortably seated, replenishing their own plates as they wish. Also, the sight of four or five tables with flowers or decorations of some sort adds to the party look as the guests come into the room.

All the food except dessert is on the sideboard or buffet. The guests serve themselves, and then sit at any one of the tables. After the used plates for this main course are removed, the desserts are brought in and put on the serving table so that the guests can then again serve themselves—or the men may serve the women guests. The coffee urn or trays with coffee pots and cups may be on the sideboard for self-service, or may be presented by a waitress in the living room.

MENU 17 (for sixteen)

MENU 18 (for sixteen)

*Eggs en Gelée
with
Truffles and Ham**

*Baby Turkeys
with
Wild Rice Stuffing*

*Spinach
with
Mushrooms and Chicory*

*Tomatoes
with
Fresh Tarragon and Dill
French Dressing*

Cold Lemon Soufflé
with
Apricot Marmalade Sauce**

Quiche Lorraine*

Boiled Tongue

Broccoli Vinaigrette

Tiny Hot Biscuits

*Raspberry Ice
with
Fresh Pineapple*

The Wine:

*A moderately dry white wine,
such as Pouilly-Fumé or Quincy
from the Loire Valley.*

The Wine:

*A white wine with this, perhaps
Pouilly-Fuissé.*

* Recipes on pages 50-51.

* Recipe on page 51.

MENU 19 (for twenty)

MENU 20 (for twenty)

*Crab and Lobster Salad
with
Sliced Avocado*

Sour Cream Dressing

*Cold Roast Beef
with
Mustard Sauce**

Whole Hot Green Beans

*Hot Indian Pudding
with
Ice Cream Sauce**

*Roast Veal
with
Carrots and Onions**

*Spinach Timbales
with
Mushrooms*

Toasted English Muffins

Applesauce Cake
with
Hot Lemon Sauce**

The Wine:

Well-chilled vin rosé.

The Wine:

Claret or a Beaujolais.

* Recipes on page 52.

* Recipes on pages 53-54.

MENU 21 (for twenty)

Shrimp Suprême*
with
Steamed Rice

Thin Slices of Corned Beef

Asparagus Casserole*

Green Salad
Anchovy Dressing

Orange Cream Tarts*

The Wine:

Tavel rosé or a California
Riesling.

* Recipes on pages 54-55.

MENU 22 (for twenty)

Billi-Bi Soup*

Herbed Roast Leg of Lamb

Grilled Tomato Halves

Lentil Salad*

Apricot Meringue*

The Wine:

A claret from a specific township
such as St.-Julien, Margaux or
St.-Estèphe.

* Recipes on pages 56-57.

MENU 23 (for twenty)   *MENU 24 (for twenty)*

Chicken with Truffles*

Baked Rice

*Eggplant, Corn, and
Tomato
Casserole**

*Salad
of
Watercress and Escarole*

Beignets Soufflés
with
Zabaglione Sauce**

Caviar-stuffed Eggs

Cold Sliced Duckling

Asparagus Vinaigrette

*Finger Sandwiches
of
Smoked Ham
with
Mustard Butter*

*Hot Rice Pudding
with
Orange Whipped Cream**

The Wine:

*A white wine—Vouvray, for ex-
ample—could be served throughout the meal.*

The Wine:

*This is a menu that calls for a red
wine—one of the California
Cabernets, or a Pinot Noir.*

* Recipes on pages 58-59.   * Recipe on page 60.

MENU 17   Eggs en Gelée with Truffles and Ham *(for 16)*

16 eggs
 2 tablespoons unflavoured gelatine
⅓ cup water
 4 cups mixed chicken and beef
   consommé

½ cup Port wine
 8 thin slices cooked ham
 3 large truffles

Poach the eggs until slightly firm for about 4 minutes in boiling salted water to which 1 tablespoon vinegar has been added. Rinse the eggs in cold water and place them on paper towels to dry. Trim whites neatly. Meanwhile, soften the gelatine in the cold water. Bring the consommé to a boil and simmer for a few minutes. Remove from the heat, add the Port, and dissolve the gelatine in the hot soup. Pour a half inch of soup into 16 ramekins and let the aspic set in the refrigerator. Cool the rest of the aspic and use it when it is beginning to jell. If it has set, melt it over hot water before using it. Dice or julienne the ham and, when the jelly in the ramekins is set, divide the ham among them. Place an egg on top of the ham and add liquid aspic almost to the top of the ramekins. Again let the aspics set in the refrigerator. Place a slice of truffle on top of each egg, fill with aspic, and let set again.

This dish may also be served as a main luncheon dish, allowing 2 eggs per person, and arranging the aspics in larger ramekins.

MENU 17   Cold Lemon Soufflé *(for 16)*

24 ladyfingers
 2 packages unflavoured gelatine
½ cup lemon juice
10 eggs
 1 cup granulated sugar

Pinch of salt
 4 teaspoons grated lemon rind
 2 cups heavy cream, whipped
   Whipped cream or apricot marmalade sauce (see below)

Cut a piece of wax paper long enough to circle two 6-cup soufflé dishes. Fold the paper lengthwise three times, then wrap it around the dishes so that the paper rises two inches above the rims. Tie securely with string beneath the rim of the dish and butter the part that faces in. Line dishes with ladyfingers, cutting them to fit the bottom of the dish, and standing them up like soldiers so that they rise above the rim of the dish, fenced in by the wax paper.

Soften the gelatine in lemon juice and dissolve over hot water. Place the eggs, the sugar, and the salt in a double boiler over simmering water. Beat for about 10 minutes until the eggs are thick, very light in colour, and fill a 12-cup sauce-pan about three-quarters full. Add the gelatine and the lemon rind and beat for a few seconds more.

Cool a little and add the whipped cream, folding in with care, and pour into the prepared soufflé dishes. The mixture should reach the top of the ladyfingers (protected by wax paper). Chill for several hours, then carefully peel off the paper. The cold soufflé should stand above the edge of the dish. Serve either with whipped cream or with apricot marmalade sauce.

APRICOT MARMALADE SAUCE

1 cup apricot preserves	2 tablespoons lemon juice
1 cup orange marmalade	4 tablespoons slivered blanched
Juice of 2 large oranges	almonds

Melt over very low heat the apricot preserves and the orange marmalade. Stir in the orange juice, the 2 tablespoons lemon juice, or more to taste, and mix well. Just before serving add the slivered blanched almonds.

MENU 18   Quiche Lorraine *(for 16)*

1 pound Canadian bacon, sliced	½ teaspoon nutmeg
4 tablespoons butter	Salt, black pepper, and cayenne
4 cups light cream	pepper
8 eggs	Two 10-inch flaky pastry shells
2 egg yolks	(see below)
4 teaspoons grated onion	1 cup grated Swiss cheese

Cut Canadian bacon in little strips and sauté in 2 tablespoons hot butter until slightly golden. Mix the cream, eggs, egg yolks, onion, nutmeg, and only a little salt (as the cheese and bacon are salty); add pepper and a dash or two of cayenne pepper. Divide the bacon between the two pastry shells, sprinkle each with ½ cup grated cheese, and fill each tart with the custard. Dot with the remaining butter and bake in a preheated medium oven (375°) for 40 to 45 minutes, or until a knife comes out clean when inserted on the side of the pie. Let stand for 10 minutes before serving as custard continues cooking for a while. If the *quiche* puffs too much while baking, prick it with the tip of a knife.

FLAKY PASTRY SHELLS

3 cups sifted flour

1 teaspoon salt

1 cup cold butter

5 tablespoons ice water, approximately

Sift flour and salt together and work the butter, cut into little pieces, into the flour until it is all little tiny lumps. Add just enough ice water to roll dough into a ball. Knead once or twice, wrap in wax paper, and let rest in the refrigerator for about 1 hour.

To make pastry shells, divide and roll out the pastry. Line two well-buttered 10-inch pie plates or flan rings; crimp the edges. Place a piece of wax paper in each and fill with raw rice or dried beans. Bake for 10 minutes in a preheated very hot oven (450°). Remove rice or beans and cool. The precooking is not essential, but does make a crisper bottom crust. The shells are now ready to be filled.

MENU 19   Mustard Sauce *(for 20)*

3 egg yolks

1 teaspoon dry mustard

2 teaspoons lemon juice

6 tablespoons Dijon mustard

3 cups heavy cream

Salt and white pepper

Beat the egg yolks with the dry mustard. Add the lemon juice slowly and beat until thick. Mix in the prepared mustard and trickle in the cream, stirring with a wooden spoon. Season with salt and pepper to taste. Refrigerate for 1 hour or more.

MENU 19   Hot Indian Pudding with Ice Cream Sauce *(for 20)*

6 cups milk

1 cup yellow corn meal

½ cup dark molasses

½ cup brown sugar

½ cup butter

1 teaspoon cinnamon

1 teaspoon ginger

½ teaspoon salt

½ pound chopped pitted dates

1 cup heavy cream, whipped

2 cups vanilla ice cream

Scald half the milk and trickle in the yellow corn meal. Stir until the mixture starts to boil. Place over boiling water and cook for 20 minutes, stirring occasionally. Add the molasses, brown sugar, butter, spices, salt, dates, and the remaining cold milk. Stir well and pour into a well-buttered baking dish. Bake in a slow oven (300°) for about 3 hours.

Serve hot with a sauce of softened ice cream with whipped cream folded into it.

MENU 20   Roast Veal with Carrots and Onions *(for 20)*

Two 5-pound boned and rolled rump roasts of veal
Bones from the roasts
2 large onions
4 whole cloves
2 carrots, quartered
30 little white onions
20 carrots, sliced crosswise
½ cup butter
2 teaspoons salt
1 teaspoon coarsely ground black pepper
Parsley for garnish

Have the butcher reserve for you the bones from the veal when he bones and rolls the rump roasts. Ask for extra veal bones if they are available.

Place all the bones in a pot and add enough water to cover well. Add the large onions, each stuck with 2 cloves, and the 2 quartered carrots. Simmer gently, skimming the liquid carefully, for several hours, or until you have about 3 cups strong veal broth. Strain and reserve the broth.

About 3 hours before you plan to serve the veal, heat oven to very hot (475°). Place the roasts in a large roasting pan surrounded by the little white onions and the sliced carrots. Spread ¼ cup softened butter over each roast and place the roasts in the oven to brown lightly, basting frequently. Be careful not to allow the butter to burn; turn the heat down a bit if necessary. Turn the meat over during the process so as to brown both sides. When the roasts are browned, season them with the salt and pepper; turn the oven to medium (350° to 375°), and continue cooking slowly, basting frequently, until well done, about 2½ hours. The vegetables will be nice and brown by this time. Transfer the roasts to another roasting pan, remove the strings, and spoon over them as much buttery fat as possible, skimmed from the vegetables. Return the veal to the oven while you finish the sauce.

Add the strong veal broth to the vegetables and reduce by simmering until rich and syrupy. Carve the roast, garnish with parsley, and serve accompanied by the sauce.

MENU 20   Applesauce Cake *(for 20)*

2 cups currants
¾ cup dark rum
4 cups sifted flour
½ teaspoon salt
4 teaspoons baking soda
2 teaspoons nutmeg
2 teaspoons cinnamon
1 teaspoon cloves

1 teaspoon allspice
2 cups dark brown sugar
1 cup sweet butter
3 eggs
1½ cups broken walnuts
4 cups hot applesauce
Hot lemon sauce (see below)

Soak the currants in the rum. Preheat oven to medium (350°). Sift together the flour, salt, soda, and all the spices. In a large bowl cream the sugar and butter; beat the eggs slightly and add to the bowl. Add the currants and walnuts, then gradually add the flour mixture alternately with the applesauce, beating well after each addition. Butter generously two large loaf pans, pour in the batter, and bake for 1 hour. Serve warm with hot lemon sauce.

HOT LEMON SAUCE

1½ cups sugar
Pinch of salt
3 egg yolks
3 tablespoons cornstarch

2 cups boiling water
1 cup lemon juice
¼ cup sweet butter
Grated rind of 2 lemons

In the top of a double boiler combine the sugar, salt, and egg yolks and beat until thick. Mix the cornstarch with a little cold water to make a smooth semi-liquid paste; add to the eggs and sugar. Slowly pour in the boiling water, stirring briskly, and add the lemon juice. Cook over simmering water, stirring until thickened. Stir in the butter, add the lemon rind, and serve. This sauce may also be served cold.

MENU 21   Shrimp Suprême *(for 20)*

4 cups raw white rice
¾ cup butter
½ cup flour
4 cups milk
2 tablespoons Worcestershire
    sauce, or more
1½ bay leaves

Salt and black pepper to taste
4 to 5 dashes cayenne pepper
1 cup tomato catsup
2 cups cream
8 pounds shrimp, cleaned and
    cooked

Boil the rice in 16 cups water for 18 minutes. Drain, rinse with cold water, and place in a colander which will fit over a large saucepan. Cover the rice and steam to finish cooking and to keep hot while sauce is being made.

Melt the butter and add the flour; cook slowly for 2 minutes. Add the milk and stir until thickened and smooth. Add Worcestershire sauce to taste, bay leaves, salt, black pepper and cayenne pepper, and the tomato catsup. Add the cream and the shrimp; heat the mixture to very hot, but do not let it boil. Serve with the hot rice.

MENU 21   Asparagus Casserole *(for 20)*

4 packages frozen jumbo asparagus spears

4 packages frozen tiny Belgian carrots, or 4 cans whole baby carrots, drained

2 pounds fresh button mushrooms, or 2 cups canned mushrooms, drained

1 cup butter

½ cup minced onion

¼ cup flour

2 cups beef bouillon

4 cups sour cream, or more

Salt and freshly ground black pepper

Cook the frozen asparagus and carrots in salted water according to the directions on the packages, keeping the asparagus firm and green. Cool under cold water; drain well. Scrub the mushrooms and dry well. Remove the stems level with the caps and mince the stems. Melt the butter and sauté the mushroom caps and stems and the onions for about 7 minutes. Add the flour and cook for 2 minutes, stirring. Add the bouillon and cook, stirring, until thickened and smooth. Add the sour cream, mix well, and season with salt and freshly ground pepper to taste. Arrange the asparagus, the carrots, and the mushrooms in sauce in layers in two well-buttered casseroles, ending with the mushrooms in sauce. Place in a preheated medium oven (350°) and bake until very hot.

MENU 21   Orange Cream Tarts *(for 20)*

12 large navel oranges

1 cup water

1¾ cups sugar

3 cups heavy cream

6 egg yolks, well beaten

Pinch of salt

4 teaspoons grated orange rind

3 tablespoons orange liqueur

2 graham-cracker piecrust shells (see below)

Cut the oranges across the sections into thin slices including the rind. Discard the ends and reserve two circular slices; cut the rest of the slices in half. Make a syrup of the water and 1 cup sugar and cook for 5 minutes. Add the orange slices and simmer gently, uncovered, for 40 minutes. Cool.

Scald the cream in the top of a double boiler. Pour the cream into the well-beaten egg yolks, stirring briskly. Return to the top of the double boiler and add the remaining ¾ cup sugar and the pinch of salt. Cook over barely simmering water in the lower part of the double boiler, stirring constantly with a wooden spoon, until the custard coats the spoon, for about 10 minutes. Add the grated orange rind and 2 tablespoons orange liqueur and cool, stirring occasionally. Pour into prepared graham-cracker piecrust shells. Cover with the halved poached orange slices placed overlapping in a circle, with a whole slice in the centre of each pie.

Reduce the syrup in which the oranges were poached until it is quite thick. Add the remaining 1 tablespoon orange liqueur and cool slightly. Spoon the syrup over the tarts to form a glaze.

GRAHAM-CRACKER PIECRUST SHELLS

1 cup butter	70 graham crackers, finely crumbled
½ cup sugar	

Let the butter soften at room temperature until it is creamy but not melted. Add other ingredients and pat into linings for two well-buttered pie plates. Bake in a preheated medium oven (375°) for 4 minutes. Cool.

MENU 22   Billi-Bi Soup (for 20)

10 pounds mussels in shells	6 parsley sprigs
5 cups dry white wine	¼ cup butter
1 cup minced shallots or onions	Salt and cayenne pepper
Top leaves from celery stalk	10 cups heavy cream

Discard any mussels that are open and any with broken shells. Remove any beard still adhering to the shells. Scrub the mussels and rinse several times to free the shells from as much sand as possible. Place the mussels and wine in a large saucepan and steam until the mussels open, about 5 minutes. Discard any shells that have not opened. Add to the broth any juices from the opened shells. Discard the shells and put the shucked mussels aside for future use. Do not use them in the soup. Use them for Francillon salad (see page 36), or serve them cold with a mustard mayonnaise, or freeze them for future use. Strain the broth through a cloth-lined sieve into a clean pot.

Meanwhile, steam the shallots, celery leaves, and parsley in the butter until limp but not brown. Add vegetables and butter to the broth with salt and cayenne pepper to taste and simmer for 5 minutes. Strain, cool, and combine with the cream. Chill for several hours and serve in chilled cups.

MENU 22   Lentil Salad *(for 20)*

Four 1-pound packages quick-cooking lentils

2 large onions, each stuck with 3 cloves

2 garlic cloves

3 teaspoons salt

Bouquet garni composed of 1 bay leaf, 2 thyme sprigs, and 4 parsley sprigs, tied in a cheesecloth bag

Shallot and parsley dressing (see below)

½ cup chopped parsley

Wash the lentils well. Place them in a large saucepan and cover with water. Add the onions, garlic, salt, and *bouquet garni.* Simmer until the lentils are tender but not mushy, about 40 minutes. Remove *bouquet garni,* garlic, and onions. Drain the lentils and cool. Pour the dressing over the lentils, toss with two forks, and put in a serving bowl. Sprinkle with chopped parsley and serve chilled.

SHALLOT AND PARSLEY DRESSING

3 teaspoons salt

1 teaspoon freshly ground black pepper, or more

½ teaspoon Dijon mustard

5 large shallots, minced

2 medium onions, or white parts of 8 scallions, minced

½ cup red-wine vinegar

1 cup olive oil

½ cup chopped parsley

Mix everything in a jar with a tightly fitting cover. Shake well before using.

MENU 22   Apricot Meringue *(for 20)*

12 egg whites

Pinch of salt

6 tablespoons sugar

3 cups apricot preserves

Juice of 1 orange

¼ cup Kirsch

Beat the egg whites with the pinch of salt in a large bowl until soft peaks are formed. Add the sugar by spoonfuls while continuing to beat to make a firm meringue. Purée in a blender, or through a sieve, the apricot preserves and dilute them with the orange juice and Kirsch. Fold gently but thoroughly into the meringue. Chill and serve.

This dessert may also be baked in a medium oven (350°) for 15 minutes and served hot.

MENU 23   Chicken with Truffles *(for 20)*

Ten 2½-pound chickens
2 onions, each stuck with 1 clove
4 celery stalks, chopped
Bouquet garni composed of bay leaf, parsley sprig, thyme sprig, and 3 peppercorns, tied in a cheesecloth bag

4 cups chicken broth
10 truffles, sliced thin
1½ cups butter
Salt and black pepper
8 shallots or 2 medium onions, chopped
Watercress

Have the butcher prepare whole chickens with unbroken skins. Be sure to have him give you the livers, hearts, gizzards, and necks of the birds.

Simmer the livers, hearts, gizzards, and necks of the chickens with the onions, celery, and *bouquet garni* in the chicken broth for about 1 hour. Strain the stock, degrease, and reserve.

Wash and wipe the chickens. With the fingers loosen the skin around the necks and insert thin slices of truffle under the skin, 2 to each side of the breast. Loosen the skin around the legs in the same way and insert 1 slice of truffle under the skin of each leg. Put 2 tablespoons butter inside the cavity of each chicken. Salt and pepper well and rub the skin liberally with butter. Place the truffled chickens in a buttered roasting pan and surround with the chopped shallots. Roast in a medium oven (350°), basting often, until the chickens are golden brown, about 1½ hours. Carve each chicken into four pieces and keep warm on a heated platter.

Pour off excess fat from the roasting pan. Deglaze with the strained chicken stock and simmer for 5 to 6 minutes, stirring continuously. Strain the sauce and add any leftover truffles, minced. Decorate the platter of chicken with watercress. Serve the sauce in a separate dish.

MENU 23   Eggplant, Corn, and Tomato Casserole *(for 20)*

4 medium eggplants

12 large tomatoes

1½ cups flour

Salt and freshly ground black pepper

1½ cups olive oil

2 garlic cloves (optional)

2 large Bermuda onions, sliced thin

12 ears of corn, or 3 packages frozen corn

1 cup bread crumbs

6 tablespoons butter

Slice unpeeled eggplants and tomatoes in half-inch slices. Mix the flour with salt and pepper and dredge the eggplant and tomato slices. Heat half the oil with the garlic. Remove the garlic when it starts to brown. Sauté the eggplant and tomatoes, turning them when slightly golden on one side and adding oil as needed. Preheat the oven to hot (400°). In two large ovenproof dishes place a layer of eggplant, then onion rings, then tomato slices, then all the corn, cut off the cob. Season each layer with salt and pepper. Repeat eggplant, onion, and tomato layers. Sprinkle top with seasoning and bread crumbs, and dot with butter. Bake for 40 minutes, or until top is golden, adding a little olive oil if it seems dry. If made ahead, cover with foil and reheat in a low oven for 20 minutes before serving.

MENU 23   Beignets Soufflés *(for 20)*

2 cups water

1 cup sweet butter

½ teaspoon salt

3 tablespoons sugar

2 cups sifted flour

10 eggs

2 teaspoons vanilla

¼ cup light rum

Vegetable fat or oil for frying

Powdered sugar

Zabaglione sauce (see below)

In a large saucepan bring to a boil the water, butter, salt, and sugar. Dump in the flour all at once and stir briskly with a wooden spoon. Keep cooking for about 5 minutes over low heat to dry out the batter. Remove from the heat and add the eggs, one at a time, beating hard each time. Add the vanilla and the rum. Heat the fat to 360° and drop the batter into the fat in walnut-size spoonfuls, cooking only a few at a time. Raise the heat a little and cook the *beignets* until they are golden on both sides. The *beignets* turn of their own accord and take about 10 minutes to cook. Cool the fat to 360° before proceeding with each next batch. Pile in a mound on a heated platter, sprinkle with powdered sugar, and serve with zabaglione sauce.

ZABAGLIONE SAUCE

12 egg yolks	2 teaspoons vanilla
2 cups sugar	¼ cup light rum
2 cups mellow white wine	

Divide the ingredients and make the sauce in two batches. In a large double boiler, over simmering water, place the egg yolks and sugar and beat with a hand beater, or an electric beater, until eggs and sugar form a ribbon when the beater is lifted out. Pour in the wine and continue beating until the sauce is foamy, adding the vanilla and the rum at the end. If the sauce cannot be served immediately, do not attempt to keep it warm or to reheat it. It is also satisfactory at room temperature.

MENU 24   Hot Rice Pudding *(for 20)*

1½ cups raw white rice	1 cup chopped candied orange peel
1½ cups sugar	3 cups heavy cream
10 cups light cream	2 tablespoons sugar
2 pinches salt	2 tablespoons orange liqueur
4 teaspoons vanilla extract	

Put ¾ cup raw rice in each of two 8-cup baking dishes. Stir 1½ cups sugar, the light cream, salt, vanilla extract, and orange peel in a bowl, then divide; put half in each baking dish, stirring to mix well with the rice. Bake, uncovered, in a preheated low oven (300°) for 2 hours, stirring two or three times. If all the liquid has not been absorbed, cook for another 30 minutes without stirring. Serve quite warm, with a bowl of heavy cream, whipped with 2 tablespoons sugar and the orange liqueur.

4

Elegant Little Tables— Buffet Service

DINNERS FOR TWENTY-FOUR

THESE are three- or four-course dinners that can be almost as elegant as a dinner with a full staff. The small tables are set as for a served dinner, with place cards, with a small scheme of decoration for each table, and with the first course on the table when dinner is announced. The guests seat themselves immediately, finding their places by the place cards.

All the main dishes are on the buffet table. After the first course is eaten, used plates are taken away, and the guests then go to the buffet table to serve themselves, or the men guests serve the women and themselves. The plates are removed after the main course, and guests then serve themselves with dessert which has been put on the cleared-off buffet table. Coffee can be served either from an urn on the buffet table or on trays in the living room after the guests leave the tables.

Among the first-course dishes which can satisfactorily be put on the table before the guests begin to eat, it is important not to include anything which looks as if it were a fractional part of a larger service; for instance, a slice of *quiche lorraine*, or a slice of caviar tart, or a serving of fish mousse. But smoked salmon, prosciutto, cold egg dishes, clams or oysters on the half shell can all await the guests with equanimity. So, also, could a hot soup, if served in little covered soup bowls.

61

MENU 25 (for twenty-four)

Hot Clear Beet Soup

Beef Bourguignon*

Parsley Potatoes

*Salad
of
Watercress and Spinach*

Coeurs à la Crème*
with
Strawberries and Cream

The Wine:

*A full-bodied Burgundy such as
Richebourg.*

MENU 26 (for twenty-four)

Curried Chicken Soup*

*Cornish Game Hens
Stuffed with Mushrooms*

Baby Snap Beans with Dill

*Mixed Green Salad of
Endive, Romaine,
Watercress*

*Hot Bread
Garlic Butter*

Gâteau Basque*
with
Cherry Sauce*

The Wine:

*A vin rosé, or Château Beyche-
velle from Bordeaux.*

MENU 27 (for twenty-four)

Jellied Tomato Clam Soup*

Hot Cheese Biscuits

Roast Veal
with
Orange Sauce*

Buttered Brussels Sprouts

Salad of Lettuce and Water
Chestnuts with Tarragon

Lady Baltimore Cake*

Brie and Blue Cheeses
Bar-le-Duc
Strawberry Jam
Melba Rounds
English Water Biscuits

The Wine:

*A fine white wine, such as Corton
Charlemagne.*

* Recipes on pages 69-70.

MENU 28 (for twenty-four)

Chicken Gumbo*

Cold Roast Quail

Tomato Aspic Ring*
with
Vegetable Salad

Hot Beaten Biscuits

Fresh Fruit with Kirsch

Cookies

The Wine:

A red wine—perhaps a claret.

* Recipes on page 71.

MENU 29 (for twenty-four)

Smoked Salmon
with
Capers and Lemon

Boeuf à la Mode*
with
Carrots and Onions

Salad
of
Endive, Chicory, Celery

Seedless Grapes
in
Sour Cream
with
Brown Sugar
and
Grand Marnier

The Wine:

A Chablis for the salmon; Côte Rôtie from the Rhone for the boeuf à la mode.

* Recipe on page 72.

MENU 30 (for twenty-four)

Individual Pizzas*

Chicken or Lobster Salad
in
Devilled-Egg Aspic Ring

Hot Corn Sticks

Chocolate Ice Cream Mould
with
Raspberry Ice Inside

Pecan Macaroons

The Wine:

A vin rosé, very cold, would enhance this menu.

* Recipe on page 73.

MENU 31 (for twenty-four)

Cold Brook Trout
Vinaigrette

Jellied Parsleyed Ham*

Cold Rice Salad*

French Bread
Tray of Cheeses

Marrons Croquettes*
with
Brandy Sauce*

The Wine:

You might serve Champagne all
through this dinner.

* Recipes on pages 74-75.

MENU 32 (for twenty-four)

Individual Onion Tarts

Chicken and
Celery Hearts*
Madeira Cream Sauce*

Parsley Potato Balls

Cold Artichokes
with Vinaigrette Sauce

Fresh Pears
Camembert Cheese

The Wine:

A good Rhine wine or a white
Loire such as Pouilly-Fumé.

* Recipes on page 76.

MENU 25   Beef Bourguignon *(for 24)*

1 pound bacon, in one piece
½ cup olive oil, or more
1½ cups flour
4 teaspoons salt
1 teaspoon black pepper
10 pounds lean beef, cut in 1½-inch pieces
4 large yellow onions, chopped
¾ cup Cognac
Bouquet garni composed of 6 garlic cloves, crushed, 1½ teaspoons thyme, 3 bay leaves, crumbled, tied in 2 cheesecloth bags

4 tablespoons tomato paste
7 cups red wine
6 cups beef bouillon, or more
   Additional salt and pepper to taste
60 tiny white onions
1 cup butter
2 tablespoons sugar
3 pounds button mushrooms, or quartered if large
½ cup chopped parsley

Remove the rind from the bacon. Cut the bacon into 1-inch sticks, ½ inch thick. Parboil and reserve the rind. Heat 2 tablespoons olive oil in a heavy frying pan and render the bacon until it browns. Remove and reserve it. Mix the flour, salt, and pepper. Dry the meat well and dredge it with the seasoned flour. Brown it on all sides in the hot fat. This will have to be done in several batches, adding oil as needed. As the meat is browned, place it in two 20-cup oven casseroles. Brown the chopped onions and add to the meat. Remove all fat from the frying pan and deglaze it with the Cognac. Pour over the meat. Add the bacon, the rind, the *bouquet garni,* and the tomato paste. Add the wine and enough bouillon to cover the meat and mix well. Taste for pepper and salt. If canned bouillon is used, salt should be used with a light hand. Cover the casseroles, bring the broth to a boil, and place in a preheated medium oven (350°). Cook for 2 hours, keeping the broth at a very slow simmer. Stir occasionally and add more bouillon if needed.

Sauté the white onions in half the butter with the sugar, shaking the pan to caramelize the onions as evenly as possible. Pour some bouillon over them and simmer, covered, for 10 to 15 minutes. The onions should remain whole. Sauté the mushrooms in the remaining butter. Add onions and mushrooms to the beef, and continue cooking for 1 more hour, or until beef is tender.

Remove bacon rind and *bouquet garni.* Remove fat from the surface, sprinkle with chopped parsley, and serve in the casseroles. This dish is improved by being prepared the day before and reheated.

MENU 25   Coeurs à la Crème *(for 24)*

2 pounds cream cheese   2 cups heavy cream
2 pounds creamed cottage cheese   ½ cup honey

Force the cottage cheese through a fine strainer. Mix well with softened cream cheese, cream, and honey. Or put all in a blender and blend until smooth. Pour into two large heart-shaped moulds with holes for drainage, lined with a dampened piece of cheesecloth large enough to fold over the cheese. Close the cheesecloth tightly over the mixture, packing it down with the hands. Place each mould on a plate to drain and chill overnight. At serving time, unmould and serve with wild strawberry preserves or fresh strawberries, and with a pitcher of sweet cream or a bowl of sour cream.

MENU 26   Curried Chicken Soup *(for 24)*

10 tablespoons butter   16 cups strong chicken broth
 3 apples, peeled and chopped   2 double chicken breasts, cooked
 6 celery stalks, chopped   and minced
1½ cups chopped onions   Salt, white pepper, and cayenne
 ½ cup curry powder, or more   pepper
 ⅔ cup sifted flour   4 cups light cream

Melt the butter in a large soup kettle and brown the apples, celery, and onions until soft. Add the curry powder and the flour, stir until smooth, and cook for a few minutes. Add the broth and stir until the mixture thickens. Put the minced chicken in a blender with enough soup to purée it. Pour back into remaining soup. Taste for seasoning, adding salt, white pepper, and cayenne pepper. Add the cream. If the soup is to be served hot, bring almost to boiling point again and serve. If the soup is to be served cold, chill for several hours before serving.

MENU 26   Gâteau Basque *(for 24)*

FILLING

4 egg yolks   2 cups scalded milk
½ cup sugar   ⅓ cup lemon juice
6 tablespoons flour   4 teaspoons grated lemon rind
2 pinches salt

Prepare the filling first, because it must be quite cold before the cake is baked.

Mix the egg yolks and sugar together in a saucepan, until they are very light. Add the flour and salt and blend well. Add the scalded milk, little by little, mixing until the mixture is smooth. Cook over low heat until the filling thickens, stirring constantly to prevent lumping. The mixture will not curdle. Strain and cool a little before adding the lemon juice and rind; then cool completely before using.

CAKE

4 cups sifted self-rising flour	4 egg yolks
¼ teaspoon salt	2 whole eggs
2 cups sugar	4 teaspoons grated lemon rind
2 cups butter, at room temperature	Cherry sauce (see below)

Preheat oven to medium (375°). Butter and flour two 9-inch springform pans. Measure all the cake ingredients, and resift the flour with the salt. Place the flour in a large bowl, and make a well. In the well place the sugar, the butter, 3 of the egg yolks, and the whole eggs, all to be mixed with either a whisk or an electric hand beater at "stir" speed. Slowly incorporate the flour with the sugar, butter, and eggs. When the mixture is light, fluffy, and stiff, stir in the lemon rind. Place a little less than half the batter in each pan. Make a shallow well in the batter and pour in the filling. Add the remaining cake batter, spreading it with a spatula, taking care not to let the filling come through. With a fork make decorative marks on the surface of the cake. Mix 1 tablespoon water with the remaining egg yolk and glaze the cakes. Bake for 35 to 40 minutes, or until golden. Serve with cherry sauce.

CHERRY SAUCE

One 1-pound, 13-ounce can Bing cherries	2 tablespoons lemon juice
	1 tablespoon grated lemon rind
2 cups seedless raspberry jelly	½ teaspoon ginger
Juice of 1 orange	

Drain the cherries, and put the juice in a saucepan with the raspberry jelly, orange juice, and lemon juice and rind. Melt the jelly over low heat, stirring occasionally. If the sauce is too sweet, add more lemon juice. Flavour with ginger, adding more to taste. Add cherries to the sauce to heat. Serve cherry sauce hot to pour over warm *gâteau basque*, or as sauce for other desserts.

MENU 27   Jellied Tomato Clam Soup *(for 24)*

8 cups tomato juice
6 cups clam juice
6 cups chicken broth
4 egg whites, slightly beaten
4 egg shells
1½ cups diced celery
1 cup chopped onions

1½ teaspoons basil
2 bay leaves
Salt and black pepper
9 tablespoons unflavoured gelatine
1¼ cups cold water
1 cup chopped chives

Put all the ingredients except the gelatine, water, and chives in a soup kettle and heat to the boiling point. Simmer for 15 minutes and strain very carefully through a fine strainer lined with a cloth dampened in cold water. Taste for seasoning and add salt and pepper if necessary. Soften the gelatine in the cold water and dissolve it in the hot broth. The broth will now be a clear delicate pink. For a darker colour carefully add a little red vegetable colouring, 1 drop at a time. Place the soup in the refrigerator to chill and set for several hours. At serving time spoon into chilled cups and sprinkle with chives.

MENU 27   Roast Veal with Orange Sauce *(for 24)*

4 teaspoons salt
1 teaspoon black pepper
1 teaspoon mace
1 teaspoon paprika
Two 6-pound rolled boneless veal roasts
¾ cup butter

1½ cups chopped shallots
3 navel oranges
1 cup sugar
1½ cups water
1½ cups white wine
3 cups beef bouillon
½ cup currant jelly

Mix salt, pepper, mace, and paprika. Wipe the roasts and rub the spices into them. Spread each roast with 4 tablespoons softened butter and butter one large or two smaller roasting pans with the remainder. Place the roasts in the buttered pans and surround them with the chopped shallots. Put into a preheated hot oven (450°) and roast for 30 minutes, basting twice. Turn the meat and roast for 10 minutes longer. Turn again, lower the heat to medium (375°), and roast about 2½ hours, lowering the heat to 350° if the drippings seem to be cooking too fast.

Pare the rind from the oranges, cut it into very fine julienne strips, and poach the strips for 5 minutes in a syrup made of the sugar and water. Strain. Remove the pith and skins from the oranges and reserve the sections.

Remove the roasts to a heated platter, cover with foil, and keep warm while making the sauce. Place the roasting pans on top of the stove, deglaze with the white wine over medium heat, add the bouillon, and simmer for 5 minutes. Strain the sauce into a saucepan, reduce it a little more, and add the currant jelly. As the jelly melts over low heat, add the strained orange strips and any extra orange juice. Slice the roasts and arrange the orange sections around the meat. Spoon a little sauce over the meat and serve the remainder in a sauce-boat. Syrup from the cooked rind may be used at some other time over fruit.

MENU 27   Lady Baltimore Cake *(for 12)*

⅔ cup butter, or margarine
2 cups sugar
1 cup milk, or water, or half and half
2½ cups flour

2½ teaspoons baking powder
5 egg whites
½ teaspoon almond extract
Lady Baltimore frosting (see below)

Cream the butter and sugar and add the liquid alternately with the flour sifted with baking powder. Fold in the beaten egg whites and last the almond extract. Bake in two well-greased and floured 8-inch cake pans in a preheated medium oven (350°) for 30 minutes, or until cake springs back to the touch. Remove from pans and cool on racks. Spread some frosting over the bottom side of one layer (as it will be flat) and cover with second layer, top side up. Frost all over.

LADY BALTIMORE FROSTING

2¼ cups sugar
6 tablespoons water
½ teaspoon cream of tartar
3 egg whites
Pinch of salt

½ cup chopped pecans
½ cup mixed dates, raisins, and candied cherries, all chopped
½ teaspoon almond extract

Put sugar, water, cream of tartar, egg whites, and salt in the top of a double boiler over boiling water. Beat with a rotary egg beater until stiff enough to stand up in peaks. It may take only 4 minutes with an electric beater. Then stir in the chopped pecans, chopped fruits, and almond extract.

MENU 28   Chicken Gumbo *(for 24)*

Two 5- to 6-pound plump tender chickens, cut up as for fricassee
Flour
6 tablespoons pure pork lard, or more
12 white onions, chopped fine
¾ pound cooked smoked ham, diced fine
12 cups chicken broth
Salt
4 to 5 chili pepper pods
Two 18-ounce cans okra
Two 18-ounce cans tomatoes
Two 4-ounce cans pimientos, drained and coarsely chopped
4 cups cooked long-grain rice
Freshly ground black pepper

Wipe the chickens with a damp cloth, dry, and dredge lightly with flour. Heat lard in an iron soup kettle and brown the chicken, a few pieces at a time. Remove the pieces as they become brown. Lower the heat and put in the onions and ham, using more lard if needed. (Use as little lard as possible to complete the browning process.) Cook for 5 minutes. Return the chicken to the kettle, add the chicken broth, salt, and chili peppers. Let simmer, covered, until the chicken is tender, about 1 hour, and then pour into a bowl to cool. (This is the halfway point and the procedure this far can be done the day before. If so, put the cooled chicken and stock in the refrigerator.)

Discard chicken skin and bones and cut the meat into large pieces. Skim all the fat from the chicken stock and discard the chili pods. Reheat the stock; drain the okra, trim off the ends, and if whole, slice into small pieces. Add okra, tomatoes, and pimientos to stock. Skim when it boils, lower the heat, and add the chicken meat. Simmer for a few minutes and serve in a large tureen. This gumbo should be very thick. Serve with fluffy dry rice seasoned with salt and freshly ground pepper.

MENU 28   Tomato Aspic Ring *(for 24)*

6½ tablespoons unflavoured gelatine
1 cup cold water
12 cups tomato juice
1 tablespoon salt
1½ teaspoons white pepper
Leaves from 3 celery stalks
4 parsley sprigs
1 tablespoon onion powder

Soften the gelatine in the cold water. Bring all the remaining ingredients to a boil in a saucepan, and simmer very slowly for 3 to 4 minutes. Strain and add the gelatine, stirring until dissolved. Pour into a 12-cup ring mould or two 6-cup moulds and chill until set. Unmould and serve plain, or fill with vegetable salad such as cooked lima beans, peas, diced celery, carrots, or other vegetables of your choice, mixed with mayonnaise.

MENU 29   Boeuf à la Mode *(for 24)*

10-pound rump of beef, tied and larded
    Red-wine marinade (see below)
6 tablespoons fat, not butter, preferably beef drippings
½ pound lean salt pork, diced and blanched

½ cup Cognac
2 calf's feet, cleaned and split
4 cups beef bouillon, or more
60 tiny carrots
4 tablespoons butter, or more
    Salt and black pepper
    Chopped parsley

Place the beef in a narrow high-sided container so the marinade will almost cover it. Pour the marinade over and marinate in the refrigerator for at least 4 hours. Turn frequently, using wooden spoons, to be sure meat is seasoned on all sides.

Drain the meat, reserving the marinade, and dry the meat well, as it will not brown if it is wet. Melt the fat and brown the meat well on all sides in a heavy casserole with a cover. Add the drained vegetables from the marinade and the salt pork, adding a little fat if needed. Pour the warmed Cognac over this and ignite it. After Cognac burns off, arrange calf's feet around meat; pour marinade and beef bouillon over so the liquid comes halfway up the meat. Cook over very low heat, after the broth comes to a simmer, either on top of the stove or in a preheated medium oven (350°), for about 4½ hours, turning the meat occasionally.

Scrub and trim the tiny carrots and cook in boiling salted water to cover for 6 to 8 minutes. Drain and brown them in butter, turning gently so they remain whole.

Remove the beef from the casserole and discard the strings. Slice the meat, arrange it on a heated serving platter surrounded by the carrots, and keep warm.

Remove fat from sauce remaining in vessel; remove calf's feet and reserve for another use. Force the sauce through a medium sieve, add salt and pepper if necessary, and reheat. Pour some sauce over the meat and sprinkle with chopped parsley. Serve the remainder of the sauce separately.

RED WINE MARINADE

7 cups red wine	8 peppercorns, crushed
½ cup red-wine vinegar	4 garlic cloves, crushed
½ cup olive oil	2 large bay leaves
1 cup chopped onions	5 whole cloves
1 cup chopped carrots	1½ teaspoons dried thyme
1 cup chopped celery	⅓ cup chopped parsley

Mix all the ingredients, stirring to moisten the vegetables and herbs. Use for beef. The marinade may be made with a dry white wine instead of red.

MENU 30   Individual Pizzas *(for 24)*

1½ packages yeast	2 cups warm water
1 teaspoon sugar	6 cups flour, measured after sifting
1½ teaspoons salt	Pizza filling (see below)

Dissolve yeast with sugar and salt in the warm water in a large bowl. Add the flour and mix. Turn onto a floured board and knead for 5 minutes. Put the ball of dough in the bowl and let it rise until double in volume, about 2 hours. Turn out again onto the board and divide into 24 little balls. Roll and pull these into 24 pancakes about 4 inches in diameter and ¼ inch thick. Place on cookie sheets and spread immediately with filling. Bake in a hot oven for 20 to 25 minutes until bubbly and hot, and serve immediately.

PIZZA FILLING

Three 6-ounce cans tomato paste	48 pimiento-stuffed green olives, sliced
One 6-ounce can water	
2 pounds Italian sausage or salami	½ cup olive oil
2 pounds mozzarella cheese	

Dilute tomato paste with water and spread on the dough rounds. Slice sausage or salami and arrange on top of tomato paste. Slice cheese into 24 pieces and put one piece on each pizza, on top of the sausage or salami slice. Decorate with olive slices and trickle over each 1 teaspoon olive oil.

MENU 31   Jellied Parsleyed Ham *(for 24)*

10-pound precooked ham
1 veal knuckle
2 calf's feet, cleaned and split
7 cups white Burgundy wine
6 shallots
Bouquet garni composed of 2 carrots, 1 large onion stuck with 3 cloves, 1 celery stalk with leaves,
pinch of tarragon, pinch of chervil, 1 garlic clove, 1 bay leaf, 10 peppercorns, all tied in a cheesecloth bag
½ cup chopped parsley
4 egg whites, slightly beaten
4 egg shells, crushed

On the day before the dinner, place everything except the parsley and the eggs in a large deep saucepan. Add enough water to cover the ham. Cover and simmer slowly for 2½ hours, or until ham is loose on the bone. Remove the ham. Strain the liquid into a clean saucepan. Clarify the broth by adding egg whites and shells; bring to a boil, stirring constantly, and then simmer for 15 minutes. Strain carefully through a wet cloth. (If calf's feet have not been used, measure the broth and add 1 tablespoon unflavoured gelatine for each 2 cups of broth. Stir to dissolve the gelatine.) Cool the broth.

Bone the ham and put into a large bowl. When the broth begins to set, mix with parsley. Pour over the ham. Chill thoroughly. Sprinkle with additional chopped parsley, slice in the bowl and serve.

MENU 31   Cold Rice Salad *(for 24)*

8 cups cooked white rice
6 tomatoes skinned, seeded, and diced
2 bunches scallions, minced
Leaves from 1 bunch of mint, chopped
1 cup finely chopped parsley
Lemon French dressing (see below)

Combine all salad ingredients in a bowl. Add dressing to salad until just moistened. Serve in an oval mound on a bed of romaine lettuce leaves on a large platter. Or make two salads on smaller round platters.

Lemon French Dressing

¾ cup lemon juice　　　　　　Salt and black pepper
1½ cups olive oil

Mix lemon juice and olive oil and add salt and pepper to taste. Use for cold rice salad, or for other salads of mixed greens or vegetables.

MENU 31　　　Marrons Croquettes *(for 24)*

4 pounds chestnuts in shells　　　Two 9-ounce jars brandied whole
1½ cups sugar　　　　　　　　　　chestnuts
2½ cups water　　　　　　　　　2 cups milk
　2-inch piece of vanilla bean　　　Bread crumbs
⅓ cup butter　　　　　　　　　　Vegetable fat or oil for frying
8 egg yolks　　　　　　　　　　　Brandy sauce (see below)

Slit the chestnut shells on the side and roast in a hot oven (400°) for 10 minutes. Remove the shells. Put the chestnuts in a large pot of cold water and slowly bring to a boil. Let them boil for 1 minute and then cool them in the water. As soon as they are cool enough to handle, but while they are still warm and wet, remove the skins. Cook the chestnuts with the sugar, 2½ cups water, and the vanilla bean until they are quite tender. Remove the vanilla bean, but scrape the seeds into the mixture. Purée the chestnuts. Dry the purée in a saucepan over high heat if it is too liquid. Add the butter and the egg yolks and cool. Divide the mixture into small portions and roll into little balls. Place a whole brandied chestnut in the center of each croquette. Dip the croquettes in milk, roll them in bread crumbs, and fry in deep fat heated to 375° until they are brown and crisp. Serve with brandy sauce.

Brandy Sauce

8 egg yolks　　　　　　　　　　2 tablespoons lemon juice
1½ cups sugar　　　　　　　　　2 tablespoons grated orange rind
1 cup orange juice　　　　　　　1 cup Cognac

Beat the egg yolks with the sugar in the top of a large double boiler until thick and light. Place over barely simmering water and beat until the mixture starts doubling in volume. Slowly add the orange juice, the lemon juice, and the orange rind. Keep beating until well heated, about 5 minutes. Remove the double boiler from the heat. Add the Cognac and keep the sauce over the hot water for about 3 minutes longer. Serve warm.

MENU 32   Chicken and Celery Hearts *(for 24)*

Six 3-pound chickens, cut in quarters
30 bunches celery trimmed to 5-inch lengths
10 cups chicken broth, or more
4 large onions, sliced
1 cup parsley sprigs
Salt and white pepper to taste
Madeira cream sauce (see below)
8 truffles, minced

Singe, wash, and dry the chickens. Trim the celery, removing heavy outer stalks. Put the chickens and celery hearts into a large cooking pot and add the broth to cover. Add onions, parsley, salt and pepper. Bring to a boil, reduce heat to simmer, and skim carefully until no more scum appears. Finish poaching the chicken, about 25 minutes altogether. If celery is not quite done, remove the chicken and keep warm. Continue simmering the celery, but keep it firm or the ribs will fall apart. Remove the celery and reserve the chicken broth to use in making Madeira cream sauce. At serving time arrange the chicken on a hot platter with the celery hearts around it. Pour some sauce over the chicken and sprinkle the top with the minced truffles. Serve the remaining sauce in a heated sauceboat.

MADEIRA CREAM SAUCE

8 cups chicken broth
½ cup white wine
1 cup butter
⅔ cup flour
Salt and white pepper
Juice of 1 lemon
6 egg yolks
2 cups heavy cream
1 cup Madeira wine

Strain the chicken broth carefully through a cloth-lined sieve so it is very clear. Put it in a large saucepan with the white wine and simmer for about 10 minutes. Melt the butter, add the flour, and cook for 3 minutes, stirring. Add the hot broth and stir until thick and smooth. Season with salt, white pepper, and lemon juice to taste. Beat the egg yolks with the cream, add a little hot sauce to them, and stir back into the sauce. After the egg yolks have been added, do not allow to boil. Add the Madeira and keep warm over hot water until ready to serve.

5 *Sixteen Buffet Luncheons*

FOR TEN TO TWENTY-FOUR

BUFFET luncheons have a place of their own on the calendar of almost everyone who entertains at all—either in town or out. They have for years been a favourite kind of country party; Frank Crowninshield, describing New York social life in the days of Ward McAllister, tells us that in the 1890's Mr. McAllister made the country luncheon a fashion for city worldlings. It was a very special kind of country luncheon; a coach-and-four filled with the *jeunesse dorée* was preceded by carts with a portable dance floor, a small band for music to dance by, and followed by a train of butlers and footmen with buckets of ice for the wines and Champagnes. That sort of extravagant luncheon was "nice but not necessary," a *grande dame* of the era is said to have said. Nice, indeed! But even if today we have no nostalgic yearning for a coach-and-four, it would be nice to find open country with room enough for a portable dance floor. The menus here are for a simpler life. One is a buffet with no special seating arrangements; one is a luncheon where guests, having served themselves, are seated at one long table. For another, guests serve themselves, then sit as they like at small tables. Finally, a carefully arranged luncheon, with place cards, the first course on the prettily decorated small tables when the guests sit down.

"FIND YOUR OWN PLACE" BUFFET,
FOR TWENTY TO TWENTY-FOUR

For these luncheons, there is no prearranged seating, but the guests serve themselves from a long serving table and then find a convenient and comfortable place to eat. These menus are planned to be eaten with ease, even standing! All the food is on the serving table except desserts, which are put there just as the guests are finishing the main course.

MENU 33 (for twenty)

Beef and Kidney Pie*

Brussels Sprouts

Glazed Carrots

Pineapple Sherbet
with
Raspberries

The Wine:

A red Bordeaux from St. Émilion will complement the hearty beef and kidney pie.

* Recipe on page 87.

MENU 34 (for twenty)

Lobster in Cucumber*
Russian Dressing*

Roquefort Cheese Soufflé*

Hot Toasted Crackers

Fresh Coconut Layer Cake

The Wine:

Champagne all through this lunch; or perhaps a still white wine—Chablis or Vouvray.

* Recipes on pages 87-88.

MENU 35 (for twenty-four)

MENU 36 (for twenty-four)

*Peas and Lima Beans
au Gratin**

*Avocado
Stuffed with Shrimp*

Deep-Dish Apple Pie

*Tomatoes
Stuffed with Crabmeat**

Chicory and Orange Salad*

Macaroon and Pear Tart*

The Wine:

A vin rosé *or a dry white wine—
Pouilly-Fumé for instance.*

The Wine:

*This is a white-wine luncheon—
a fresh Muscadet or an Alsatian
Riesling.*

* Recipe on page 89.

* Recipes on pages 89-90.

BUFFET AT ONE LONG TABLE—FOR TEN TO TWELVE

The long table might be under green trees, or in a city dining room. The guests are seated, and the foods are on a separate serving table, from which they serve themselves. Convenience in eating is not necessarily a limitation in choosing menus for this plan, as the guests will be as comfortable at table as if it were a served luncheon. The carbonada criolla in menu 38 is a sort of glorified stew which can be served on regular plates; here the salad may require a separate plate.

MENU 37 (for ten)

MENU 38 (for ten)

Hot Green Noodles*
with
Cold Pâté

Mixed Vegetable Salad

Bowl of Cut Fresh Fruit
with
Champagne

Little Cakes

The Wine:

Either white or red—a Bordeaux or an Italian Valpolicella.

Carbonada Criolla*

French Bread

Sliced Tomato Salad
with
Basil and Parsley
Chiffonade Dressing

Orange and Lemon Mousse
with
Curaçao Sauce

The Wine:

For this luncheon a red wine—a California Zinfandel, or a red Bordeaux from the Médoc.

* Recipe on page 91.

* Recipe on page 92.

MENU 39 (for twelve)

Hot Spinach Soufflé
with
Mushroom Sauce

Breast of Chicken
in
*Tarragon Aspic**

Zucchini Salad
French Dressing

Bing Cherries Flambé

The Wine:

A white Swiss wine —a Johannis-
berg du Valais or a Neuchâtel—
would be a good choice here.

* Recipe on page 92.

MENU 40 (for twelve)

Smoked Salmon
with
*Hot Boiled Potatoes**

Dry Toast

*Apricot "Omelette"**

The Wine:

A white wine is indicated, a
Montrachet or, less expensive, a
Petit Chablis.

* Recipes on pages 93-94.

SMALL TABLES, CASUAL SEATING, FOR SIXTEEN TO TWENTY

In this plan, as in the similar buffet dinner, the guests will be at small tables, but will serve themselves from a long serving table or buffet. The food is planned to be eaten while comfortably seated at table, so the choice of the menu is not limited to easy-to-eat foods. Menu 42 and menu 44 are suggested for luncheons which may be the chief meal of the day—such a day as a Sunday in the country.

MENU 41 (for sixteen)   *MENU 42 (for twenty)*

Grilled Mushroom Caps with Slivers of Smoked Turkey	*Boeuf à la Mode en Gelée**
*Eggplant Casserole**	*Salade Schiaparelli**
Lemon Sherbet with Sliced Oranges and Apricot Brandy Sauce	*Cheeses*
	Macaroon Tart
Café Diable	
The Wine:	**The Wine:**
A light red wine, such as Château Kirwan from Bordeaux.	*This is a red-wine luncheon—a St. Émilion or California Pinot Noir.*

* Recipe on page 94.   * Recipes on pages 95-96.

MENU 43 (for twenty)

MENU 44 (for twenty)

Chicken in Aspic
with
Ham Cornucopias
Filled with Vegetables*

Salad
of
Endive and White Grapes

Peaches, Nectarines
Pears, Fresh Berries
in
Thin Custard Sauce

Veal Spezzatino*

Zucchini with Butter

Boston Lettuce Salad
Cream and
Mustard Dressing

Popovers

Cold Chocolate Soufflé
with
Orange Marmalade Sauce

Italian Coffee
with
Cinnamon

The Wine:

A white wine or a rosé—Pouilly-
Fumé or Meursault for the white;
Tavel for the rosé.

The Wine:

Either white or red, or both,
might be served—Italian Soave
for the white; a Chianti the red.

* Recipe on page 97.

* Recipe on page 98.

TWENTY-FOUR GUESTS AT PRETTY, SMALL TABLES

These menus are planned to be eaten exactly as if they were completely served luncheons. In each instance, the first course is already on the table when the guests find their place cards and are seated. After this course, the used plates are taken away and the guests serve themselves, or the men guests serve the ladies. These are all fairly nourishing menus, and menus 45 to 48 might be used for dinner instead of luncheon.

MENU 45 (for twenty-four)

Melon Quarters

Curried Chicken*

*Braised Tongue
Served with
Puréed Spinach*

*Watercress and
Tomato Salad*

Hot Rolls and Butter

Fruit Compote Brûlée*

The Wine:

Champagne, a red Rhone, or beer.

* Recipes on pages 98-99.

MENU 46 (for twenty-four)

Cold Tomato Consommé

Caviar Tart

Roast Quail on Hominy*

Green Salad with Cheeses

Bite-sized Fruit Tarts

The Wine:

A Chablis for the caviar, and a claret, such as Château Léoville-Las-Cases, for the quail and the cheeses.

* Recipe on page 99.

MENU 47 (for twenty-four)

Halves of Cold Lobster
with
Shrimp and Watercress
Mayonnaise

Chicken Breasts
with
Wild Rice and Chestnuts*

Vanilla Ice Cream
and
Strawberries

The Wine:

This luncheon deserves a charming white wine: an Italian Soave,
a Moselle, or a Pouilly-Fuissé.

* Recipe on page 100.

MENU 48 (for twenty-four)

Cold Curried Eggs

Fish Tetrazzini*

Hot Muffins

Mixed Green Salad
of Lettuce, Romaine,
Chicory, Endive

Baba Ring
with
Compote of Fresh Fruits

Madeleines

The Wine:

A dry white wine with the fish—
a Puligny-Montrachet or a
Meursault.

* Recipe on page 101.

MENU 33   Beef and Kidney Pie *(for 20)*

8 pounds stew beef, cut in 1-inch cubes
30 lamb kidneys
¼ cup olive oil
1 cup butter
1 cup flour
Salt and black pepper
1 cup chopped onions

Bouquet garni composed of bay leaf, 4 parsley sprigs, garlic clove, and 8 peppercorns, tied in a cheesecloth bag
3 tablespoons tomato paste
6 cups strong beef bouillon
¾ cup Madeira
Puff pastry (see page 138)

Wipe the meat carefully. Trim and wipe the kidneys, but do not wash. Leave the kidneys whole but remove any fat or filaments.

Heat olive oil and half the butter in a heavy-bottomed cooking pot or saucepan. Dredge the beef with the flour mixed with salt and pepper. Brown quickly in the hot fat, shaking and turning to brown evenly. Add the onions and brown, adding butter and oil if necessary. This may have to be done in separate batches, as large amounts of meat seared at one time will render juice which will steam and prevent browning. Add *bouquet garni*, tomato paste, bouillon, and enough water to cover. Stir well and bring to a boil. Lower the heat and simmer for 1¾ hours, or until meat is tender.

Melt ½ cup butter in another pan; when foaming put in the kidneys in batches of 8 or 10. Shake the pan so the kidneys are coated with butter. Cook each batch for about 3 minutes only, then add them to the beef. Add wine. Remove the *bouquet garni* and taste for seasoning. Add additional salt and pepper if necessary.

Pour the stew into two buttered deep 12-cup oven dishes. Preheat the oven to very hot (425°). Cover the stew with rolled-out puff pastry, made well ahead of time, just ready to be smoothed on. Prick well with a fork, and bake for about 25 minutes, or until well puffed and golden.

The stew may also be cooked in advance. If so, reheat it and put on the pastry to brown about 30 minutes before serving.

MENU 34   Lobster in Cucumber *(for 20)*

20 young cucumbers, about 7 to 8 inches long
3 pounds cooked lobster meat, cut in small pieces

1½ cups minced raw celery
Russian dressing (see below)
6 tablespoons minced parsley
6 tablespoons minced dill

Peel the cucumbers. Cut in half and hollow out to make 40 shallow boats. Or cut a slice lengthwise from the top of each cucumber and hollow out to make 20 deeper boats. Mix lobster meat, minced celery, and 4 cups of the dressing. Fill the cucumber boats, piling the lobster salad high. Sprinkle each boat with mixed parsley and dill. Chill. Serve on a leaf or two of lettuce. Serve more dressing separately.

RUSSIAN DRESSING

1 small onion
Juice of 2 limes
4½ cups mayonnaise

1½ cups chili sauce
Salt, black pepper, cayenne pepper

Mince the onion in a bowl until it is almost puréed. Turn the purée into a cloth dampened with cold water and press out all the juice into a larger bowl. Add lime juice, mayonnaise, and chili sauce, and mix well. Season to taste with salt, black pepper, and cayenne pepper.

MENU 34   Roquefort Cheese Soufflé (for 20)

3 cups Roquefort cheese
2 tablespoons unflavoured gelatine
½ cup cold water
6 egg yolks, beaten
2 cups milk

3 tablespoons Cognac
1 tablespoon Worcestershire sauce
Black pepper
6 egg whites
2 cups heavy cream

Prepare two soufflé dishes with buttered paper collars. Tie the paper around so that it extends 2 inches above the dish.

Put the cheese through the finest blade of a meat grinder before measuring. Soften the gelatine in the cold water. Make a custard of the beaten egg yolks and the milk by cooking in a double boiler over hot water until the custard coats a spoon. Add the gelatine, stir until dissolved, and cool the custard. Combine the custard with the Roquefort cheese and put the whole mixture through a fine strainer. Add Cognac and Worcestershire sauce, and season to taste with black pepper. Beat egg whites stiff. Whip cream firm. Fold egg whites, then whipped cream into the cheese custard and pour into the prepared soufflé dishes. Let the soufflés stand in the refrigerator for 4 to 5 hours or overnight.

At serving time, carefully remove the paper collars. The soufflé will stand firmly above the dishes. Sprinkle with paprika and serve with hot toasted crackers.

MENU 35 Peas and Lima Beans au Gratin *(for 24)*

1¼ cups butter
¾ cup sifted flour
6 cups milk
   Salt and black pepper
   Few dashes Tabasco

2 cups heavy cream
2 cups freshly grated Parmesan cheese
6 cups cooked peas
6 cups cooked baby lima beans

Melt 1 cup of the butter, add the flour, and cook carefully without browning. Add the milk and cook over low heat, stirring, until thickened and smooth. Season to taste with salt, black pepper, and Tabasco. Add the cream and 1½ cups of the cheese. Mix with the peas and lima beans and pour into two buttered 10- or 12-cup baking dishes. Sprinkle with remaining cheese and dot with butter. At serving time, bake in a preheated hot oven (400°) for about 20 minutes, or until golden and bubbly.

MENU 36 Tomatoes Stuffed with Crabmeat *(for 24)*

24 ripe tomatoes
 4 pounds cooked crabmeat
1½ cups minced celery
 4 cups mayonnaise
¾ cup sour cream

Salt and black pepper
3 green peppers, minced
4 dozen lettuce leaves
24 lime or lemon wedges

Cut a slice off the stem end of each tomato and scoop out the pulp and seeds. Season with salt and invert to drain. Clean the crabmeat carefully to remove any cartilage or hard particles. Mix with celery. Combine the mayonnaise and sour cream. Mix the dressing with the crabmeat, seasoning to taste with salt and pepper. Fill the tomato shells and sprinkle with the minced peppers. Arrange the filled tomatoes on lettuce leaves and garnish with lime or lemon wedges.

MENU 36 Chicory and Orange Salad *(for 24)*

8 heads of chicory
2 celery hearts, cut in julienne
1 bunch of beets, cooked and grated

4 navel oranges
Herb dressing (see below)

Use only the white hearts of the chicory, each separated into three pieces. Use the green leaves on another occasion. (They may be cooked and puréed like spinach.) Place one piece of chicory heart on each salad plate and arrange little heaps of julienned celery and grated beets over the chicory. Carefully peel and seed the oranges and divide them into skinless sections. Put orange sections in the centre of each salad. Pour well-mixed herb dressing over all.

HERB DRESSING

6 eggs, hard boiled
2 cups olive oil
⅔ cup lemon juice
1 tablespoon prepared mustard
  (mild)

Salt and freshly ground black
pepper
1 tablespoon mixed *fines herbes*

Chop the hard-boiled eggs and mix them with the oil, lemon juice, mustard, and salt and pepper to taste. Add the *fines herbes*. These may be a mixture of chervil, tarragon, parsley, and basil in proportions to taste; or other herbs may be used. Stir in the herbs to moisten them and shake the dressing well.

MENU 36 Macaroon and Pear Tart *(for 24)*

15 eggs, separated
2½ cups sugar
1⅓ cups sifted flour
6 cups milk
⅓ cup dark rum, or more to taste

3 sweet tart pastry shells (see
  below)
24 canned pear halves, drained
30 macaroons, crumbled
⅔ cup very fine granulated sugar

Beat egg yolks with the 2½ cups sugar until thick and very light in colour. Add the flour and beat until smooth. Scald the milk and pour into the flour, beating hard. Cook over very low heat, stirring, until the mixture is thickened and boiling. Stir briskly until the custard is very smooth. Remove from the heat and add rum. Stir often while the custard cools.

When the custard is cool, pour some into each tart shell. Arrange the pears in concentric circles on the custard and sprinkle them with macaroon crumbs. Pour the remaining custard over the pears.

Beat the egg whites until they start to form soft peaks. Add the ⅔ cup fine sugar gradually and keep beating until the meringue is stiff and glossy. Pile the meringue on the tarts, making sure to touch the crust all around. Bake in a preheated moderate oven (350°) for 15 minutes. Serve warm or cold.

SWEET TART PASTRY SHELLS

6 cups sifted flour	1½ cups butter, cut into little
1 teaspoon salt	pieces
½ cup sugar	Ice water
3 egg yolks	

Sift the flour, salt, and sugar into a bowl. Make a well and add the egg yolks and butter. Work into a dough, adding ice water little by little just until the dough forms a ball. Chill the ball of dough for 2 hours. Butter three 11-inch pie plates. Preheat oven to hot (400°). Roll out the dough and line pie plates loosely. Make high edges and flute them. Line the dough with wax paper and fill with raw rice or beans. Bake for 15 minutes, lower the heat to medium (350°), and bake until golden, about 20 minutes. Remove the rice or beans and the wax paper and cool. The tart shells are now ready to be filled.

MENU 37   Hot Green Noodles with Cold Pâté *(for 10)*

2 pounds green noodles	1 cup freshly grated Parmesan
1 cup sweet butter	cheese
8 ounces pâté, very cold and firm	5 truffles, minced

Boil the noodles briskly in water to cover, until tender. Drain; put them into the bowl in which they are to be served; toss with butter cut in small pieces, and with the cold pâté cut into little cubes; mix quickly. Sprinkle with the cheese and the truffles. This is a dish that should be eaten immediately, while the noodles are still very hot and the pâté unmelted. It is good with any pâté, from the finest Strasbourg to any of the various canned liver pastes.

MENU 38   Carbonada Criolla *(for 10)*

6 tablespoons butter, approximately
2 garlic cloves
3½ pounds top round of beef, cut into 1½-inch cubes
1 large onion, chopped
2 large tomatoes, chopped
1 large green pepper, diced
1 teaspoon sugar
Salt and black pepper
5 white potatoes, coarsely chopped
5 small sweet potatoes
3 cups beef bouillon
6 ears of corn, cut off the cob, or 2 packages frozen corn
5 peaches, peeled and cut up

Melt the butter in a large Dutch oven or heavy 24-cup saucepan. Sauté the garlic cloves until brown and remove. Add the beef and brown well. Then add the chopped onion and brown for a few minutes. Add the tomatoes, green pepper, sugar, salt, and pepper. Cook for 35 to 40 minutes. Add the white potatoes, sweet potatoes, and the bouillon. Simmer for 20 minutes. Add the cut corn and the peaches; cook for 15 minutes more, or until all the vegetables are cooked and the meat is tender. Correct the seasoning and serve. If the mixture gets a little dry during cooking, add a little more bouillon or water.

MENU 39   Breast of Chicken in Tarragon Aspic *(for 12)*

6 double chicken breasts, poached
5 tablespoons unflavoured gelatine
1 cup dry white wine
8 cups strong clear chicken broth
1 bunch fresh tarragon, or 1 tablespoon dried tarragon
Salt and white pepper
6 hard-boiled eggs, sliced
One 4-ounce can pimientos
Watercress
Green mayonnaise (see below)

Cut the poached chicken into julienne strips. Soften the gelatine in the white wine. Heat the chicken broth with the tarragon but do not boil. (If the broth is not clear, clarify it with the egg whites and crushed shells as it is being heated.)

Strain the broth, discard the tarragon, and add the softened gelatine to the hot broth to dissolve. Season to taste with salt and pepper and cool.

Pour a half inch of aspic into two 8-cup moulds rinsed in cold water. Arrange egg slices with perfect yolk centres on the aspic. Cover with a little aspic and chill to set. Drain the pimientos, cut into julienne, and mix with the chicken. Put a layer of chicken and pimiento in each mould. Pour in aspic to cover and chill again. Keep adding chicken and aspic until the moulds are full. Chill for several hours. Turn out by dipping the moulds into hot water for a few seconds, then run a thin knife blade around the sides of the aspic. Place platters on the moulds and invert. Place watercress in tufts around the aspics. Serve green mayonnaise separately in a sauceboat.

Green Mayonnaise

½ cup watercress leaves   2 cups mayonnaise
⅓ cup parsley sprigs   ½ cup sour cream

Blanch the watercress leaves and parsley sprigs by pouring boiling water over them. Leave the greens for 2 minutes, then drain thoroughly. Mince the leaves and sprigs finely and add to the mayonnaise which has been blended with the sour cream. Serve with aspic dishes.

MENU 40   Smoked Salmon with Hot Boiled Potatoes (for 12)

36 uniform new potatoes   12 lemon wedges
   Sweet butter balls   24 slices of smoked salmon
¾ cup chopped parsley

Boil the potatoes in their jackets. Serve with the sweet butter balls and a bowl of chopped parsley. Put lemon wedges around the platter of salmon. Have peppermills filled with fresh peppercorns on the table for seasoning the salmon. This is a Scandinavian dish, and it is a hearty and delicious surprise for a luncheon.

MENU 40   Apricot "Omelette" *(for 12)*

1½ cups milk
1½ cups heavy cream
  6 tablespoons sugar
  1 cup butter
  3 cups flour

12 eggs
 1 teaspoon salt
 2 cups apricot jam
   Powdered sugar

This dessert is based on cream-puff paste. For easier handling, divide the ingredients into two batches and make the paste twice. Fill two cake pans with each batch.

Scald milk, cream, sugar, and butter. Dump in the flour all at once and cook until the pastry leaves the sides of the pan. Stir briskly for 5 minutes over medium heat. Cool a little and beat in the eggs one at a time. Cool. Add salt and continue beating thoroughly. Pour into four buttered 8-inch cake pans and bake in a preheated medium oven (350°) for 40 minutes. If beads of moisture show on the surface, bake a little longer. Turn off the oven and leave the cake for a few minutes. Remove from the oven, take out the cake pans, and cool on racks. Spread four of the pastries with apricot jam and cover each with one of remaining pastries. Sprinkle with sugar and serve warm.

MENU 41   Eggplant Casserole *(for 16)*

 4 medium eggplants
12 medium tomatoes
 1 cup olive oil
 4 pounds ground round steak with
   all fat removed

1½ pounds Swiss cheese, sliced
 2 tablespoons dried sweet basil
   Salt and black pepper

Slice eggplant without peeling. Salt slightly and let stand for 2 hours. Press the slices to remove all water. Slice and drain the tomatoes. Then sauté eggplant in olive oil until golden brown. In a casserole place a half-inch layer of the eggplant. Cover this with a half-inch layer of the ground round steak. On top of this place a half-inch layer of the sliced tomatoes. Add a half-inch layer of sliced cheese. Repeat, ending with the cheese. Season each layer with sweet basil and a little salt and pepper. Bake in a preheated medium oven (350°) for 30 to 45 minutes, depending upon how well done you wish the meat to be.

MENU 42 Boeuf à la Mode en Gelée *(for 20)*

Red-wine marinade (see page 73)
Pinch of ginger
⅛ teaspoon nutmeg
8-pound bottom round or rump of beef, tied and larded
5 tablespoons fat, not butter, preferably beef drippings
2 onions, sliced
6 large carrots, sliced
½ cup brandy

2 calf's feet, cleaned and split
Bouquet garni composed of 6 peppercorns, 3 whole cloves, 2 garlic cloves, 2 parsley sprigs, 2 thyme sprigs, and 1 bay leaf, tied in a cheesecloth bag
4 cups beef bouillon
36 small whole carrots
36 small white onions
Salt and black pepper

Mix the marinade, adding ginger and nutmeg, and place the larded beef into it. Marinate the beef for 24 hours, turning frequently. Drain the meat, reserving the marinade, and dry the meat carefully. Brown the meat on all sides in the beef drippings; this will take about 30 minutes. Brown the sliced onions and carrots a little. Place the browned meat in an iron kettle or Dutch oven. Heat the brandy, pour it over the meat, and ignite it. Arrange the browned onions and carrots, the calf's feet, and the *bouquet garni* around the meat. Pour the reserved marinade and the beef bouillon over all. Bring the liquid to a boil and remove any scum. Turn the heat down to a simmer and cook slowly for about 4½ hours. The meat should be very tender.

Scrape the whole carrots and peel the white onions and simmer them separately in salted water to cover until just tender.

When the meat is done, let it remain in the juices for 20 minutes. Then remove the beef and calf's feet and dry them. Discard the *bouquet garni*. Strain the stock and remove the fat. If necessary, clarify the stock with egg white. Taste for seasoning and add salt and black pepper if desired.

(If calf's feet were not available, measure the liquid and use 1 tablespoon unflavoured gelatine for each 2 cups stock. Soften the gelatine in a little cold water and dissolve it in the hot stock.)

Cool the stock. When it is beginning to jell, pour a thin layer of the aspic into a large deep oval dish or mould and place it in the refrigerator. At this point, test to be sure the jelly has the proper consistency. If too little gelatine has been extracted from the calf's feet, it may be necessary to add a little gelatine. When the jelly is solid, decorate with the cooked whole carrots and small onions, and with the meat from the calf's feet cut into lozenges. Add other vegetables such as cooked peas or beans if you wish. Add a little liquid jelly to fix the vegetables. Cut the beef into thin even slices. When the jelly over the vegetables is solid, arrange the meat slices in the dish so that they overlap each other. Spread the remainder of the jelly over the meat and place the dish in the refrigerator for a few hours. Unmould and serve.

MENU 42   Salade Schiaparelli *(for 20)*

6 heads young romaine lettuce
6 tomatoes, skinned, seeded and cut into wedges
2 celery hearts, cut into thin strips
1½ bunches watercress
2 cups olive oil
½ cup lemon juice
8 anchovy fillets

2 teaspoons salt
½ teaspoon black pepper
2 tablespoons chopped parsley
¼ teaspoon each of dried marjoram, thyme, tarragon, and chervil
2 garlic cloves
1½ cups bread cubes
4 eggs

Pull the romaine leaves apart, add the tomatoes, the celery hearts, and the watercress with the thick stems cut off. Put back in the refrigerator in a bowl covered with wax paper.

Make a dressing of 1½ cups olive oil, the lemon juice, anchovy fillets, salt, pepper, parsley, and the dried herbs. Heat the remaining ½ cup olive oil for 3 minutes. Peel the garlic cloves and cut in half, reserving one piece. Drop the rest into the oil and sauté for 3 minutes. Remove and discard the garlic. Put bread cubes into the oil and cook until the cubes are golden brown. Boil the eggs for 3 minutes; shell, cool, and put in the refrigerator. Cool the bread cubes.

Rub a large salad bowl with the remaining half garlic clove. Put in the greens, tomatoes, and dressing; toss thoroughly and then add bread cubes. Toss again, and at the last moment put in the eggs, which have been cut into quarters. Mix gently, and serve.

MENU 43   Chicken in Aspic with
Ham Cornucopias, Vegetable-filled
(for 20)

10 double chicken breasts

16 cups chicken broth

3 egg whites

4 tablespoons unflavoured gelatine

⅔ cup cold water

3 cups mayonnaise

Five 7-ounce cans *purée de foie gras*

20 large stuffed green olives

20 slices boiled ham

4 cups mixed cooked vegetables (baby lima beans, peas, diced carrots, diced string beans)

Place the chicken breasts in two pots and add the well-seasoned chicken broth, adding additional water if necessary to cover. Simmer for 20 to 25 minutes until tender, or longer if the breasts are very large. Drain and cool the chicken. Clarify the stock with the slightly beaten egg whites. Soften the gelatine in the cold water and dissolve it in 8 cups of the hot stock. Cool this aspic and put aside. Reserve the remaining chicken stock for some other use.

Remove skins and bones from the chicken breasts and place breasts on cake racks over platters. Mix 3 cups of the aspic with the mayonnaise. Spread the breasts with *purée de foie gras*. With a spoon, spread aspic mayonnaise on the breasts, over the *foie gras*, allowing any excess aspic to drip into the platters. Chill, and repeat several times until breasts are well coated with aspic. Slice the olives; dip the slices in clear aspic and arrange them as decorations on the chicken. Paint with clear aspic and chill again.

Cut the ham in neat triangles. Use special cornucopia moulds, or make moulds of rolled paper about the size of a paper cup. Paint the inside with clear aspic and insert a ham slice dipped in aspic. Chill until set. Mix the remaining aspic mayonnaise with the vegetables. Fill the ham cornucopias with the vegetables and chill again. All should be very cold.

At serving time, arrange the chicken breasts in circles on platters. Unmould the ham cornucopias by wrapping the outside of the moulds quickly in a warm wet cloth, or by peeling off the rolled paper moulds. Place ham around chicken, with wide ends facing out. Dice the remaining clear aspic and arrange the cubes on the platter around the chicken and ham.

MENU 44   Veal Spezzatino *(for 20)*

8 pounds boned shoulder of veal	2 tablespoons butter
1 cup olive oil	2 teaspoons dried orégano
5 medium onions	3 bay leaves
3 garlic cloves	3 cups dry white wine
¾ cup fresh Italian parsley	6 cups beef bouillon
32 button mushroom caps	Salt and black pepper
Five 1-pound cans tomatoes, or	
20 ripe tomatoes, seeded	

Cut the veal into bite-sized strips. Heat the olive oil in a large skillet and put in the veal in batches and lightly brown it. Chop the onions, garlic, and parsley very fine and put them into the skillet in which the veal was browned. Add the mushroom caps, cover, and simmer the vegetables for 10 minutes. Then add the tomatoes, butter, orégano, bay leaves, wine, and bouillon. Season to taste with salt and pepper. Mix with the browned veal and divide the mixture between two large saucepans. Cook uncovered over low heat for 1 hour, or until the veal is very tender.

MENU 45   Curried Chicken *(for 24)*

Five 3-pound chickens	⅓ cup Madras curry
1 cup butter, or more	4 cups chicken broth
4 large onions, chopped fine	4 very ripe bananas, mashed
4 unpeeled apples, chopped fine	2 cups scalded cream
Salt and black pepper	

Cut each chicken into 8 pieces, reserving the backs and necks to make broth for another occasion. Heat the butter in a heavy iron pan. Sauté the chicken pieces in batches until brown on one side; turn, add the chopped onions and apples, and cook until all are golden. Season with salt and pepper. Mix the curry with enough broth to make a thin paste, about ½ cup, and add to the chicken. Cook the mixture a minute or two to blend in the seasonings, then add the remaining broth and the bananas. Stir smooth, cover, and cook over low heat for 30 to 40 minutes, or until the chicken is tender. If the sauce becomes too dry, add a little more broth. Remove the chicken to a heated platter, leaving the sauce in the pan. Pour the cream into the sauce and simmer for 2 minutes. Pour over the chicken and serve.

MENU 45   Fruit Compote Brûlée *(for 24)*

Two 1-pound, 13-ounce cans Elberta peaches
Two 1-pound, 13-ounce cans apricot halves
One 1-pound, 13-ounce can Bing cherries
One 1-pound, 13-ounce can pitted prunes or plums

1 lemon, juice and grated rind
3 oranges, juice and grated rind
2 cups brown sugar
3 cups heavy cream
4 tablespoons sugar
3 teaspoons vanilla extract

Preheat oven to low (325°). Drain the fruit, reserving the syrup for some other use. Mix the fruit and pack into two casseroles or deep pyrex dishes. Bake for 1 hour. Mix the rinds and juices of the lemon and oranges and divide between the fruit casseroles. Cook for 5 minutes longer. Cover with brown sugar, so no fruit shows, and put under the broiler to caramelize. Whip the cream and add the 4 tablespoons sugar and vanilla extract. Serve the fruit hot or cold with bowls of the whipped cream.

MENU 46   Roast Quail on Hominy *(for 24)*

4 cups uncooked hominy grits
16 cups cold water
4 teaspoons salt
½ cup sugar
½ cup boiling water

36 quail
2 cups butter
2 cups beef bouillon
Salt and black pepper
1 cup heavy cream

This is a recipe to celebrate huntsman's luck!

First cook the hominy in the cold water with the salt. Boil, stirring frequently, for one hour, until the consistency of thick pudding.

Preheat the oven to very hot (475°). Make caramel by cooking the sugar slowly until very dark brown; then add the boiling water and continue to cook until the sugar and water make a thick syrup. Sprinkle this caramel on the quail to make a pretty brown; put a lump of butter on each bird. Put the birds in an open roasting pan. Roast them for 18 to 20 minutes, basting constantly with the bouillon. Salt and pepper them as they become brown. When the birds are cooked, remove them from the roasting pan and keep hot. Use the juices in the pan to make the sauce, adding the rest of the bouillon, the cream to give consistency, and the rest of the caramel to give colour. Cook over low heat until the sauce is thickened.

Serve the quail on two platters; make a mound or nest of hominy for each platter. Arrange the quail on top of the hominy and pour the sauce around the platter. If there is any sauce remaining, serve it separately.

MENU 47   Chicken Breasts with Wild Rice and Chestnuts *(for 24)*

½ cup honey	1 cup chopped shallots or onions
⅔ cup soy sauce	1½ cups chicken broth
¼ cup water	4 cups raw wild rice
12 double chicken breasts	10 cups cold water
1½ cups butter	2 teaspoons salt
Salt and black pepper	6 cups cooked whole chestnuts
1 tablespoon ginger	

Combine the honey, soy sauce, and water. Use a pastry brush to paint the chicken breasts, inside first, with this sauce. Place the chicken in shallow roasting pans, skin side down. Dot with ½ cup butter and broil for 10 minutes, basting once or twice with more sauce. Season the breasts with salt and pepper and half the ginger and turn skin side up. Again brush the pieces with sauce and dot with ½ cup butter. Broil for 10 minutes longer and season again with salt and pepper and the remaining ginger. Add the shallots and bake the chicken in a preheated medium oven (350°) for 25 minutes, or until tender. Keep basting with sauce and add chicken broth to the pan as needed to keep the meat moist.

Wash the rice in cold water until the water is clear. Put the grain into two large pots and add 5 cups cold water and a teaspoon of salt to each. Bring to a boil, turn down the heat, and simmer, uncovered, for 15 to 18 minutes. Do not overcook; the rice should be firm.

Drain freshly cooked or canned chestnuts and sauté them in the remaining ½ cup butter, shaking the pan to turn the chestnuts. Add more butter if needed. Combine the sautéed nuts and butter with the wild rice. Pile the mixture in domes in the centre of two platters and surround with the chicken breasts. Pour the pan sauce over the chicken. Decorate the platters with watercress or parsley.

MENU 48   Fish Tetrazzini *(for 24)*

4 pounds crab claws	4 cups milk
5 cups chicken broth	4 cups heavy cream
4 dozen canned Norwegian hali-	⅓ cup curry powder
but balls	Salt and black pepper
1½ cups butter	3 pounds vermicelli
1 cup sifted flour	

Remove the small piece of shell that remains on the crab claws, either fresh or frozen. Simmer the meat in seasoned chicken broth for about 10 minutes. Remove the crabmeat and strain the liquid. Heat the halibut balls in their own juice and add to the crabmeat. Make a cream sauce. Melt the butter in a saucepan, add the flour, and stir smooth. Gradually add the strained chicken broth and the heated milk and cream. Stir until thickened and smooth. Season with curry powder, salt, and pepper. Combine with the crabmeat.

Cook the vermicelli according to directions on the package. Line two oval 16-cup oven dishes with the drained vermicelli. Pour the fish into the centre and over the vermicelli. Glaze in a very hot oven (450°) for 3 to 4 minutes.

6

Buffet Parties
on the Grand Scale

ENTERTAINING two or three hundred people, or even seventy-five, at supper or dinner is not a social duty that falls often to many people. When it does, experience is, not unexpectedly, of prime importance—your own experience or that of other successful hostesses whose ideas about food, drink, service and general logistics have been developed, party by party, to a high degree of workability.

Here are five plans for very big buffet parties: two of them from ambassadorial circles where entertaining in a variety of circumstances is a part of life; the third is a big, big supper dance, for which a talented young married pair threw open their whole house; the fourth party is a buffet supper which is given once a year by a New York host and hostess whose entertaining experience is probably as varied as that of many ambassadors; the fifth is a buffet breakfast before a special event, but its plan could be helpful in other circumstances as well.

Four of these big parties have a point in common—each one has been done over and over by the hostess until the giving becomes easier each time, and the repetition of the pattern is part of the charm.

No recipes are given for these menus, as the necessary professional aides for such parties are unlikely to need, or be willing to use, recipes not their own.

THE SMORGASBORD SUPPER
FOR TWO HUNDRED TO THREE HUNDRED GUESTS

This party was a regular feature for many years at one of the most popular embassies in Washington. It might begin at nine o'clock, with guests coming and going until midnight. The choice of this sort of entertainment is peculiarly suited to Washington life, as cocktail parties given there often last until nine o'clock, when many of the embassy guests will begin to arrive for the dinner/supper. Then, too, Washington dinners *per se* are rarely late affairs, many of them ending at half past ten or a quarter to eleven. This makes it possible for guests at those dinners to arrive before midnight at an embassy party, for a glass and a touch of smorgasbord. The party system, at this particular embassy, that proved successful for so many years can be adopted by others who have large and flexible areas; it is not recommended if the guests will be cramped for space, or unable to eat with at least a small degree of comfort. In the embassy in Washington, which was a large four-storey house, the first floor was given over to the kitchen, with an ample butler's pantry, and the dining room. In another house, the rooms used might be the living room, dining room, and library, if they are contiguous rooms and if the doors can comfortably be left open to permit freedom of circulation, which is the basis of this party. Or the plan might be useful for a big country party with small tables for guests spilling out of the house to the terraces and the lawns.

In this embassy two very long tables were set up running the length of the large polished kitchen, and on these two tables was set out a dazzling variety of smorgasbord. This array of foods was the work, during the two or three days before the party, of the embassy chef and two able helpers. The last day's cooking was done in an auxiliary kitchen in the cellar, to make possible the polished spotlessness of the big kitchen the night of the party. In addition to the size of the galaxy of smorgasbord, the arrangement of the various foods was dazzling too. Colours were considered in juxtaposition, meats were decorated with various greens, small dishes of unexpected tidbits and plates of Danish breads punctuated the big platters and bowls.

The smorgasbord constituted the entire meal with the exception of dessert. As the guests entered the room where the food was laid out, they took up their silver, plates, and napkins. They then served themselves from as many dishes as they wished, and proceeded to the dining room where, with plate in one hand, they were served with a glass of Champagne, vodka, aquavit, or beer for the other hand. They then proceeded to seat themselves at any of the many small tables placed about the dining room. (In your case it might be the dining room, the living room, and the library.) The plates to which the guests had served themselves would contain several appetizers, a main course of meat such as sliced ham or Danish meatballs, and perhaps two or three touches of various kinds of salad. Seated at the small tables, the guests ate supper with the accompaniment of beer or Champagne to which they had previously been served. Waiters made the round of the tables, refilling the glasses. Eventually, these waiters removed the plates from which the smorgasbord had been eaten and served the guests with dessert. In contrast to the great variety of food on the buffet, constantly replenished from the butler's pantry, there was often only one dessert, never more than two, and the hostess took especial care that the dessert be likely to have universal acceptance. After eating, the guests might move upstairs where there was usually music of one kind or another, but it was not customary for many guests to stay the whole evening.

Here is a menu for one of these vast buffet suppers, which were possible only because of the size of the rooms, the availability of a number of waiters, meticulous planning based on long experience, a responsible, authoritative kitchen head, and the predictable flow of guests beginning about nine o'clock, waxing and waning until half past twelve or one.

MENU 49

*Hot Roast Beef
with French-fried Onions*

Chicken Curry Salad

*Salad of
Small Danish Shrimp*

Ham with Pineapple Slices

Pâté

Cucumber Salad

Pickled Beets

*Hot Pork Loin with
Apple Rings, Red Cabbage*

Fruit Salad

Hot Danish Meatballs

Green Salad

Tongue with Italian Salad

Cheeses

Dessert:

*Chopped Fruits with
Brandy or Kirsch
Sprinkled with
Toasted Almonds*

THE BUFFET DE GARE
FOR FIFTY TO SIXTY GUESTS

Another embassy party plan, using quite a different system, was also successful, but was not undertaken for as large a company as the smorgasbord supper described in the preceding pages. The French hostess called it a *"buffet de gare"* in nostalgic reminiscence of the impressive romantic railroad-station dining rooms of the 1890's. Polished wood and polished brass, long tables and "community dishes" of the good foods were the attractions of this system—a little like an old-fashioned French *pension*. Again, this plan calls for a room of some size—a large dining room, or two rooms which open up into each other. In the *buffet de gare* party there were two tables set for sixteen each; guests came and went throughout the evening and supper was served continuously from nine o'clock until two in the morning. Set out on each table were platters of *boeuf à la mode en gelée*, cold chicken tarragon, brilliantly green salads, and a *salade Olivier* (a mixture of potato, chicken, and diced dill pickle). Added to these were cheeses, and fresh fruits placed on the tables in bowls—both decorations and delights. Champagne was served throughout the meal until the fruits and cheeses, when red or white Bordeaux wines were offered. The guests sat down whenever they liked, wherever they liked, or whenever there was a vacant place, and served themselves. With all the advantages of an ordinary buffet, this plan avoids the major buffet hazards—the problem of balancing plates and glasses, and of carrying one's plate about. The food on the table was continuously replenished and as places were vacated they were reset for the next guest. The usefulness of this plan is obvious, but a large room or rooms, long tables, and attentive waiters are necessary in this scheme.

Here is another suggestion for a possible menu for the *buffet de gare*.

MENU 50

Cold Smoked Trout

Hot Chicken in Casserole

Ravioli in Casserole
with
Tomato and Beef Sauce

Salad
of
Baby Beets and Endive

Cheeses
Olivers, Water Biscuits
Melba Rounds, Rye Crisp

Bowl of Fruits

THE SUPPER DANCE
FOR TWO HUNDRED AND FIFTY GUESTS

For a big supper dance, one talented young New York hostess and her husband threw their whole house open for the party. Some of the furniture was moved out (there are moving firms who will take some of the furniture and store it in their vans overnight), and every room in the house was turned into a room for entertaining. In this particular instance, the house was decorated throughout with a brilliant printed cotton— hundreds of yards of it were draped over the usual curtains, hung inside the closets, even made into napkins and covers for the dozens of little tables scattered about.

The food was not elaborate, but it was continual and plentiful. As the guests came in, about half past ten, a cold buffet was ready and waiting: cold salmon with green sauce, sliced baked ham, French bread, and a big bowl of green salad which was constantly replenished with fresh greens. Later on, about midnight or a little after, from chafing dishes on the same dining room console, the waiters served hot curry and rice. For dessert there was a choice of Viennese pastries or pineapple and strawberries with Kirsch. And to those who stayed the course, that is, until half past four, a breakfast of scrambled eggs and sausages, toast and coffee was served in *buffet de gare* style; people ate in groups at small tables scattered throughout the party rooms. This same plan could be used successfully for much smaller parties.

At this party, there were two bands—one which specialized in "hot" music; for a smaller party, one of the orchestras might alternate with records or, if there is a piano, simply with piano music.

Here are two other menus which might be served at such a party.

MENU 51

Cold Buffet:

Smoked Trout

*Thin Slices
of
Rare Roast Beef*

Hot Buffet:

Risotto with Chicken Livers

Italian Bread Sticks

Green Salad

Dessert:

*Sections
of
Orange and Grapefruit
Sprinkled with Rum*

Thin Lacy Cookies

MENU 52

Cold Buffet:

Lobster and Chicken Salad

Beaten Biscuits

Stuffed Eggs

Hot Buffet:

*Casseroles of Lasagne
with
Beef and Tomato Sauce*

Dessert:

*Mixed Slices and Shreds
of
Fresh Pineapple
with
Orange Liqueur*

THE IMPRESARIO'S HOLIDAY PARTY
FOR SEVENTY GUESTS

This is an annual New Year party, but its plan could serve at any time of the year, and for a party of half the size. Its success is based on meticulous pre-planning, with no attempt at exotic food, but the best of its kind and plenty of it. Also, in the mind of the host, it is indispensable that the Champagne, which is served throughout the evening, be of the very best mark.

The guests are invited, always, just after Thanksgiving. The invitations read:

Mr. and Mrs. Anderson Parris, junior
request the pleasure of
the company of
Mr. and Mrs. Beecher*
at a small dance
on Friday, the thirty-first of December
at ten o'clock
Three East Third Street

R.s.v.p.

* Written by hand.

After the guests arrive, have put away their wraps, and are ready to go into the ballroom, a waiter offers a tray of Champagne glasses. For this party, people usually arrive fairly promptly, and by half past ten the floor is full of dancers. For those who would like Champagne during the dancing, there is a serving table in the hallway to which they can go; but drinks are not served throughout the rooms during the dancing until just before supper time. Dancing and Champagne go on until close to midnight.

There is no such thing as people drifting in for supper when they feel like it. Supper is served at midnight; everyone is seated, without confusion. While the dancing goes on in the wide spaces of the ballroom, the living room, and music room; the supper tables for six—twelve of them—are set up, and set, in the library, dining room, and foyer, and around the edges of the ballroom. Although this is a buffet supper, there is a place card at each place, and a beguiling, non-interfering decoration on every table. In a word, this is not a catch-as-catch-can, as buffets can sometimes turn out to be, but a fairly controlled, elegant evening.

As the hour for the supper approaches, waiters pass through the rooms with trays of filled glasses for those who are not already drinking, and with bottles of Champagne to refill the glasses of those who have already visited the serving table in the hallway. Glasses in hand, the guests go to their tables and, having found their places, leave the glasses on the table and go to one of the two long buffet tables which have been arranged —one in the dining room and the other at the end of the living room; a quick change, this, but not too difficult, as the dancing has died down temporarily. Throughout the meal, the guests serve themselves to food and the waiters refill the Champagne glasses.

After the seated supper, dancing goes on for as long as the guests feel lively; food is not served again, but Champagne is continual. Having once eaten, the guests are presumably ready either for more dancing or for going home.

Here is a menu for one of these annual holiday parties. As you see, there is nothing extraordinary in the choice of food; the success is simply because it is all expertly prepared and effectively presented. The scrambled eggs and bacon are sizzling in chafing dishes; so are the small frankfurters. The cold meats are served on separate platters, each decorated with a different green—parsley, watercress, or tarragon. The endive and beet salads have wreaths of beet slices around the edge, interspersed with touches of green herbs. The green salads are in enormous silver bowls and are artfully composed of different shades of green. The tomato aspic, filled with chicken salad, is a decoration in itself.

MENU 53

Scrambled Eggs and Bacon

Small Hot Frankfurters

Boeuf à la Mode en Gelée

Smoked Turkey

Prosciutto

Endive and Beet Salad

Mixed Green Salad

*Chicken Salad
in Tomato Aspic Ring*

Roquefort Cheese Soufflé

*Ice Cream in Moulds
Vanilla and Coffee
Rum and Peach*

Cheesecake ‑

Chocolate Mousse Cake

Lemon Sugar Cake

*Fresh Fruit Compote
with Scoops of Sherbet*

THE OUTDOOR BUFFET BREAKFAST
FOR TWO HUNDRED

When does breakfast become luncheon? One answer is, in Louisville, on Derby Day, in Kentucky. Louisville is filled with hostesses of mark, and many of them have established a certain kind of party which remains almost as true to form as the Derby itself, season after season.

One afternoon julep party for about two hundred is given out of doors at one of the magnificent farms which surround Louisville. Home-smoked Kentucky ham with beaten biscuits and thin cucumber sandwiches accompany the Bourbon. There are many pre-Derby luncheons where turkey, chicken, crab meat, sweetbreads, and mahogany-dark Kentucky ham appear, along with Bibb lettuce (a Kentucky origination), home-grown asparagus, and home-grown strawberries.

Even for two hundred guests, the parties are rarely "catered"; the food is home cooked by the household staff with free-lance waiters and helpers called in.

One distinguished Kentucky citizen and his beautiful Virginian wife have a Derby Day Breakfast every year on that fateful Saturday. It begins at about eleven o'clock; hours are as flexible as the race horses; people come and go for hours and many guests go direct to the track from this party, feeling, in any case, sustained for the excitement to come.

Although this is a very special party for a very special event, its plan could be useful in other circumstances. But part of the charm is in the fact that this delicious though fairly uncomplicated food is eaten out of doors under the big trees on the lawn, with dozens of pots of pink geraniums all about. Guests are seated at small, pink-covered tables after they have served themselves from the long buffet table, which is also covered with pink tablecloths.

Here is what these hospitable people have served more than once to their one hundred fifty to two hundred guests:

MENU 54

Turkey Hash

Corncakes with Lacy Edges

*Pitchers
of
Melted Butter
and
Maple Syrup*

Kentucky Bacon

*Green and Red
Fried Tomatoes*

*Strawberries
with
Thick Sour Cream*

*Black Coffee
in
Breakfast Cups*

PART TWO

The

Seated

Dinner

Parties

The dinner party at home remains the backbone of entertaining all across America. The weekday luncheon party has never had the acceptance here that it has had in Paris and London, because American men will so rarely make themselves available. Sunday luncheons can be delightful (they are discussed later in this book), but the most flattering, the most hospitable invitation that can be given is an invitation to a dinner party at the hostess' house.

The daughter of California's Governor Pacheco, Mrs. William Tevis, wrote in her own cookbook, in the 1860's, that if she sat down to dinner at half past six and rose before midnight, she considered that the dinner was a failure. "Either," she said, "the service had been rushed or one or two of the proper eighteen courses had been dropped."

Happily, fashions in dinner parties change, and as drastically different as the 1860 dinner customs seem, it is a fact that fashions in entertaining change more gradually than fashions in decorating or in clothes. But they do change, imperceptibly at any given moment, but noticeably when viewed over a period of even fifteen years or so. Menus have become simpler, smaller, more calorie-conscious; pre-dinner drinking is markedly less; wines are more carefully chosen; service becomes simpler as fewer servers are available. And as useful, as pleasant as is the accepted custom of the buffet dinner (discussed elsewhere in these pages), the seated dinner party at home remains of first importance.

In the following pages are plans for little dinners for eight to ten people; for the elegant black-tie dinner for twelve to twenty-four guests or more; a brief notation about the increasingly rare formal dinner; and ideas and menus for holiday parties.

1 The Little Dinners

FOR EIGHT TO TEN

THE dinner for eight or ten is perhaps the most hospitable of all dinners, for there is the opportunity for real conversation, the chance to establish some sort of person-to-person feeling which can result in a stimulating evening. One of the world's distinguished hostesses fixes on eight as the ideal size. Others reduce even that number, and maintain that a dinner for six offers an opportunity for perfection—agreeable conversation, superb food, and a flattering intimacy for the guests not possible at a larger party. Brillat-Savarin thought six was the right number. Whether dinners for eight or ten are the *summum bonum* in entertaining, remains, necessarily, a matter of opinion; but they are the most frequent form of dinner-giving from Maine to California, from Canada to Texas. For a dinner of this size, talk is usually the centre of the evening—that, and the food, which *should* star.

Here are twelve menus for just that kind of dinner, enough to carry a reasonably active hostess through a winter season. Each menu is different, but not violently so; none is exotic or likely to be boring to the men at the table. None of these menus seems to represent a determination to be unusual, rather a desire to please, a special regard for the guests. And since the size of the dinner party indicates that the hostess knows at least most of the guests fairly well, she is in a position to tailor the dinner plan somewhat to her guests' known preferences.

118

MENU 55 (for eight)

Green Turtle Soup
with
Sherry and Curry

Breast
of
Guinea Hen Smitane*

Currant Jelly

Green Bean Salad
with
Cubed Cheese

Chocolate Mint Soufflé*

The Wine:

*The best red wine you can find—
but not too heavy; Château Haut-
Brion would be excellent.*

---

* Recipes on page 125.

MENU 56 (for eight)

Carrot Soufflé
with
Cream and Honey*

Shad Roe
with
White Wine*

Spinach
with
Mushrooms and Madeira

Green Salad

Pistachio Mousse

The Wine:

*A white Rhone, such as Hermi-
tage Blanc.*

---

* Recipes on page 126.

MENU 57 (for eight)

*Prosciutto
with
Melon or Figs*

*Squabs
Stuffed with Wild Rice
with
Honey and Soy Sauce*

Lettuce with Fresh Mint

*Brown Bread
with
Herb Butter*

*English Trifle**

The Wine:

*A full-bodied Vouvray would be
pleasant.*

* Recipe on page 127.

MENU 58 (for eight)

*Spinach Soup**

Roast Loin of Pork

*Red Cabbage with Apples**

Parsley Potatoes

*Coffee Cream**

Warm Macaroons

The Wine:

*A Grenache or Gamay rosé from
California.*

* Recipes on pages 128-129.

MENU 59 (for eight to ten)   *MENU 60 (for ten)*

*Rabbit Négaunée**

Currant Jelly

Rolls

*Green Salad
with
Pomegranate Seeds*

*Liederkranz Mould**
Crackers and Bread Sticks

*Apples Porcupine**

The Wine:

*An excellent wine for this menu
would be a red Burgundy such
as Vosne-Romanée.*

*Ham Mousse Ring
Filled with Vegetables**

*Saddle of Lamb
à l'Orientale**

*Rice Pilaff**

Maple Ice Cream Mould

Little Cakes

The Wine:

*This menu would be enhanced
by a claret such as Château
Cheval Blanc.*

* Recipes on pages 130-131.   * Recipes on pages 131-133.

MENU 61 (for ten)

Clam Stew*

Quarter-size Hot Biscuits

Chicken Tarragon

Deep-dish Green Pea Tart

Potatoes Anna*

Apricots Colbert*

The Wine:

A white Burgundy, or a vin rosé.

* Recipes on pages 133-134.

MENU 62 (for ten)

Clear Oxtail Soup

Pheasants in Cream*

Buttered Broccoli

Endive
French Dressing

Cheese Ramekins*

Orange Sections
with
Curaçao

The Wine:

*A red Bordeaux would be good
with both the pheasants and the
cheese.*

* Recipes on pages 135-136.

MENU 63 (for ten)

Jellied Essence of Tomato
Parsley and Basil Garnish

Cheese Straws
English Water Biscuits

Soufflé of Sole*
with
Shrimp and
Mushroom Sauce*

Roast Lamb en Croûte*

Thin-Sliced Cucumbers
Fresh Dill
French Dressing

Sliced Pears
Black and White Grapes
with Slivered Almonds
and Kirsch

The Wine:

White wine such as Pouilly-Fumé or a fine Piesporter from the Moselle with the sole; and a claret, such as Château Talbot, with the lamb.

---

* Recipes on pages 137-138.

MENU 64 (for ten)

Grilled Mushrooms
Stuffed with Minced
Clams*

Roast Tenderloin of Beef

Baby Okra

Tiny Carrots

Potato Balls

Popovers

Lemon Mousse*

The Wine:

A red Burgundy or red Bordeaux with the beef. Champagne would be pleasant with the dessert.

---

* Recipes on page 139.

MENU 65 (for ten)

Curried Crab Soup*

Savoury Roast Veal*

Green Peas, French Style*

Gratin of Potatoes

Meringues Glacées

The Wine:

A vin rosé, or a white Burgundy.

* Recipes on pages 140-141.

MENU 66 (for ten)

Striped Bass in Aspic*

Broiled Venison Steaks*

Currant Jelly

Fried Hominy Squares

Green Beans
in
Mustard Cream*

Orange Sherbet
Vanilla Ice Cream
over
Strawberries in Cointreau

The Wine:

Serve a dry white wine, a Chablis, with the fish; a red Burgundy such as Grands-Echézeaux with the venison.

* Recipes on pages 141-143.

MENU 55   Breast of Guinea Hen Smitane *(for 8)*

2 cups raw wild rice	1 cup raisins, soaked in boiling
4 cups beef bouillon	water
½ cup butter	1 tablespoon sweet paprika
8 guinea hen breasts	1 tablespoon flour
Salt and black pepper	2 cups sour cream

Wash the wild rice until the water is quite clear. Simmer in the bouillon for 18 minutes, or until the liquid is absorbed, adding more bouillon if the rice becomes dry before done. Stir in gently 2 tablespoons of the butter and keep warm until serving time.

Sauté the guinea hen breasts, skin side down, in 6 tablespoons hot melted butter until quite golden. Season with salt and pepper, turn, brown on the other side, and season. Remove to a hot platter and keep warm. Add the drained raisins to the sauté pan, and add the paprika, flour, and cream. Stir well to deglaze the pan; if cream separates, add a little fresh cream. Simmer for 3 to 4 minutes, add salt and pepper to taste, and pour the mixture over the birds. Surround with the buttered wild rice and serve immediately.

MENU 55   Chocolate Mint Soufflé *(for 8)*

6 ounces unsweetened chocolate	3 teaspoons peppermint extract
¼ cup hot water	⅛ teaspoon salt
⅓ cup flour	12 egg whites
2 cups milk	1½ cups heavy cream
1½ cups sugar	3 tablespoons fine granulated
6 tablespoons butter	sugar
2 teaspoons grated lemon rind	1 teaspoon vanilla
8 egg yolks	

Preheat the oven to medium (350°); butter and sugar two 6-cup soufflé dishes. Melt the chocolate slowly with the hot water in a double boiler over barely simmering water. Meanwhile stir the flour into a little of the cold milk in a saucepan. Add the remaining milk gradually, stirring to keep smooth. Cook, stirring constantly, until thick and smooth. Add the 1½ cups sugar, stir until melted, then add the butter and lemon rind. Beat the egg yolks until thick and lemon-coloured; add the yolks to the milk, along with the peppermint extract and the melted chocolate. Add the salt to the egg whites in a large bowl and beat until stiff and glossy, but not dry. Fold one third of the egg whites into the chocolate mixture, thoroughly but carefully. Pour this into the remaining egg whites and carefully fold in again, turning the bowl until well mixed. Pour into the prepared soufflé dishes and bake for 40 minutes. Serve immediately with the heavy cream, whipped, sweetened with the 3 tablespoons fine sugar, and flavoured with the vanilla.

MENU 56   Carrot Soufflé *(for 8)*

1½ cups puréed carrots (about 1 to   ½ cup butter
   1½ pounds raw carrots)   5 tablespoons flour
⅛ teaspoon cloves   1½ cups light cream
2 tablespoons honey   6 egg yolks
   Salt and white pepper to taste   8 egg whites, beaten stiff

Season the carrots with the ground cloves and add the honey, salt, and pepper. Butter an 8-cup soufflé dish with 2 tablespoons of the butter and preheat the oven to medium (350°). Make a *roux* with the rest of the butter and the flour; cook it for a minute or two and add the cream. Stir until smooth over low heat. Beat in the egg yolks, one at a time, and add the puréed carrots. Taste for salt and pepper. Pour all this into a large mixing bowl. When cool, add a quarter of the stiffly beaten egg whites and mix well. Add remaining whites and fold carefully with a lifting motion, turning the bowl to blend well. Pour into the soufflé dish and bake for 35 minutes, until brown and well puffed.

MENU 56   Shad Roe with White Wine *(for 8)*

4 large pairs of shad roe   ½ cup dry white wine
3 lemons   8 pieces of toast, sautéed in butter
1 cup butter   ¼ cup chopped parsley
   Salt and white pepper   Parsley sprigs for garnish

Very gently and carefully separate the pairs of roe, cutting the membrane with a scissors. Pat dry with paper towels. Squeeze one lemon, and strain the juice over the roe. Melt one third of the butter in a large heavy skillet that will hold all the roe, or in two smaller ones. Poach the roe in butter. Do not let it cook too fast, as this could break the membrane holding the eggs, which would look unattractive. Cook it slowly for 15 minutes, uncovered, basting frequently with the butter; season with salt and pepper. Add the wine and simmer, uncovered, for 5 minutes more. Dot with the remaining butter and put under the broiler, 3 inches from the source of heat, to brown the top. Arrange the roe on the toast on a serving platter and pour the pan juices over all. Sprinkle with parsley. Cut the remaining lemons into 8 wedges and arrange around the roe. Put tufts of parsley at each end of the platter.

If the roe is small, count on one pair per person and do not split the pair before poaching.

MENU 57   English Trifle *(for 8)*

7- or 8-inch spongecake, sliced in three layers, or 2½ dozen ladyfingers
2 cups seedless raspberry jam
4 bananas
8 fresh peaches
¼ cup maraschino liqueur
1 cup Sherry
English custard (see below)
1 cup heavy cream
Angelica
Crystallized violets

Line the bottom of a large bowl, about 12-cup size, with dry spongecake or ladyfingers, spongecake preferred. Over the first layer spread raspberry jam, sliced bananas, and sliced fresh peaches; pour half the maraschino liqueur and Sherry over all. Then spread several spoonfuls of the custard on top of the fruit. Place a second layer of the spongecake over this, repeat the fruit layer, and again add liqueur, Sherry, and custard. The top layer should be spongecake, with only custard on top. Put the bowl in the refrigerator to mellow until next day, or for several hours. Before serving, whip the cream and spread it over the top irregularly, leaving space for custard to show. In these spaces put small pieces of angelica and crystallized violets, and serve.

ENGLISH CUSTARD

4 cups milk	¾ cup sugar
2-inch piece of vanilla bean	6 egg yolks

In the top of a 6-cup double boiler scald the milk with the sugar and vanilla bean. Meanwhile, beat the egg yolks to mix well. Slowly pour the sweetened and scalded milk into the beaten eggs, stirring briskly. Return to the top of the double boiler and cook over barely simmering water, stirring constantly, until the mixture coats the spoon, about 10 minutes. Strain into a bowl to cool. Open the vanilla bean, scrape the seeds into custard, and stir. If not using vanilla bean, add 2 teaspoons vanilla extract, or to taste, after the custard is thickened and off the heat.

MENU 58   Spinach Soup *(for 8)*

6 tablespoons butter	4 cups hot chicken broth
1 small onion, minced	4 cups milk
1 pound spinach, cleaned and chopped	¼ cup flour
	3 egg yolks
1 teaspoon salt	1 cup light cream
½ teaspoon black pepper	1 cup salted whipped cream
⅛ teaspoon nutmeg	

Melt the butter in a large saucepan, add the minced onion, and cook slowly until transparent but not browned. Add the roughly chopped spinach and let it get quite limp in the butter, turning it over and over, and adding more butter if needed. Sprinkle with the salt, pepper, and nutmeg. Stir in the hot chicken broth and simmer, covered, for 15 minutes. Purée through a sieve or in a blender and return to a clean pan. Combine ½ cup cold milk with the flour, and slowly stir smooth. Add remaining milk to the puréed spinach and heat. Correct the seasoning if necessary and add the milk and flour mixture, bit by bit, to the soup, stirring until thickened and boiling. Simmer over low heat for about 5 to 7 minutes. Beat the egg yolks into the light cream, pour a little hot soup into them, stir smooth, and pour back into the soup. Stir until the soup is on the verge of boiling, but do not let it boil. Serve in heated plates with a tablespoon of salted whipped cream garnishing each serving.

MENU 58   Red Cabbage with Apples *(for 8)*

1 large head of red cabbage, or 2 small ones	6 tart apples
2 tablespoons vinegar	1 bay leaf
2 onions	4 cloves
3 tablespoons butter	2 peppercorns
3 tablespoons bacon fat	Salt
1 cup red wine	Juice of ½ lemon

Discard coarse or damaged outside leaves but do not wash the cabbage; slice very fine. Stuff it all into an enamel container; add the vinegar, stir, and leave for 20 minutes. Chop up the onions and brown them slowly in a saucepan, using 2 tablespoons butter and all the bacon fat. When the onions are brown, put them, with as much of the cabbage as can be held comfortably at first, into a big soup kettle. (The reason for using a soup kettle is that it has high sides and will hold the bulk.) Cook for a few minutes, turning and stirring the cabbage; then add more cabbage as the first cabbage becomes limp with cooking. When all cabbage has been put into the kettle and has become limp, add the wine. Turn and stir carefully and add the apples, peeled, cored, and sliced or quartered, the bay leaf, cloves, peppercorns, and a little salt. Cover loosely, and cook over very low heat for 30 minutes, or until the cabbage and the apples are tender and the moisture is absorbed. Stir from time to time; add lemon juice and salt to taste. The cabbage reheats well. Just before serving add 1 tablespoon butter.

MENU 58   Coffee Cream *(for 8)*

6 egg yolks	½ cup water
¾ cup sugar	3 cups heavy cream
1½ cups strong cold coffee	Slivered almonds
2 tablespoons unflavoured gelatine	

Beat together the egg yolks and the sugar until the yolks are quite pale; add the coffee. Cook in a double boiler over just simmering water until the mixture reaches a soft custardy consistency, stirring all the time. Soften the gelatine in the cold water. Take egg mixture off the heat and stir in the gelatine. Chill the mixture, but not long enough to have it set firmly. Whip the cream until it is very stiff and firm and fold it into the chilled coffee custard. Pour the whole mixture into a melon mould and put it in the refrigerator to set. Unmould at serving time by putting a cloth, wrung out in hot water, over the mould. Sprinkle slivered almonds over the top, and serve.

MENU 59   Rabbit Négaunée *(for 8 to 10)*

4 cups raw wild rice, washed and drained
4 packaged frozen rabbits, cut for frying
Salt and black pepper
¼ teaspoon ginger
1½ cups butter
8 cups beef bouillon

2 cups claret or Burgundy
2 bunches scallions, white part only, cut up
1½ pounds mushrooms, sliced
1 tablespoon chopped parsley or chervil
½ teaspoon dried rosemary
½ teaspoon dried marjoram

Put the wild rice in the bottom of a large buttered casserole. Defrost the pieces of rabbit, reserving kidneys and livers, and season with salt, pepper, and ginger. Brown the pieces in 1 cup of the butter, and put them into the casserole on top of the rice. Add the bouillon. In the same pan in which the rabbit has been browned, sauté the livers and kidneys until well done, cut them up, and put them into the casserole. Add the wine. Brown the scallions and mushrooms slightly in the remaining butter, and add them to the rabbit and the rice, with the herbs and more salt and pepper. Cook in a medium oven (350°) for approximately 1 hour, or until most of the liquid has been absorbed and the rabbit is tender. If liquid is absorbed and the rice seems dry before the rabbit is done, add a little wine or bouillon.

MENU 59   Liederkranz Mould *(for 8 to 10)*

5 Liederkranz cheeses
(20 ounces)
2 cups dry white wine

2½ cups sweet butter
½ cup brandy
¾ cup fine dry bread crumbs

Put the cheese in a bowl and pour wine over it. Cover and let soak overnight. Drain the cheese, discard the wine, and mash and mix the cheese with the softened butter. When well blended, add the brandy. Put into an oiled mould and chill. Unmould at serving time and cover all over with bread crumbs.

MENU 59   Apples Porcupine *(for 8 to 10)*

8 to 10 large pitted prunes	3 egg whites
1½ cups Port wine	¼ cup sugar
8 to 10 large baking apples	1½ teaspoons vanilla extract
¾ cup brown sugar	½ cup slivered almonds
¼ cup butter	1½ cups heavy cream

Soak the prunes in Port wine to cover for several hours or overnight. If any wine is unabsorbed, drain and add to the rest of the Port. Core the apples and place a prune in each cavity. Fill the apples with brown sugar and place them in a well-buttered baking pan. Sprinkle with remaining brown sugar, dot with butter, and add the Port. Bake for 1 hour in a hot oven (400°), basting with pan syrup a few times. Beat the egg whites until firm, add 2 tablespoons sugar and 1 teaspoon vanilla, and beat until very stiff. Reduce the oven heat to low (300°) and take out the apples. Let the apples cool a little, swirl the meringue on them, and stud with the slivered almonds. Return to the oven and bake for about 15 minutes, or until the meringue is delicately golden and the almonds slightly toasted. Serve warm with a bowl of whipped cream, sweetened with the remaining 2 tablespoons sugar and flavoured with the remaining ½ teaspoon vanilla.

MENU 60   Ham Mousse Ring Filled with Vegetables *(for 10)*

3 tablespoons butter	Cayenne pepper
3 tablespoons flour	Salt
1½ cups chicken broth	2 egg whites, beaten stiff
2 egg yolks, beaten	1 cup heavy cream, whipped
2 tablespoons unflavoured gela-tine	6 cups cooked vegetables
¾ cup cold water	1 cup French dressing
4 tablespoons medium dry Sherry	½ cup sour cream
3½ cups ground cooked ham	½ cup mayonnaise

Melt the butter in a large saucepan. Add the flour and cook slowly for 2 minutes. Pour in the chicken broth and stir over low heat until thick and smooth. Remove from the heat and stir slowly into the beaten egg yolks. Soften the gelatine in the cold water and dissolve it in the hot sauce; add the Sherry and the ham. Season with cayenne and with salt if needed. Cool the mixture to lukewarm, then fold in the stiffly beaten egg whites and the whipped cream. Wash a 10-cup ring mould in cold water, then fill with the ham mousse; chill for several hours until firm. At serving time unmould onto a platter. Use two or more kinds of vegetables—peas, baby lima beans, diced carrots, potatoes, or beets—cooked and cooled. Combine them and mix with the French dressing. Fill the ring with vegetables and pile the remaining vegetables around the ring. Serve with a sauce made with the sour cream and mayonnaise mixed together.

MENU 60   Saddle of Lamb à l'Orientale (for 10)

2 double racks of lamb	½ cup bread crumbs
2 tablespoons butter	1 garlic clove, minced
1 teaspoon dried thyme	1 cup olive oil
2½ teaspoons salt	1 large eggplant
¾ teaspoon black pepper	½ cup sifted flour
6 shallots, or 3 medium onions	1½ cups beef bouillon
10 large tomatoes	10 watercress sprigs

Preheat the oven to very hot (450°). Have the butcher leave the lamb racks whole, trim the fat away from chop bones, and make the bones about two inches shorter, so that the racks rest on the bones while roasting. Mix the butter with the thyme, 1½ teaspoons salt, and ½ teaspoon pepper, and rub the lamb racks with the mixture. Butter a roasting pan generously, place the lamb racks in the pan side by side, and surround with the shallots. Roast for 15 minutes, then lower the heat to medium (375°). Continue roasting for 25 to 30 minutes more if lamb is to be rare; and for an additional 10 to 15 minutes for medium to well done.

Cut a slice from the tops of the tomatoes and press out the juice and the seeds. Mix the bread crumbs with the minced garlic and spread the mixture on the cut side of the tomatoes. Sprinkle with salt and pepper and trickle ¼ cup olive oil on them. Bake in a flat pan, with a little more olive oil added, for 25 minutes.

Slice the eggplant ½ inch thick; there should be 10 slices, as nearly the same size as possible. Salt the slices and leave them, weighted, for 30 minutes. Mix the flour with the remaining 1 teaspoon salt and ¼ teaspoon pepper. Dry the eggplant slices and dip them in the seasoned flour. Heat ¼ cup olive oil in a heavy frying pan and sauté the eggplant until golden on both sides, adding the remaining oil as needed. Keep hot.

Remove lamb from the oven to a heated platter, slice the meat between the bones, and return to the turned-off oven to keep warm. Pour the beef bouillon into the roasting pan and simmer, scraping up all the little brown particles in the pan. Strain and serve in a sauceboat. Arrange the eggplant slices, each with a tomato on it, around the meat. Add watercress sprigs for decoration.

MENU 60   Rice Pilaff *(for 10)*

2 cups raw white rice	½ teaspoon saffron
4 cups beef bouillon	3 tablespoons pine nuts

If beef bouillon is well seasoned, no salt is necessary. Simmer the rice, covered, in the beef bouillon with ½ teaspoon saffron for 20 to 25 minutes. Rice should absorb all of the liquid, but if some remains after 25 minutes, drain. Put the cooked rice in colander over boiling water to steam, uncovered, for 10 minutes. Before serving, mix with pine nuts.

MENU 61   Clam Stew *(for 10)*

6 tablespoons butter	¼ teaspoon nutmeg
1 leek, white part only, sliced	Salt and white pepper
2 onions, chopped fine	1 cup light cream
3 pints shucked clams	Paprika
5 cups milk	3 tablespoons chopped chives

About 7 to 8 dozen clams in their shells will give 3 pints shucked. Ask your fish dealer to open them for you.

Melt the butter in a 16-cup saucepan and steam the white part of the leek and the finely chopped onions until soft. Add the liquid from the clams, the milk, nutmeg, and salt and pepper to taste. Add the clams, whole or chopped, then the cream; bring to a simmer and cook for 3 to 4 minutes. Serve immediately, with a dusting of paprika and chopped chives.

MENU 61   Potatoes Anna *(for 10)*

10 large Idaho potatoes   1 cup butter, melted
  Salt and freshly ground black   Parsley sprigs
  pepper

Butter generously two 9-inch pie plates. Peel the potatoes and cut them evenly into slices ¼ inch thick or less. Leave in salted ice water for 30 minutes. Dry thoroughly and arrange overlapping layers in the pie plates, salting each layer and sprinkling with freshly ground pepper and melted butter. Bake in a preheated very hot oven (425°) for 40 minutes, or until a fork goes through the potatoes easily and they are crusty and golden. Invert on round serving platters, put a few tufts of parsley around them, and serve cut in wedge-shaped pieces.

MENU 61   Apricots Colbert *(for 10)*

½ cup raw white rice   ½ cup melted butter
1½ cups milk   1 cup fine bread or cake crumbs
 3 tablespoons sugar   1 cup clarified butter
¼ teaspoon salt   Apricot sauce (see below)
 1 teaspoon vanilla extract
  Three 1-pound, 13-ounce cans
  large apricot halves

Make a rice pudding: Wash the rice and put it in a saucepan with the milk, sugar, salt, and vanilla extract. Bring the mixture to a boil and simmer over low heat for 25 minutes until the rice is tender and the liquid absorbed. Keep the pudding firm so it will hold its shape. Or make rice pudding from packaged mix. There should be 1½ cups pudding.

Drain the apricots, reserving the syrup for the sauce. There should be 48 halves. Gently dry the apricots with paper towels. Put 1 tablespoon of the rice pudding in each of the 24 apricot halves, cover with the remaining fruit, and gently press together. Roll the fruit in melted butter and then in the fine crumbs. Sauté in the clarified butter, turning gently so the fruit becomes golden brown all over. Serve with hot apricot sauce.

APRICOT SAUCE

Apricot syrup from three 1-
pound, 13-ounce cans apricot
halves
½ cup apricot nectar

½ cup apricot preserves
½ cup orange marmalade
Lemon juice
¼ cup Kirsch

Put the apricot syrup and apricot nectar in the top of a large double boiler. Add
the preserves and marmalade and melt over simmering water until a smooth sauce
is obtained. If too sweet, add lemon juice to taste. At serving time, reheat over
hot water and add the Kirsch.

MENU 62   Pheasants in Cream *(for 10)*

5 pheasants
2 carrots, chopped
2 onions, sliced thin
3 celery stalks, chopped
¼ cup olive oil
½ cup butter
Bouquet garni composed of parsley
   sprigs, 1 bay leaf, and 2 peppercorns

6 cups chicken broth, or more
   Salt and black pepper
10 strips of lean bacon
14 shallots or scallions, chopped
½ cup Cognac
1 cup heavy cream

Only breasts and second joints are served. Other portions of the birds are used
in making stock for the sauce. Cut off the second joints and drumsticks from
the body of the pheasants; divide backs from breasts, leaving the breasts attached to centre bones. Brown the backs and drumsticks, carrots, onions, and
celery in oil and half the butter. When well browned, add the *bouquet garni* and
chicken broth to cover. Simmer gently for about 2 hours, covered. Strain, and
reserve the stock, which should by then be reduced to about 3 cups.

   Rub pheasant breasts and second joints with salt and pepper. Cut the bacon
strips in half and tie a piece across each pheasant piece. Brown these pieces
carefully in the remaining butter in a baking dish. Add the chopped shallots.
When meat and shallots are well browned, pour the heated Cognac over them;
ignite the spirit and burn off. After the flame subsides, add the reserved stock

and cook, uncovered, in a medium oven (375°) for 30 minutes, basting frequently. Add the heated heavy cream and cook for another 20 minutes, basting all the time. The sauce should not be thickened further.

Remove the pheasant pieces, discard the bacon and ties, cut breasts from centre bones and divide in two. Place each half breast on top of a second joint on a hot platter and pour the sauce over them.

MENU 62   Cheese Ramekins *(for 10)*

Tart pastry (see below)
4 egg yolks
1 tablespoon flour
1 cup milk
1 cup heavy cream

Salt and cayenne pepper
½ teaspoon nutmeg
½ cup grated Swiss cheese
2 tablespoons Kirsch

Line 10 individual tart pans with tart pastry and keep them cold. Preheat oven to very hot (450°). Beat the egg yolks with the flour until smooth. Scald the milk and cream and pour slowly into the eggs, stirring briskly. Season with salt, cayenne pepper, and nutmeg; add the grated cheese and the Kirsch. Pour the mixture into the pastry-lined tart pans, place these on cookie sheets, and bake for 10 minutes. Lower the heat to medium (350°) and bake until the pastry is golden and the custard is set. These tarts may be made ahead of time and reheated later.

TART PASTRY

2 cups sifted flour
½ teaspoon salt
½ cup butter

3 tablespoons vegetable shortening
1 egg yolk

Resift the flour with the salt onto a board or into a bowl, and make a well in the centre. Put in the butter, cut into small pieces, the shortening, and the egg yolk. Work with the tips of the fingers and add the smallest amount of ice water needed to be able to roll the pastry into a ball. (It may not need any water.) Chill the pastry and keep cold until ready to use.

MENU 63   Soufflé of Sole *(for 10)*

2 cups dry white wine	6 tablespoons flour
10 fillets of sole (about 3 pounds)	2 cups milk
1 onion, chopped	3 dashes cayenne pepper
2 celery stalks, chopped	8 egg yolks, well beaten
2 teaspoons salt	12 egg whites, beaten stiff
½ teaspoon black pepper	Shrimp and mushroom sauce
½ cup butter	(see below)

Pour the wine over the fish, onion, and celery in a shallow wide pan; add enough water so the fish is covered. Add 1½ teaspoons salt and the black pepper. Bring to a simmer and cook gently until the fish is just tender, about 7 to 8 minutes. Drain, and reserve the broth to make sauce. Flake enough fish to make 2 cups. Butter two 6-cup soufflé dishes with 2 tablespoons of the butter and line them with the remaining cooked fillets of sole. Make a cream sauce with the remaining butter, the flour, milk, remaining salt, and cayenne pepper. Cook the sauce, stirring constantly, until thickened and smooth. Add the well-beaten egg yolks and stir in the 2 cups of flaked fish. Taste for seasoning. Fold in thoroughly one third of the stiffly beaten egg whites, then more gently fold in the remainder. Pour into the prepared soufflé dishes, and bake in a pre-heated medium oven (350°) for 35 to 40 minutes. Serve immediately with a sauceboat of shrimp and mushroom sauce.

Shrimp and Mushroom Sauce

½ pound mushrooms, sliced	2 cups fish broth
7 tablespoons butter	½ cup heavy cream
Juice of ½ lemon	Salt and black pepper
¼ cup flour	1 pound cooked shrimp, cut up

Simmer the mushrooms in a very little salted water with 1 tablespoon butter and the lemon juice for about 8 minutes. Drain well and reserve the broth. Melt 4 tablespoons of the butter, add the flour, and cook for a minute or two. Add the fish and mushroom broths. Stir, cooking slowly until thickened. Add the cream, correct the seasoning, and fold in the shrimp and mushrooms. Dot the surface of the sauce with the remaining 2 tablespoons butter. Keep the sauce hot over hot water and stir in the butter just before serving.

MENU 63   Roast Lamb en Croûte *(for 10)*

¼ cup butter	8 shallots or scallions, chopped
2 small legs of lamb without chops, about 5 pounds each	½ cup white wine
	2 cups beef bouillon
Salt and black pepper	Puff pastry (see below)
½ teaspoon dried tarragon	2 egg yolks

Preheat the oven to very hot (450°). Generously butter a large roasting pan. Rub the legs of lamb with salt, pepper, and tarragon. Place in the roasting pan with the shallots, and roast for 25 minutes. Lower the heat to medium (350°) and cook for 30 minutes longer without opening the oven door. Remove the meat to a platter, to cool the surface. Deglaze the roasting pan with the white wine, add the bouillon, and simmer for about 8 minutes. Strain and reserve.

Turn the oven up to 450° again. Divide the pastry in two, and roll out. Place each leg, meaty side down, on a sheet of pastry rolled to ¼-inch thickness and wide enough to cover the lamb, with a slight lapover. Wrap lamb in pastry and seal the ends. Place the roasts on cookie sheets, with lapped pastry side down. Beat the egg yolks with 1 tablespoon water and paint the pastry with it. Make a slit or two in the pastry for steam to escape. Put the lamb in the oven. After 10 minutes, turn the heat down to medium (375°). Watch carefully that the pastry does not brown too fast. Bake for 20 minutes longer, or until pastry is golden. Carve like a regular leg of lamb, cutting in slices toward the bone. Reheat wine and bouillon mixture and serve in a sauceboat.

Lamb *en croûte* can also be made with simple pie pastry, but puff pastry makes a more interesting dish.

PUFF PASTRY

2 cups sweet butter	2 teaspoons salt
4 cups sifted flour	1½ cups water

Work the butter in ice water until waxy. Make a square cake of it and chill. Sift the flour with the salt and add the water, a little at a time, until the dough has the same consistency as the butter. This may not use up all the water, but use no more than is needed. Chill the dough for 30 minutes. Roll it out on a well-floured board, leaving the centre quite thick. Place the butter in the middle of the dough, and fold the edges over the butter so the cover is as thick as the underneath part. Roll out with a well-floured rolling pin in quick straight-ahead motions until a long narrow strip is obtained, about ½ inch thick and 18 inches long. Fold one third of this strip over, then bring the opposite end over this so there are three layers of dough. Roll edges very gently to seal. Give the pastry a quarter turn so edges face you, and repeat rolling out and folding in three. Chill again for 30 minutes. Repeat two more turns and chill again. Roll out, turn, and fold twice more. Chill for 30 minutes, roll out, and use. The two last rollings out should be done just before the pastry is to be used.

MENU 64   Grilled Mushrooms Stuffed with
Minced Clams *(for 10)*

4½ ounces cream cheese
    7-ounce can minced clams
  1 small onion, minced
    Salt and freshly ground black
    pepper

1 egg, beaten
40 large mushroom caps
½ cup bread crumbs
1 cup butter
10 slices of white bread

Soften the cheese and stir with the clams, onion, salt to taste, a generous amount of freshly ground pepper, and enough of the beaten egg to give a semifirm texture. Pile high inside the mushroom caps, sprinkle with bread crumbs, and dot with ½ cup of the butter. Heat ¼ cup of the butter in a shallow pan, arrange the mushroom caps in the pan, and simmer over medium heat for about 4 minutes. Then put the mushrooms under the broiler at a distance of 4 inches from the source of heat and grill until puffed and delicately golden. Cut crusts from the bread slices, trim the slices into squares, and brown them in the remaining butter. Serve 4 mushroom caps per person on a square of sautéed bread. Pour any butter remaining in the pan over the mushrooms.

MENU 64   Lemon Mousse *(for 10)*

¾ cup sugar
¼ cup water
½ cup lemon juice
 8 eggs, separated

Grated rind of 2 lemons
1 cup heavy cream
2 navel oranges, or 12 crystallized
    violets

In the top of a large double boiler melt the sugar with the water and lemon juice. Simmer for 5 minutes. Beat the egg yolks and add a little hot sugar syrup to the eggs, stirring briskly. Add the egg yolks to the rest of the sugar syrup and cook, stirring, over barely simmering water until thickened. Put the top of the double boiler into a pan of cold water to cool. Whip the egg whites very stiff. Stir lemon rind into the cooled syrup and fold in the egg whites. Whip the cream stiff and fold it into the lemon and egg-white mixture. Pour into one or two silver or crystal bowls and chill. When the mousse has set, arrange skinless orange sections or crystallized violets to look like a star in the centre of the mould. Serve very cold.

MENU 65   Curried Crab Soup *(for 10)*

¼ cup butter	8 cups milk
1 onion, minced	Salt and black pepper
2 tablespoons minced celery	2 cups fresh crabmeat
3 tablespoons flour	1 cup heavy cream
2 tablespoons curry powder	½ cup minced chives
½ teaspoon nutmeg	Sprinkling of paprika
2 tablespoons tomato paste	

Melt the butter in a deep saucepan, add the minced onion and celery, and cook without browning until transparent. Add the flour and cook for a minute without browning. Add the curry powder and nutmeg, and simmer for a minute longer; add the tomato paste, stir smooth, and pour in the milk. Stir until thickened and smooth. Season with salt and pepper to taste. Add the crabmeat, carefully picked over for any hard particles, and flaked. Add the cream, bring to a simmer, and serve very hot with a sprinkling of chives and paprika.

MENU 65   Savoury Roast Veal *(for 10)*

5- to 6-pound rump of veal	1 onion, sliced
½ cup butter	2 garlic cloves, minced
2 teaspoons salt	½ teaspoon mace
1 teaspoon freshly ground pepper	1 cup light beef bouillon
½ cup chopped parsley	1 cup light cream

Have the butcher leave the veal untied. Mix 6 tablespoons butter with 1 teaspoon salt, ½ teaspoon pepper, and half the parsley. Rub it well into the meat, roll the roast, and tie it. Butter the roasting pan with the remaining butter and place the veal in the pan with the onion and garlic. Sprinkle with the remaining salt and pepper and the mace. Preheat the oven to very hot (450°) and roast the meat for 30 minutes. Add the bouillon to the pan, lower the heat to medium (350°), and roast for 1½ hours, basting often. Remove the roast to a heated platter and cover with foil to keep warm. Deglaze the pan with the cream, simmer for 5 minutes, and strain this sauce. Slice the veal, pour a spoon or two of the sauce over it, and sprinkle the remaining ¼ cup parsley over the meat. Serve sauce separately.

MENU 65   Green Peas, French Style *(for 10)*

24 tiny white onions	1 teaspoon salt
6 pounds fresh peas, or 4 packages frozen peas	1 cup water
	¼ cup butter
1 head Boston lettuce	White pepper
4 teaspoons sugar	3 tablespoons heavy cream

Plunge the onions into boiling water for 5 minutes. Rinse under cold water, and peel off the outer skins. Shell the peas. Pull the lettuce apart and wash the leaves. Put the onions, peas, and lettuce in a saucepan and sprinkle with sugar and salt. Add the water and 2 tablespoons of the butter. Cover the pan and simmer until the peas are tender, about 15 minutes if the peas are fresh. Be careful not to overcook, but there should be no liquid left. Season with additional salt, if necessary, and pepper to taste. Add the remaining butter and the cream and serve right away.

MENU 66   Striped Bass in Aspic *(for 10)*

6- or 7-pound bass	2 teaspoons salt
3 tablespoons butter	3 egg whites and shells
1 large onion, sliced	1½ tablespoons unflavoured gelatine
1 carrot, diced	
2 celery stalks, diced	Lemon wedges
1½ cups dry white wine	Hard-boiled egg halves
5¼ cups cold water	Cucumber boats
Bouquet garni composed of parsley sprigs, thyme sprig, 1 bay leaf, and 4 peppercorns, tied in a cheesecloth bag	Sauce gribiche (see below)

Have the fish dealer clean the fish, but leave it whole. If you have a vessel large enough to hold the fish with its head still attached, keep the head as the whole fish makes an impressive dish.

Melt the butter and steam the vegetables in it until soft. Add the wine and 2 cups of the water, the *bouquet garni,* and the salt. Simmer for 25 minutes. Now add 3 cups of the water and pour all this liquid into a large oval vessel, large enough to hold the fish without breaking it. Wrap the fish well in cheesecloth and put it on a rack in the vessel. Have long ends on the cheesecloth to make it easy to lift out the cooked fish. The fish should be covered with liquid; add more water if necessary. Bring the liquid to a bare simmer and continue to cook very slowly for 7 minutes per pound, or until the fish flakes at the touch of a fork. Remove from the kettle with great care, transfer to the serving platter, and unwrap. Very gently remove the skin. Cool.

Simmer the fish broth until it is reduced to 4 cups and cool. Discard the *bouquet garni.* Beat the egg whites slightly to break up a little and add them with the crushed egg shells to the cold broth. Bring to a boil, stirring constantly, and simmer again for 10 minutes. Soften the gelatine in the remaining ¼ cup cold water, add it to the hot liquid, and pour all through the finest strainer into a bowl. Taste for seasoning and add additional salt and pepper if needed. Chill. When the aspic starts to set, spoon it over the fish until it is entirely coated. Break up any remaining aspic with a fork and arrange it around the fish. Decorate the platter with lemon wedges, hard-boiled egg halves, and cucumber boats filled with sauce gribiche. Serve additional sauce gribiche separately.

SAUCE GRIBICHE

3 hard-boiled eggs	⅓ cup chopped gherkins
1 teaspoon dry mustard	2 tablespoons chopped capers
1 cup olive oil	1 tablespoon chopped parsley
3 tablespoons white-wine vinegar	2 teaspoons chopped chives
1 teaspoon salt	1 teaspoon dried tarragon
3 dashes cayenne pepper	

Make a mayonnaise: Mash until smooth the hard-boiled egg yolks and the mustard; add oil very slowly, alternating with vinegar to taste. Season with salt and cayenne pepper. When all the oil has been added, put in all the remaining ingredients and the hard-boiled egg whites, chopped up.

MENU 66   Broiled Venison Steaks *(for 10)*

3 or 4 venison steaks, 1½ inches   Olive oil
  thick   Salt
Juniper berry marinade (see below)

Marinate the steaks in juniper berry marinade for 24 hours before using, adding additional olive oil if necessary so that the steaks really soak it up. Broil to desired degree of doneness (many prefer venison fairly well done), basting often with the marinade. Season the steaks with salt when they are done on one side and then later on the other side.

JUNIPER BERRY MARINADE

½ cup olive oil   8 juniper berries, crushed
 2 cups red wine   Black pepper
12 peppercorns

Mix all ingredients. Do not add salt, for salt in the marinade draws out the juice. Use for venison steaks and for other game.

MENU 66   Green Beans in Mustard Cream *(for 10)*

2½ pounds green beans   1 teaspoon salt
¼ cup butter   ¼ teaspoon black pepper
1 small onion, minced   2 egg yolks
3 tablespoons flour   2 tablespoons prepared mustard,
1 teaspoon dry mustard   or more to taste
3 cups light cream   ½ cup chopped parsley

Slice the beans lengthwise. Plunge them into boiling salted water and bring quickly back to a full boil. Cook over high heat for 10 minutes, keeping the beans firm and green. Drain and keep hot.

Melt the butter and gently cook the onion until transparent. Add the flour and simmer a little. Stir in the dry mustard and pour in 2½ cups of the cream. Cook slowly, stirring, until thickened. Season with the salt and pepper. Beat the egg yolks with the last ½ cup of cream, and gradually add some hot sauce to the mixture, stirring all the time. Add the warmed egg yolks to the balance of the sauce and cook, stirring, over low heat for 5 minutes. Stir in the prepared mustard gradually, adding more or less to taste. Combine with the green beans and serve with the chopped parsley sprinkled on top.

2

The "Circumstantial" Dinner

FOR TWELVE TO TWENTY-FOUR

THE ELEGANT BLACK-TIE DINNER

The twelve- to twenty-four-guest seated dinner, usually black tie (less frequently white tie), is by its nature more impersonal than the smaller dinner, and is the most "circumstantial" dinner one can give, short of the really formal dinner. It is often, these days, followed by some sort of arranged entertainment—by music from a new pianist or a singing guest, by dancing, or by a private cinema showing. Some guests may slip into a prepared setting for bridge in a quiet room. At a dinner of this size, the guests rarely expect simply to sit about and talk after coffee. Or such a dinner may be a prelude to a bigger event—a museum opening, a benefit ball, or a private dance. If the dinner is part of a gay, long evening, the food can be planned with that in mind.

Here, fourteen menus for seated black-tie dinners for twelve to twenty-four guests. In these days few houses can seat twenty-four guests at one table, or even at two tables. Four tables of six is a usual solution, or one table of twelve and two of six. For this larger guest list, there is more leeway in the choice of menus than for almost any other sort of dinner.

MENU 67 (for twelve)

Caviar in Aspic*
Hot Toast

Fillet of Beef en Croûte

Braised Endive

Watercress Salad

Chocolate-Hazelnut Cream*

The Wine:

Bonnes Mares or Musigny.

*Recipes on page 156.

MENU 68 (for twelve)

Hot Crabmeat Mornay*

Roast Capon
with
Sausage and Bread Stuffing

Brussels Sprouts
with
Buttered Chestnuts

Romaine Salad
with
Sliced Oranges

Austrian Nockerln*
with
Vanilla Sauce*

The Wine:

Champagne throughout.

* Recipes on pages 157-158.

MENU 69 (for sixteen)

Consommé Stracciatelle*

Boeuf à la Mode*

Salad
of
Escarole, Lettuce, Beets

Cheese Mousse

Burnt Almond Chiffon Pie*

The Wine:

A red Burgundy such as an estate-bottled Pommard.

* Recipes on pages 72 and 158.

MENU 70 (for sixteen)

Lobster Bisque*
with
Artichoke Toast

Roast Veal
with
Mushrooms, en Croûte*

Carrots Vichy

Broccoli Vinaigrette

Flaming Cherries
with
Orange Sections

The Wine:

A white Burgundy—Batard Montrachet or Meursault Perrières.

* Recipes on pages 159-160.

MENU 71 (for sixteen)

Fillet of Sole
in
Chablis Sauce*

Roast Goose with Peaches*

Baked Zucchini*

Bibb Lettuce
Oil and Vinegar Dressing

Tomme de Savoie Cheese
Golden Puff Crackers

Coffee Walnut Roll*

The Wine:

Offer a grand cru Chablis with the sole and a fine Hermitage from the Rhone Valley with the goose and the cheese.

* Recipes on pages 161-163.

MENU 72 (for eighteen)

Tomato and Dill Soup*

French Bread with Herbs

Crown Roasts of Lamb
with
Barley Pilaff*

Green Beans
and
Onion Rings

Endive Salad
Roquefort Dressing

Tarte Tatin*

The Wine:

A great château-bottled claret such as Château Lafite Rothschild or Château Latour.

* Recipes on pages 164-165.

MENU 73 (for eighteen)

Consommé with Okra*

Roast Duckling
with
Cherries*

Green Peas French Style

Baked Hominy Grits*

Green Salad with Cheeses

Praline Bavarian Cream
with
Strawberries*

The Wine:

A glass of Amontillado Sherry with the soup; a red Burgundy such as Chambertin with the duckling.

* Recipes on pages 166-167.

MENU 74 (for twenty)

Purée Saint-Germain*

Coq au Vin*

Braised Endive

New Potatoes with Dill

Little Croissants

Lime Ice Ring
with
Fresh Pineapple in Rum

The Wine:

This chicken is cooked with red wine, so a claret would be a good choice.

* Recipes on pages 168-169.

MENU 75 (for twenty)

Shrimp in Sauce Piquante*

Sauté of Chicken Breasts*
on
Cracked Wheat Pilaff*

New Peas and Baby Onions

Cognac Cream*
on
Toasted Spongecake

The Wine:

A white wine of the Montrachet family is excellent with this menu.

* Recipes on pages 170-171.

MENU 76 (for twenty)

Cold Borscht*

Braised Young Turkeys in Champagne*

Purée of Chestnuts*

Spiced Crab Apples

Asparagus Vinaigrette

Honey Mousse

The Wine:

Champagne would make this a memorable menu, served throughout.

* Recipes on pages 172-173.

MENU 77 (for twenty-four)

Oysters Rockefeller*

Pheasant en Casserole*
with
Sea Grape Jelly

Brown Rice Ring
with
Baby Brussels Sprouts*

French Peach Halves
with
Slivered Almonds
and
Raspberry Sauce

Cookies

The Wine:

Serve a Chablis with the oysters, and a full red Burgundy, such as Vosne-Romanée la Grande Rue, with the pheasant.

* Recipes on pages 174-175.

MENU 78 (for twenty-four)

Egg and Caviar Mousse*

Roast Beef
with
Artichoke Bottoms
with
Bread-crumb Stuffing

French Peas and
Mushrooms

Green Salad

Flaming Ginger Pancakes*

The Wine:

A small glass of vodka might accompany the mousse. Serve a full-bodied red wine with the beef, perhaps a Pomerol, such as Château Pétrus.

* Recipes on page 176.

MENU 79 (for twenty-four)   *MENU 80 (for twenty-four)*

Lobster Bordelaise*

*Roast Loin of Young Veal
with
Tarragon Sauce**

Braised Chestnuts

Puréed Carrots

Raspberries Frangipane*

Oysters in Sherry*

*Braised Stuffed
Shoulder of Lamb
with
Truffles**

*Green Salad
with
Camembert Cheese*

Tarte à l'Orange*

The Wine:

*A distinguished white Bordeaux
—Château Haut-Brion-Blanc—
would be perfect.*

The Wine:

*With the lamb a Beaujolais, or a
Pommard or Beaune if you feel a
little more extravagant.*

* Recipes on pages 177-179.   * Recipes on pages 179-181.

THE FORMAL DINNER PARTY

The essence of formal entertaining is a strict observance of tradition. Someone has said that traditions are "group efforts to keep the unexpected from happening," and for a formal dinner, the choice of menus is half dictated already. Great originality is not expected; it's a little like a man's tail coat: perfection in the classic pattern is the aim.

If you have a single qualm about attempting this rigidly dictated event, don't do it. You will remember Mr. Morgan's answer to the young man who asked whether he (Mr. Morgan) thought the young man could afford a yacht. Mr. Morgan's answer was: "If you have to ask, you can't." The very elegant black-tie dinners described in the preceding section meet almost all of the situations for which one might consider a formal dinner; these black-tie dinners dispense with a few of the rites without lessening the pleasure—or the compliment to the guests. So, if the procedures of a formal dinner tend to discourage the hostess, it is well to lay aside the idea. But on certain specified occasions, the formal dinner is the expected. It is marked by third person invitations; guests in full evening dress; a card for each man guest as he arrives, telling him who his dinner partner is; the ritual of the butler's announcing each guest as he or she enters the room where the hostess is receiving. Sixteen guests is the usual minimum; they are seated at one table; the menu is written in French; all place cards bear the full names of the guests; there are five to seven courses and at least three wines. The table is covered with a cloth, set with candles and flowers or decorative centrepieces; and the serving of the dinner follows a classic pattern, with two menservants for every eight guests. The butler pours the wine and supervises generally.

Here are three menu variations within the conventional framework of a formal dinner. Recipes are not given, as here one presupposes an able chef who prefers his own way. These menus were composed by a famous private chef responsible over many years for great formal dinners in a distinguished household.

MENU 81

MENU 82

Caviar

Vodka

Borscht à la Russe

Sherry
(Amontillado)

Saumon Froid, Sauce Verte

Château Haut-
Brion-Blanc

Pintades Rôties

Clos de Vougeot

Pommes Dauphine

Épinards en Branche

Aspic de Roquefort
à la Mayonnaise

Glace Pralinée

Veuve Clicquot

Huîtres en Coquille

Vouvray

Oxtail Soup

Sherry
(Amontillado)

Turbot au Court-Bouillon

Johannisberger
Roselack
Spätlese

Filet de Boeuf Richelieu
Sauce Madère

Château Lafite

Asperges, Sauce Mousseline

Mousse aux Fraises

Champagne,
Blanc de Blancs
(Château Salon)

Fruit

MENU 83

Clams on Half Shell

Tortue Verte

Sherry
(Amontillado)

Pompano Bercy

Chevalier
Montrachet

Selle d'Agneau

Hermitage
(Clos Sizeranne)

Aspic de Foie Gras

Salade d'Endive

Glace Nesselrode

Champagne,
Dom Perignon

MENU 67   Caviar in Aspic *(for 12)*

2½ tablespoons unflavoured
gelatine
4 cups mild chicken broth

8 ounces caviar
6 hard-boiled eggs
1 bunch of watercress

Soften the gelatine in the chicken broth for a few minutes, then dissolve over heat. Scrape the caviar into a 6-cup ring mould. Spoon ¼ to ½ cup of the broth over the caviar and shake the mould until the caviar is level all around. Place in refrigerator. Separate the hard-boiled eggs and mince the whites and yolks separately. When the gelatine is set on the caviar, sprinkle the egg whites on top of the caviar, repeat the spooning and shaking processes with more broth, and again return to refrigerator. When this layer has set, do the same thing with the egg yolks. When the egg-yolk layer has set, fill the mould with the remaining aspic broth. Leave the mould in the refrigerator for 1 hour to set firmly. Now unmould carefully onto a round or square silver dish and decorate the centre of the ring with just the tops of the watercress. Serve with hot toast, lemon, and small glasses of vodka.

MENU 67   Chocolate-Hazelnut Cream *(for 12)*

1 cup shelled hazelnuts
12 ounces semisweet chocolate bits
4 ounces unsweetened chocolate,
cut into small chunks

2 cups light cream
½ cup milk
Dash of salt
8 egg yolks

You will need a blender for this. Into it dump the hazelnuts and run the motor until the nuts are reduced to a powder. Loosen this thoroughly with a rubber spatula or spoon. On the top of it place the semisweet and the unsweetened chocolate pieces. Heat the cream and the milk together, but do not boil, then pour it into the blender. This is the only cooking involved. Add the dash of salt. Now hold the top of the blender in place with your hand and turn the motor to high. When the racket has stopped and the mixture sounds smooth, pour in the 8 egg yolks. Let run for another half minute, then pour into *pots-de-crème* dishes or Champagne glasses. Chill in the refrigerator, but remove 1 hour before serving.

MENU 68   Hot Crabmeat Mornay *(for 12)*

2 pounds lump crab, cooked
⅓ cup brandy
6 tablespoons butter
¼ cup flour
2 cups chicken broth
2 egg yolks
½ cup heavy cream
3 truffles, minced fine
¼ teaspoon nutmeg
½ cup mixed grated Parmesan and Gruyère cheese
Salt and black pepper

Place the crabmeat in a shallow pan; pour the brandy over it. Marinate for 2 hours, stirring frequently. Melt 4 tablespoons of the butter in the top of a large double boiler. When hot and foaming, add the flour; stir in well and cook it without browning for 2 minutes. Remove the pan from the heat and gradually add the broth, stirring until well blended. Cook over low heat, stirring, until it is smooth and thick. Simmer this *velouté* for 20 minutes, stirring occasionally. (If it must wait before being used, butter the surface to prevent a crust from forming.) Beat the egg yolks with the cream and add to the sauce. Bring to a boil again, stirring. Add the truffles, the nutmeg, and the cheese, stirring until the cheese is incorporated in the sauce. Correct the seasoning and add the crabmeat and brandy. Add the remaining butter, stir smooth, and transfer to a chafing dish to serve. If the dish must wait, keep it hot over hot, not boiling, water until time to serve.

MENU 68   Austrian Nockerln *(for 12)*

16 eggs
⅔ cup butter
½ cup sugar
¼ cup flour
Large pinch of salt
2 cups boiling milk
3 teaspoons vanilla

Have all the ingredients at room temperature except the milk. Preheat the oven to medium (350°). Separate the egg yolks from the whites. Cream the butter and sugar together. Beat the yolks until light and thick, and then add the butter and sugar mixture and 3 tablespoons of the flour. Mix well. Add the pinch of salt to the whites and beat until very stiff and nearly dry. Dust with the last tablespoon of flour and add the egg-yolk mixture. Fold together well but gently. Pour 1 cup of the boiling milk, flavoured with the vanilla, into each of 2 deep oval baking dishes. With a very large kitchen spoon take spoonfuls of custard mixture and pile into each dish in three distinct, high mounds. Bake for 5 minutes, or until golden. Serve warm with vanilla sauce.

VANILLA SAUCE

4 cups light cream	½ cup sugar
8 egg yolks	2 teaspoons vanilla extract
Pinch of salt	

Scald the cream in the top part of a double boiler. Beat the egg yolks until light. Add the salt and the sugar. Pour a little of the hot cream into the eggs, stirring briskly, and pour this mixture back into the remaining cream. Cook over just simmering water, stirring all the time with a wooden spoon, until the mixture just coats the spoon. Pour into a bowl. Add vanilla extract. Serve warm with Austrian *Nockerln* or other desserts.

MENU 69   Consommé Stracciatelle *(for 16)*

8 large eggs	1 cup semolina or farina
1½ cups freshly grated Parmesan cheese	16 cups chicken or beef consommé

The consommé should be very strong, well flavoured, and very clear. Place the eggs, freshly grated Parmesan cheese, and semolina or farina in a bowl, add 2 cups consommé, and beat the mixture smooth. Heat the remaining consommé to the boiling point and dribble in the egg mixture, beating together gently. Continue stirring while the soup simmers, for about 4 to 5 minutes. Serve immediately in hot plates or cups.

MENU 69   Burnt Almond Chiffon Pie *(for 16)*

Two 10-inch flaky pastry shells (see page 52)	¾ cup sugar
	Pinch of salt
2½ tablespoons unflavoured gelatine	4 eggs, separated
⅓ cup cold water	3½ cups heavy cream
3 cups milk	4½ teaspoons vanilla extract
	1 cup slivered toasted almonds

Follow the directions for flaky pastry shells (p. 52), but continue to bake the shells for 15 minutes longer in a very hot oven (450°) until they are crisp and golden brown. Cool completely before filling.

Soften the gelatine in the cold water. In the top of a double boiler scald the milk with ¼ cup of the sugar and the pinch of salt; cool slightly. In a bowl beat the egg yolks until very pale, then pour the scalded milk into the bowl, stirring briskly into the yolks. Return mixture to the top of the double boiler, and place over the bottom part containing barely simmering water. Cook over very low heat, stirring until the custard coats the spoon, about 8 to 10 minutes. Remove from the heat, add the gelatine, and stir until dissolved. Cool. Beat the egg whites until very stiff. Whip 2 cups heavy cream with 6 tablespoons sugar. When the custard begins to set, fold in the stiffly beaten egg whites, then the whipped cream and 3 teaspoons vanilla extract. Last, fold in the toasted almonds. Divide the mixture between the two baked pastry shells, and chill until quite set, or for several hours. At serving time, whip the remaining 1½ cups cream, sweeten with the remaining 2 tablespoons sugar, and fold in 1½ teaspoons vanilla extract. Swirl the whipped cream on top of pies.

MENU 70   Lobster Bisque *(for 16)*

Six 1½-pound lobsters
10 tablespoons butter
 2 carrots, diced
 4 celery stalks, diced
 2 large onions, minced
 6 tablespoons brandy
 1 cup dry white wine
16 cups fish stock (see p. 160)

Bouquet garni composed of 1 bay leaf, ¼ teaspoon thyme, 4 parsley sprigs
Salt and freshly ground white pepper
Cayenne pepper
 6 tablespoons raw white rice
 2 cups heavy cream

Cut up the live lobsters and remove sac and vein, or have the fish dealer do it. Do this at the last moment before beginning the preparation so that the lobster can be cooked as soon as possible after it is cut up. Melt the butter and simmer the vegetables until they are soft. Add the lobster pieces and cook for 10 minutes. Add the brandy, white wine, half the stock or broth and the *bouquet garni*. Season with salt, freshly ground white pepper, and a few dashes of cayenne pepper. Simmer for 10 or more minutes. Meanwhile, cook the rice in the remaining broth until very soft. Remove lobster from heat and discard *bouquet garni*. Remove the meat from the shell, dice half the meat very small, and reserve. Put the remaining lobster meat twice through the finest blade of a meat grinder, then purée through a sieve or in a blender with the vegetables, the rice, and the broth. Return this purée to a saucepan; taste for seasoning, add the cream, and heat. Serve very hot in heated cups with some of the reserved diced lobster in each cup.

FISH STOCK

¾ cup butter	4 bay leaves
6 celery stalks, sliced	12 peppercorns
6 carrots, sliced	2 tablespoons salt
4 medium onions, chopped	½ teaspoon dried thyme
5 to 6 pounds raw fish carcasses or bones	½ teaspoon dried tarragon
	4 cups dry white wine
8 parsley sprigs	14 cups water

In a large kettle melt the butter and add the vegetables. Simmer until the vegetables are soft. Coarsely chop the fish carcasses or bones and add them to the vegetables. Or use 1 to 2 pounds fish in place of part of the bones to obtain a richer stock. Simmer for 10 minutes longer without browning the mixture. Add the herbs and spices and pour in the wine and water. Stir well, cover, and simmer gently for 30 to 40 minutes. Strain the stock through a cloth-lined sieve. Make this stock a day ahead and store it overnight in the refrigerator. The fat will rise to the surface and can easily be removed. Makes about 16 cups of stock.

MENU 70   Roast Veal with Mushrooms, en Croûte *(for 16)*

Two 6-pound loins of veal, rolled and tied	3 celery stalks, chopped
	1 cup dry white wine
4 teaspoons salt	2 pounds mushrooms, minced
1 teaspoon mace	½ cup chopped parsley
1½ teaspoons black pepper	Flaky pastry (see below)
1 cup butter	2 egg yolks
1½ cups chopped shallots or onions	2 cups beef bouillon
3 carrots, chopped	

Preheat the oven to very hot (425°). Wipe the meat carefully. Mix 3 teaspoons of the salt, the mace, 1 teaspoon of the pepper, and ½ cup of the butter and spread on the meat. Place in a large well-buttered roasting pan or two smaller ones. Surround each roast with ½ cup shallots and half the carrots and celery. Roast for 30 minutes in the very hot oven. Reduce the heat to medium (350°), add the wine, and continue roasting for 1½ hours, basting the meat with the pan juices. Turn meat over midway through the roasting period. Remove from the oven, and cool the meat until the surface is barely warm to the touch. While the meat cools, sauté the remaining ½ cup shallots in the remaining butter; after 3 minutes add the mushrooms and sauté until all liquid has evaporated. Season with the remaining salt and pepper, add the parsley, and cool.

Raise the oven heat to very hot (425°) again. Divide the pastry in two and roll out each half into a more or less square shape, about ¼ inch thick. Place half the cooked mushroom mixture on each square of the pastry, then put the meat on the pastry, top side down, and wrap it with the mushrooms next to the meat, sealing the pastry edges with a little water. Now turn the pastry-covered meat over onto baking sheets, so the sealed edges are underneath. Put a plain wide pastry tube, buttered, into the centre. Make a few holes over the surface of the pastry with a fork. Beat the egg yolks with 2 teaspoons cold water and paint the surface with the mixture, with a pastry brush. Bake for 35 to 40 minutes, or until golden. Meanwhile, deglaze the roasting pans with the broth and simmer for 5 to 6 minutes. Strain this sauce and keep hot. At serving time, pour a little of the sauce into the crust through the pastry tube; then remove the tube. Place the veal *en croûte* on platters. Display this beautiful dish to the guests, then slice for serving and serve the remaining sauce separately.

FLAKY PASTRY

5 cups sifted flour	2 cups butter
2 teaspoons salt	6 to 10 tablespoons cold water

Resift the flour with the salt into a large bowl. With the finger tips quickly work the butter into the flour until the mixture looks like coarse corn meal. Add just enough cold water to have a soft pliable pastry that holds together in a ball. This might be 6 to 8 or even more tablespoons of water, depending on the absorbing quality of the flour. Chill until needed.

MENU 71   Fillet of Sole in Chablis Sauce *(for 16)*

16 fillets of sole	1 lemon, grated rind and juice
1 cup butter	1 pound mushrooms, sliced
2 teaspoons salt	1 garlic clove, minced (optional)
½ teaspoon white pepper	½ cup chopped parsley
3 sprinklings of cayenne pepper	4 cups Chablis wine, or other dry
6 shallots, minced	white wine
1 medium onion, sliced	

Preheat oven to hot (400°). Butter generously two wide shallow oven dishes. Double the sole fillets to half their length and arrange them in the dishes, overlapping slightly. Dot well with ¾ cup of the butter, and sprinkle with salt, white pepper, and cayenne pepper. Add the shallots and onion, lemon juice and rind, and cover with the sliced mushrooms. Add the minced garlic, if used, and half the parsley. Add the Chablis, or a good dry white wine, or Champagne. Cover with a piece of buttered wax paper and bake for 20 to 25 minutes, or until the fish is opaque and flakes at the touch of a fork. Do not overcook. Transfer the fillets to serving platters and keep warm. Combine remaining contents of the two baking dishes and reduce over high heat by a third. Swirl in remaining ¼ cup butter, pour over the fish, sprinkle with remaining parsley, and serve immediately.

MENU 71   Roast Goose with Peaches *(for 16)*

1 pound dried peaches	⅔ cup pine nuts
1 cup tawney Port wine	2 teaspoons dried sage
2 cups cracked wheat	Salt and black pepper
4 cups cold water	2½ cups beef bouillon
Two 10-pound geese	30 canned Elberta peach halves
1 cup butter	¼ cup Cognac
4 medium onions, chopped	¼ cup orange liqueur
4 celery stalks, chopped	

Soak the dried peaches overnight in the Port wine. Drain, reserving any Port wine that is not absorbed. Soak the cracked wheat in 4 cups cold water for 2 hours, until well expanded, and drain. Singe the geese with great care, and wipe inside and out. Melt ½ cup of the butter in a large frying pan and cook the onions and the celery until tender and slightly golden. Remove from the heat and add the soaked and drained cracked wheat and peaches, the pine nuts, sage, a little salt, and a generous amount of pepper. Season the inside of each goose with salt and pepper, and stuff the geese with the cracked-wheat stuffing. Tie the legs and close the opening by sewing, or cover it with foil. Prick the birds all over with a fork. Place the birds on racks in a large roasting pan, or two smaller pans, and roast in a hot oven (400°) for 30 minutes. Lower the heat to medium (350°) and pour off all the fat in the pan. Pour 1 cup bouillon and some of the reserved Port wine from the peaches over each bird. Continue roasting for 1½ hours, basting every 15 minutes. Test bird by wiggling leg: if it moves easily, bird is done. Place the birds on hot platters and cover with foil to keep warm. Pour off all fat from the pans and discard; deglaze the pans with remaining ½ cup bouillon, strain, and keep hot. Melt remaining butter in a separate pan and sauté the peach halves until heated through. Carve the birds, arrange on platters, and arrange the sautéed peach halves around the meat. Keep warm. Add strained broth from the roasting pan to the butter and juices in the sauté pan, heat to blend, and pour over the goose. There will be only a small amount of this buttery sauce. Heat Cognac and orange liqueur, pour over the peaches, ignite, and serve flaming.

MENU 71   Baked Zucchini (for 16)

8 large zucchini squash
1 cup butter
2 small onions, minced
1 pound mushrooms, minced

Salt and freshly ground black pepper
1 cup bread crumbs
1 garlic clove, minced
1 cup grated Gruyère cheese

Wash and scrub zucchini. Remove stem ends and blossom ends. Cut in half crosswise. Place in boiling salted water to cover and boil for 5 minutes. Remove and drain well. Cool a little for easy handling. Cut each half in two lengthwise. Scoop out seeds and reserve. Melt half the butter and sauté the onions for 2 minutes. Add the minced mushrooms and sauté for 8 minutes, adding more butter if needed. Season with salt and freshly ground pepper. Remove from the heat and add the bread crumbs and the minced garlic. Add half the cheese and the zucchini seeds. Mix well and use to stuff zucchini shells. Put the zucchini into well-buttered baking dishes, sprinkle with remaining cheese, and dot with remaining butter. Bake in a preheated hot oven (400°) for about 20 minutes, or until golden. Transfer to serving platters and serve hot.

MENU 71   Coffee Walnut Roll (for 16)

10 eggs, separated
2⅓ cups fine granulated sugar
½ cup ground walnuts
⅓ cup powdered coffee
2 tablespoons flour

⅛ teaspoon salt
Powdered sugar
3 cups heavy cream, whipped
1 tablespoon vanilla
2 tablespoons Cognac

Preheat the oven to medium (375°). Butter two 10- by 15-inch jelly-roll pans. Spread wax paper in the pans and butter the paper. Beat the egg yolks with

1½ cups sugar until thick and pale. Mix walnuts, coffee, and flour. Stir gently into eggs and sugar. Add salt to the egg whites and whip until they form soft peaks. Add ½ cup sugar and beat until stiff but not dry. Gently fold the whites into the yolks. Pour into the prepared pans, spread batter evenly, and bake for 15 minutes, or until edges brown and shrink slightly. Invert on a cloth sprinkled with powdered sugar. Peel off the wax paper and roll up the cake on its length. Cool, covered with the cloth. Mix the whipped cream with the vanilla, remaining sugar, and Cognac. When cool, unroll the cake, spread with the filling, and roll up. Trim uneven ends and sprinkle with additional powdered sugar.

MENU 72   Tomato and Dill Soup *(for 18)*

½ cup vegetable oil
¼ cup butter
5 medium onions, finely chopped
1 garlic clove, pierced by a wooden toothpick
14 firm medium tomatoes
4 heaping tablespoons tomato paste

½ cup potato flour, or wheat flour
12 cups chicken broth
4 cups light cream
Salt and freshly ground white pepper
¾ cup chopped fresh dill

Heat the oil and butter in a 24-cup saucepan. Add the onion and garlic and cook slowly without browning. Chop the tomatoes with their skins on, and when the onions are transparent, in about 10 minutes, add the tomatoes to them. Cook them quickly for 4 to 5 minutes, stirring to turn them over in the butter and oil. Remove from the heat and discard the garlic clove. Add tomato paste and flour and stir smooth; add the broth little by little. Replace over low heat and cook slowly, stirring, until thickened and smooth. Simmer gently for 5 minutes. Rub through a fine sieve, or put through a blender and then through a fine sieve, so as to remove the seeds and skins. Add the cream and salt and freshly ground pepper to taste. Last, stir in ½ cup of the dill and chill the soup for several hours. Serve in chilled cups with the remaining dill sprinkled on top. This soup may also be served hot.

MENU 72   Crown Roasts of Lamb with Barley Pilaff *(for 18)*

Four 12-rib crown roasts of lamb
Salt and freshly ground black pepper

Barley pilaff (see below)

Have the butcher prepare four crown roasts, made from rib chops, that have been trimmed of all fat, so the bones look like Frenched lamb chops. Cover the bone tips with foil to prevent charring. Preheat the oven to very hot (450°). Place meat in roasting pans, season with salt and pepper, and roast for 15 minutes. Lower the heat to medium (350°) and continue roasting for 45 minutes for rare lamb, up to 1 hour or more for well done, depending on the size of the chops. The usual portion is two ribs per person. When the meat is done, place the roasts on platters and fill the centre with barley pilaff. Place ruffled paper frills on the bone tips and serve immediately.

BARLEY PILAFF

1 cup butter	1 teaspoon freshly ground black
1½ cups chopped shallots or onions	pepper
6 cups pearl barley	1 cup chopped parsley
12 cups light beef bouillon	

Melt the butter in a 24-cup saucepan and gently stew the shallots. Add the barley and the broth heated to the boiling point. Grind the black pepper into the pot. Stir well, cover, and bring to a boil. Lower the heat so the broth just simmers and cook for 50 minutes to 1 hour, or until barley is tender to taste and liquid is absorbed. Add water if broth cooks away too fast. Taste the pilaff and add salt and additional pepper, if necessary. If the broth is well seasoned, salt may not be needed. Toss with chopped parsley. Use to fill racks of lamb or to serve with other meats.

MENU 72   Tarte Tatin (for 18)

4½ cups sifted flour	½ cup grated blanched almonds
4¾ cups sugar	6 pounds firm green apples,
1½ teaspoons salt	peeled, cored, and divided into
3 egg yolks	eighths
3 cups sweet butter	4 pounds firm pears, peeled, cored,
⅔ cup vegetable shortening	and divided into eighths
2 tablespoons grated lemon rind	1 cup sliced blanched almonds

Resift flour with 3 tablespoons sugar and the salt into a large cool bowl. Make a well in the flour and put in the egg yolks, half the butter cut up, the vegetable shortening, lemon rind, and grated almonds. With the tips of the fingers quickly work the flour into the butter and yolks, bit by bit, until smooth dough is obtained. If necessary, add a little ice water, the least amount necessary, to form a ball of the dough. Chill well for 2 hours.

Spread a good ¼ inch of butter in three 12-inch heatproof glass pie plates (glass so you can see what is going on when fruit cooks). Pour ½ cup sugar evenly over the butter in each pie plate. Mix the fruit with the remaining 3 cups sugar and divide among the buttered and sugared pie plates, dotting with remaining butter as you pile. Preheat oven to very hot (450°). Divide and roll out the pastry in 3 large rounds. Cover the fruit so the pastry overlaps the rim of the plate by a half inch. Press loosely to the side of the plate. Bake for 20 minutes, then reduce heat to medium (350°). Continue to bake until apples look done. Slip a thin knife under the pastry and test. If there is a lot of juice, place pie plates on an asbestos mat on top of the stove and reduce the juice over low heat. Cool a little. Place platters gently over the pastry and invert to remove tarts. Sprinkle with the sliced almonds and serve warm.

MENU 73   Consommé with Okra *(for 18)*

20 okra pods	Salt and black pepper
16 cups strong beef consommé	1 cup Sherry, or to taste

Slice the okra pods, discarding ends. Simmer pods in boiling salted water to cover, for about 25 minutes; drain. Bring the beef consommé to a boil, add the okra, and simmer for a minute or two. Season with salt and pepper to taste. Add the Sherry and serve.

MENU 73   Roast Duckling with Cherries *(for 18)*

Eight 3- to 4-pound ducklings	2 cups tawney Port wine, or more
Salt and black pepper	3 cups light beef bouillon
2 large onions, quartered	3 tablespoons cornstarch
8 celery tops with leaves	Two 1-pound cans sour cherries,
2 large apples, quartered	drained
8 teaspoons butter	

Preheat the oven to hot (400°). Wipe the ducks dry. Prick the skin all over with a fork so that fat will run out while cooking. Rub the inside of each duck with salt and pepper. Place a piece of onion, a celery stalk, and a section of apple in each duck and add about 1 teaspoon butter to each. Place the ducks on racks in roasting pans and roast for 30 minutes. Pour off the fat from the pans and discard. Divide 1½ cups of Port wine among the pans, and season the outside of the ducks with salt and pepper. Reduce the oven heat to medium (350°) and roast the ducks for about 2 hours more, basting frequently with the wine. Remove the ducks from the pans, letting the juices from inside the ducks run into the pans. Carve the ducks, arrange on platters, and keep warm.

Skim the fat from the pans. Add the bouillon to the remaining juices and heat on top of the stove, stirring with a spoon to deglaze the pans. Strain the pan liquid into a saucepan. Add a little cold water to the cornstarch in a cup, stirring until smooth. Add a little of the hot bouillon to the cup, then stir cornstarch mixture slowly into the bouillon in the saucepan, stirring until smooth and thickened. Add the drained cherries and the remaining ½ cup of Port wine, or more to taste, to make the finished sauce, and heat through. Serve over and around the carved duck.

MENU 73   Baked Hominy Grits *(for 18)*

11 cups water	3 eggs
1 tablespoon salt	7 tablespoons butter
3 cups hominy grits	

Bring the water and the salt to a boil. Sprinkle the hominy into the water, stirring all the time. When the grits are all moistened and well mixed with the water, reduce the heat and simmer, stirring often, for 25 to 30 minutes, or until hominy is too thick to stir easily. Butter two large and deep oven dishes. Add the eggs to the hominy one by one, whipping well with a spoon after each addition. Add the butter. Taste for seasoning and add additional salt, if needed. Pour the hominy into the buttered dishes and bake in a preheated medium oven (375°) for 25 minutes, or until slightly puffed and golden. Serve hot.

MENU 73   Praline Bavarian Cream with Strawberries *(for 18)*

3 cups light cream	3 cups heavy cream
2-inch piece of vanilla bean	Praline powder (see below)
8 egg yolks	3 quarts whole strawberries with long stems
1 cup sugar	Powdered sugar
2 tablespoons unflavoured gelatine	
⅓ cup cold water	

Scald the light cream with vanilla bean. Beat the egg yolks and sugar together until very light. Pour the scalded cream into the egg-yolk mixture, stirring constantly. Pour mixture back into the top of a large double boiler and cook over barely simmering water, stirring, until the custard coats the spoon. Lift out the vanilla bean and scrape the seeds into the custard. Soften the gelatine in the water, then dissolve it in the hot custard. Cool the custard.

Whip the heavy cream very stiff. Fold the whipped cream and the praline powder into the cooled custard. Pour into two 6-cup moulds, preferably ring moulds, that have been rinsed in cold water, and chill for several hours or overnight. At serving time unmould onto large platters and fill and surround the Bavarian creams with the well-washed unhulled strawberries, well-sprinkled with powdered sugar.

PRALINE POWDER

1 cup chopped unbleached almonds	½ cup sugar

Bring the unblanched almonds and the sugar to a boil, stirring constantly, and continue cooking, until the sugar turns a deep gold. Pour onto a well-greased marble slab or into a well-buttered large shallow heatproof dish. Cool. When quite cold, break up the praline and reduce to a powder by pounding in a mortar or by wrapping in a firm cloth and crushing with a rolling pin.

MENU 74   Purée Saint-Germain *(for 20)*

½ cup butter	8 cups shelled fresh peas, or de-frosted frozen peas
3 large leeks, white part only, chopped	2 teaspoons dried chervil
2 large onions, chopped	1 teaspoon sugar
2 heads Boston lettuce, shredded	Salt and black pepper
3 large Idaho potatoes, peeled and sliced thin	3 cups light cream
10 cups chicken broth	1 cup heavy cream

Melt the butter in a 32-cup soup kettle. Add the leeks, onions, and the lettuce. Simmer in the butter until soft without browning, about 10 minutes. Add the potatoes and 4 cups of the chicken broth. Simmer for 20 minutes, add the peas and chervil, and remaining broth. Bring to a boil and simmer until the peas are just done and tender, 15 to 20 minutes if using fresh peas, about 5 minutes if using frozen peas. Purée the soup through a fine sieve or in a blender. Return to the washed saucepan and season with the sugar and with salt and pepper to taste. If the soup is very thick, add a little more chicken broth, stirring to blend well. Add the light cream and heat to the boiling point, stirring a little. Whip the heavy cream and stir in a little salt. Serve the soup in hot plates and float a heaping tablespoon of whipped cream on each serving.

MENU 74   Coq au Vin *(for 20)*

Six 3-pound chickens, disjointed as for frying

2 cups butter

½ pound salt pork, cut into 1-inch strips

1 cup Armagnac or Cognac

Bouquet garni composed of 4 garlic cloves, 2 bay leaves, 2 thyme sprigs, 12 parsley sprigs, and 6 peppercorns, tied in 2 cheesecloth bags

7 cups red wine

½ cup olive oil

40 little white onions

2 pounds mushrooms

Salt and black pepper

½ cup flour

Beef bouillon if needed

½ cup chopped parsley

Wipe the chicken pieces carefully. Melt ½ cup butter in each of two 12-cup heatproof casseroles. Divide the cut-up salt pork between the two casseroles and brown. Remove the pork with a slotted spoon and reserve. Brown the chicken in the casseroles over medium heat, turning to brown on all sides, and adding additional butter or oil if needed. Heat the Armagnac or Cognac and pour ½ cup over the chicken pieces in each casserole. Ignite it and let it burn out. Add a *bouquet garni* and part of the diced cooked pork to each casserole, pour the wine over the chicken, cover and simmer for 25 minutes, or until tender.

In a separate pan heat the oil and gently brown the peeled onions, side by side, shaking the pan and turning to cook evenly. This will take about 20 minutes. Meanwhile, sauté the mushrooms in ½ cup butter, whole if they are button mushrooms, quartered if they are large. Season with salt and pepper, and add to the chicken. Add the little browned onions. Season the cooking liquid to taste and simmer, uncovered, for at least 5 minutes. Remove chicken pieces, onions, mushrooms, and salt pork to serving platters or casseroles.

Make some *beurre manié* by creaming ½ cup butter with the flour until it is a smooth paste. Discard the *bouquets garnis* and strain the sauce from both casseroles into a large saucepan. Add *beurre manié* slowly to the wine sauce, stirring to blend. If sauce needs stretching, add a little bouillon. Simmer, stirring, until smooth and thickened, about 5 minutes. Pour the sauce over the birds and sprinkle them with chopped parsley.

MENU 75   Shrimp in Sauce Piquante *(for 20)*

6 large shrimp per person, cooked
  and cleaned
6 cups mayonnaise
1 cup hot catsup, or more to taste
3 limes, juice only
7½-ounce jar sour gherkins,
  chopped

2 tablespoons chopped capers
½ cup Scotch whisky
½ cup chopped chives
½ cup sour cream
  Salt and black pepper
  Cayenne pepper
3 heads chicory

Depending on the size of the shrimp, you will need 7 to 10 pounds shrimp. Mix all the sauce ingredients in a large bowl; season with salt and pepper and a few dashes of cayenne pepper to taste. Fold in the shrimp. Separate the chicory, reserving the green outer leaves for another use. Put the little white leaves on plates, or in shrimp cocktail glasses, and arrange the sauced shrimp on the chicory.

MENU 75   Sauté of Chicken Breasts on
Cracked Wheat Pilaff *(for 20)*

10 large double chicken breasts
  Flour for dredging
  Salt and black pepper
2 cups butter

1½ cups beef bouillon
⅔ cup Cognac
  Cracked wheat pilaff
  (see below)

Cut away the bones from the chicken breasts. Dry well and dredge with flour seasoned with salt and pepper. Shake off any excess flour. Melt 1 cup butter in a large skillet and sauté the chicken breasts in batches, over high heat, turning to brown evenly on all sides. Melt the remaining 1 cup butter, but do not heat, and divide it between two other large pans. As the chicken breasts brown, put them into the buttered pans in a single layer. Deglaze the skillet with the bouillon, stirring well to melt all the brown residue into a little clear sauce. Add Cognac, and divide the sauce between the pans of chicken. Cover the pans tightly, using foil if the pans do not have covers. Reduce the heat and continue cooking until tender, about 15 to 20 minutes. Remove the lids, increase heat a little, and cook for 5 minutes more, turning the chicken until it is brown and crisp. Serve on a bed of wheat pilaff with any remaining sauce poured over.

CRACKED WHEAT PILAFF

6 cups cracked wheat
1 cup butter
1½ cups chopped onion
12 cups light beef bouillon

Salt and black pepper
1 cup pine nuts
½ cup chopped parsley

Soak the wheat in cold water for 1 hour. Melt ½ cup butter in a 16-cup saucepan and cook the onion until transparent. Drain the wheat very well, add to the onion, and cook for a minute or two. Bring the beef bouillon to a boil and add to the wheat and onion. Stir once, cover, and bring to a boil. Lower the heat and simmer for 15 minutes, or until the wheat is tender and the bouillon absorbed. If needed, add more bouillon to finish cooking. Season with salt and pepper. Sauté the pine nuts in the remaining ½ cup butter. Add to the wheat along with the chopped parsley and toss together.

MENU 75   Cognac Cream on Toasted Spongecake *(for 20)*

10 eggs, separated
1½ cups confectioners' sugar
¾ cup Cognac
3 cups heavy cream
2 tablespoons unflavoured gelatine

2 tablespoons cold water
2 tablespoons hot water
20 slices spongecake, lightly toasted
Garnish of candied fruit, slivered almonds, or pistachio nuts

Separate eggs. Beat egg whites until very stiff. Beat egg yolks with sugar until sugar dissolves, then add Cognac, and beat again to mix thoroughly. Beat the cream until stiff enough to hold the print of a fork. Sprinkle the gelatine over 2 tablespoons cold water in a cup; add 2 tablespoons hot water; stir until the gelatine has dissolved, then add to the egg-yolk mixture. Add the whipped cream to the egg-yolk mixture, and finally fold in the beaten egg whites very gently. Chill in the refrigerator for several hours until set. To serve, spoon over slices of toasted spongecake on individual plates. Garnish each serving with candied fruit, slivered almonds, or pistachio nuts.

MENU 76   Cold Borscht *(for 20)*

16 cups strong beef bouillon
1 large onion, sliced
8 cups julienned raw beets, about 4 pounds
5 cups water
  Salt and black pepper

2 tablespoons sugar, or more to taste
3 lemons, juice only, or 4 tablespoons red-wine vinegar
1 cup chopped dill
20 thin lemon slices

Bring beef bouillon to a boil with the sliced onion in a saucepan. Simmer until the onion is soft, then discard onion. Meanwhile, in a separate pan, boil the sliced beets in the water for about 20 minutes. Do not overcook or they will lose their colour. Drain and combine with the bouillon. Season with salt, a generous amount of pepper, the sugar, and the lemon juice or vinegar, the last added gradually until a slight sweet and sour taste is achieved. This may require more sugar. Heat to the boiling point, then remove from the heat and cool. Chill in the refrigerator for 2 hours. Serve with a good sprinkling of chopped dill and a slice of lemon in each soup plate; this can also be served hot.

MENU 76   Braised Young Turkeys in Champagne *(for 20)*

3 cups Champagne, or dry white wine
1 cup butter
  Two 10-pound turkeys, trussed and wiped dry
  Salt and black pepper
2 small carrots, chopped
1 large onion, chopped

6 shallots or 1 more onion, chopped
3 celery stalks, chopped
2 cups beef bouillon
½ cup Cognac
1½ cups heavy cream
8 black truffles, minced

Preheat the oven to medium (350°). Simmer the Champagne to reduce to 2½ cups. Melt the butter in two very large frying pans, large enough to brown the turkeys. Brown the birds well on all sides. Season them with salt and pepper, inside and out, and transfer them to well-buttered roasting pans with covers. Arrange the vegetables around them. Pour any butter in the frying pans over the vegetables, or, if necessary, add more, enough so the vegetables do not burn. Place in the oven and roast, covered, for 30 minutes. Add the Champagne and continue roasting for 1½ hours, basting every 15 minutes. Uncover and continue roasting for another 45 minutes, test birds for doneness by moving a leg. If it moves freely, the birds are done. Remove turkeys to hot platters and keep warm under foil.

Place roasting pans on the stove over medium heat. Add bouillon and simmer for 10 minutes, scraping up any brown residue left in the pan. Strain into a saucepan, add Cognac and cream, and heat to the boiling point. Add the minced truffles and any liquor in the cans, to make sauce. Carve the birds and arrange on the serving platters. Pour a little sauce over them, and serve the remainder in heated sauceboats.

MENU 76   Purée of Chestnuts (for 20)

5 pounds chestnuts in shells
¼ cup olive oil
6 cups light beef bouillon
⅔ cup butter

Salt and freshly ground black pepper
¾ cup heavy cream, approximately

Preheat the oven to medium (350°). Make cuts in the shape of a cross on the flat side of each chestnut, and place the nuts in a large shallow pan with the oil. The nuts will be coated with a thin film of oil as they are shaken in the pan. Roast them in the oven for 20 to 25 minutes, or until all the shells have curled open around the cuts. Remove the shells and skins. If the skins are difficult to remove, put the chestnuts into a large pot of cold water and bring to a boil. Let them boil for 1 minute and then cool them in the water. Skin the nuts as soon as they are cool enough to handle. It does not matter if the chestnuts break. Put the shelled and skinned nuts in a large saucepan with the beef bouillon, adding water to cover if necessary. Simmer until the chestnuts are very tender. Mash them and put them through a fine strainer, using just enough of the liquid in which they were cooked to make chestnuts smooth. Add the butter, a little salt to taste, and a lot of freshly ground black pepper. Add the cream gradually. Do not let the purée become too liquid. Heat, stirring with a wooden spoon, and serve immediately.

MENU 77   Oysters Rockefeller
(for 24; 6 oysters per serving)

12 dozen oysters	1 cup minced parsley
Rock salt	1 cup Pernod
2 cups butter	2 cups bread crumbs
1½ cups minced shallots or scallions	Salt, black pepper, cayenne
1 cup minced celery	pepper
3 cups finely chopped raw spinach	

Have the fish dealer open the oysters, discarding the flat side of the shell, but retaining each oyster in its curved shell. Fill ovenproof pie plates or shallow pans with rock salt. Place the oysters in their shells on these beds of salt. Melt 1 cup butter in a saucepan and cook the shallots and the celery without browning. Add the spinach and parsley and turn them in the hot butter until they are wilted but still bright green. Remove from the heat and add the remaining 1 cup butter, the Pernod, and the bread crumbs, and season to taste with salt, black pepper, and cayenne pepper. Purée the sauce in a blender and divide it among the oysters. Place the salt-filled pans containing the oysters in a preheated hot oven (450°) and bake until bubbly, about 6 minutes. Serve immediately.

MENU 77   Pheasant en Casserole *(for 24)*

1 cup butter	3 celery stalks with leaves,
½ cup olive oil	chopped
8 pheasants, cut in quarters	2 large bay leaves, crumbled
1½ cups chopped shallots or onions	2½ cups white wine
2 large garlic cloves, minced	1 cup beef bouillon
Salt and freshly ground black	2 cups heavy cream
pepper	½ cup Cognac
	½ cup minced chives

Melt the butter and oil in 2 or more large casseroles with lids, dividing the butter and oil evenly between them. (A little oil prevents the butter from burning.) When the fat is hot, brown the well-dried and quartered birds, turning them to brown evenly on all sides. At the last turn, divide the shallots between the casseroles and brown. The whole browning procedure should take about 20 minutes or more. Add the garlic, and season with salt and some fresh grindings of whole black pepper. Add half the chopped celery and a crumbled bay leaf to each casserole, pour the wine over the birds, and cover. Simmer slowly for about 25 minutes; add a little beef bouillon if the pheasant becomes too dry, but do not let the birds swim in liquid. Test for doneness by pricking with a fork in the leg joint of the bird; if the juice is pink, let the birds cook for a few minutes longer. Remove the pheasant pieces to a heated serving platter. Reduce the liquid in the casseroles a little. Add the cream, then the Cognac, and bring to a boil, stirring loose all the browned pieces in the bottoms of the pans. Add the chopped chives and pour the sauce over the birds. Or arrange birds in clean casseroles, pour the sauce over them, and serve in the casseroles.

MENU 77   Brown Rice Ring with
Baby Brussels Sprouts *(for 24)*

2½ cups butter	Black pepper
3 large onions, chopped	12 cups boiling beef bouillon
6 celery stalks, chopped fine	8 pints baby Brussels sprouts
6 cups raw rice	Salt
1 tablespoon sweet paprika	

Divide 1 cup butter between two 16-cup saucepans. Put half the onions and celery into each saucepan and simmer until golden and cooked through. Add 3 cups rice to each saucepan, and add more butter if the vegetables have absorbed it all. Brown the rice very well, stirring all the time to prevent scorching. Stir in the paprika and some pepper. When well browned, in about 10 minutes, pour 6 cups boiling bouillon into each pot of rice, stir once thoroughly, and bring to a boil again. Lower the heat and simmer, uncovered, until tender, about 15 minutes. Add more bouillon if needed but all the moisture must be absorbed. Butter three 8-cup ring moulds and pack with the rice. Keep hot in a low oven (300°). Meantime, boil the Brussels sprouts in salted water for 10 minutes, or until just tender. Brown the remaining 1½ cups butter and pour over the Brussels sprouts. Unmould the rice at serving time and fill the rings with the sprouts and brown butter.

MENU 78   Egg and Caviar Mousse *(for 24)*

5 tablespoons unflavoured gelatine
1 cup cold water
24 large eggs, hard boiled
2 medium onions, grated
5 cups mayonnaise

10 ounces black caviar
3 tablespoons Worcestershire
  sauce, more or less to taste
Freshly ground black pepper
2 cups heavy cream, whipped

Soften the gelatine in the cold water and dissolve it in the top of a double boiler. Cool. Put the eggs through a fine strainer and combine with all the remaining ingredients, except the whipped cream, adding Worcestershire to taste. Salt will not be needed, as even the very best caviar has a little, and the mayonnaise will be salty, too. Add the cooled gelatine and fold in the well-whipped cream. Rinse two 8-cup moulds in cold water and divide the mixture between them. Unmould at serving time. The mousse may be served surrounded by cherry tomatoes. A nice accompaniment is very thin rye-bread sandwiches made with sweet butter.

MENU 78   Flaming Ginger Pancakes *(for 24)*

4 cups twice-sifted flour
¼ cup sugar
⅛ teaspoon salt
8 whole eggs
4 egg yolks

6 cups milk
½ cup browned butter
⅓ cup Cognac
1 cup clarified butter
Ginger pastry cream (see below)

Sift the flour and measure, resift with sugar and salt, place in a bowl and make a well in the centre of the flour. Put the whole eggs and the extra yolks in the well and mix thoroughly. Gradually add small amounts of milk, mixing till smooth, then add the rest of the milk. The mixture should be shiny. Add the cooled butter which has been browned lightly, not burnt. More milk may be added, as the batter should have the consistency of thick cream. Add the Cognac and allow to rest for 2 hours before cooking.

Heat a 5-inch French crêpe pan until a drop of water sizzles when dropped on it. Put a teaspoon of clarified butter in the pan and immediately add a scant kitchen spoonful (about 1½ tablespoons) of crêpe batter, tilting the pan so the batter spreads evenly and quickly over the bottom of the pan. Cook, shaking the pan over the heat until crêpe is golden, about 1 minute. Turn crêpe over, adding a little butter, and cook 30 seconds. Always have the pan very hot, and use just enough batter to make very thin crêpes. Stack pancakes one on top of the other. This mixture will make 60 to 70 pancakes, depending on the size of the eggs, and the size of the pan. Pancakes may be made ahead of time. (They may even be made days ahead and frozen, to be defrosted, filled and heated at serving time.)

GINGER PASTRY CREAM

4½ cups milk	12 egg yolks
Few grains of salt	¾ cup butter
2-inch piece vanilla bean or 1 tablespoon vanilla extract	3 14-ounce jars minced preserved ginger
1½ cups sugar	¾ cup Cognac or more
¾ cup flour	2 cups orange juice

Scald the milk with the salt and vanilla bean. Place the sugar, flour, and egg yolks in a saucepan and work together until well blended, smooth and light in colour. Remove vanilla pod and scrape the seeds into the milk. Gradually add the scalded milk to the sugar and egg mixture, working smooth and stirring all the time. Cook over a low flame until it boils. If not using the vanilla bean, flavour with 1 tablespoon vanilla extract and stir in ½ cup butter. Dot the surface with butter to prevent a crust from forming. Mince half the ginger and add (without the syrup) to the custard. Add 3 tablespoons or more of Cognac. Fill pancakes with this mixture, roll into cylinders, and heat in a buttered chafing dish. Chop the remaining ginger, mix with the ginger syrup and orange juice. Heat and pour the hot ginger syrup over the pancakes, then add the remaining Cognac, warmed, and light it. Serve flaming.

MENU 79   Lobster Bordelaise *(for 24)*

2 cups butter	1 teaspoon dried tarragon
⅓ cup olive oil	Twelve 2-pound live lobsters, cut in chunks with claws cracked
2 large onions, chopped	
4 large carrots, chopped fine	⅔ cup Cognac
6 shallots, chopped	4 cups dry white wine
6 celery stalks, chopped fine	Two 6-ounce cans tomato paste
1 teaspoon salt	3 cups fish stock (see page 160) or clam juice
½ teaspoon black pepper	
2 bay leaves	Cayenne pepper
1 teaspoon dried thyme	1 cup chopped parsley

In each of two large frying pans, melt ½ cup of the butter and half of the olive oil. When hot, add chopped onions, carrots, shallots, celery, 1 teaspoon salt, ½ teaspoon pepper, bay leaves, thyme, and tarragon. Simmer over low heat, stirring occasionally, for about 25 minutes. Add ¼ cup more butter to each pan of vegetables and add the lobster. Sauté until the shells turn red. Remove from the heat, pour Cognac over the lobsters, and ignite. When the flaming Cognac dies down, add the wine and simmer for a few minutes. Add tomato paste and fish stock. Stir well, cover, and simmer for 10 to 15 minutes. Transfer the lobster to serving dishes.

Correct the seasoning of the sauce, add cayenne, and bring to a boil. Remove from the heat, add remaining ½ cup of butter, and stir in. Strain the sauce over the lobster and sprinkle with parsley.

MENU 79   Roast Loin of Young Veal with Tarragon Sauce (for 24)

Two 6-pound leg of veal roasts	2 large onions, chopped
8 veal kidneys	1½ cups white wine
1½ cups butter	3 cups beef bouillon
1½ teaspoons black pepper	1½ cups heavy cream
2 teaspoons sage	2 tablespoons chopped fresh tarragon
2 teaspoons mace	
1 teaspoon dried thyme	Braised chestnuts
2 tablespoons salt	Glazed onions
4 carrots, sliced	Chopped parsley
4 celery stalks, chopped	

Have butcher bone the veal roasts and roll them around the veal kidneys, using 4 kidneys for each roast.

Preheat the oven to medium (350°). Wipe the meat carefully, then spread with a mixture of 1 cup butter, the pepper, sage, mace, thyme, and salt. Spread remaining ½ cup butter in a large roasting pan (or two smaller pans), and place the roasts in it. Arrange the prepared vegetables around the meat, pour on the wine, and roast for about 3 hours, basting frequently, or until the juices run clear when the meat is pricked deep with a fork. Remove the meat and keep warm.

Pour bouillon into the roasting pan. Deglaze and loosen all little brown particles. Simmer for 5 minutes. Strain into a saucepan. Spoon off most of the fat. Add the cream and tarragon and simmer for a few minutes to complete the sauce.

Slice the meat and arrange braised chestnuts and glazed onions around it. Sprinkle with parsley. Serve the sauce separately.

MENU 79   Raspberries Frangipane *(for 24)*

15 egg yolks
 1 cup sugar
⅛ teaspoon salt
⅔ cup flour
 8 cups milk
   Three 2-inch pieces of vanilla
   bean

½ cup butter
24 macaroons, crumbled
10 pints fresh raspberries
 4 cups heavy cream
½ cup Kirsch

In a large bowl beat the egg yolks, ⅔ cup of the sugar, and the salt with a French whisk until light. Whisk in the flour. Meanwhile, scald the milk with vanilla bean. Pour the scalded milk gradually into the eggs, whisking fast. Open the vanilla bean and scrape the seeds into the custard. Pour the custard back into the saucepan and cook, stirring, until the mixture is very thick. Stir in the butter and the crumbled macaroons. Cover with piece of buttered wax paper and cool.

Mound the cold custard in serving bowls and pile raspberries over it. Whip the cream stiff and fold in remaining sugar and the Kirsch. Spoon the whipped cream over the raspberries and serve.

This dessert also could be made with strawberries.

MENU 80   Oysters in Sherry *(for 24)*

12 dozen oysters
12 dozen oyster shells
 2 cups butter
 8 shallots or 2 medium onions,
   minced

1 cup Amontillado Sherry, or
  more to taste
8 cups heavy cream
  Salt and freshly ground black
  pepper
½ cup fine bread crumbs

Remove oysters from shells, or have your fish dealer do this, but be sure he sends you half the shells. Drain the juice, strain, and reserve it. Melt half the butter in large iron skillets. Sauté the oysters over medium heat, shaking the pans frequently, and turning the oysters over. Sauté until all have been slightly poached in the butter. Remove from the heat and keep warm. In another pan, melt 2 tablespoons butter and simmer the shallots without browning. When they are transparent, add the Sherry and the oyster juices and any liquor from the poached oysters. Reduce this sauce by simmering over low heat for at least 10 minutes. Add the cream and reduce again to thicken the sauce. Season to taste with salt and black pepper.

Meanwhile, scrub one half shell for each oyster. Coat the shells with some of the sauce. Place an oyster on each shell and coat with a generous amount of sauce. Cut remaining butter into tiny dots. Sprinkle a very few bread crumbs on each oyster and add a few dots of butter. Glaze in batches of 30 or more for 2 to 3 minutes under a hot broiler. When half the oysters have been browned, begin serving. Continue browning and serve each batch as soon as finished.

MENU 80   **Braised Stuffed Shoulder of Lamb with Truffles** *(for 24)*

4 shoulders of lamb, about 3 pounds each	3 carrots, chopped
Four 1-ounce cans truffles, diced fine	4 garlic cloves, minced
1½ pounds fine sausage meat	1½ cups white wine
½ pound white bread with crusts removed	1 cup dry Port wine
1 cup milk, approximately	Salt and black pepper
½ cup butter	3 cups strong beef bouillon, or more if needed
2 large onions, chopped	1½ tablespoons arrowroot or cornstarch

Have the butcher bone the shoulders of lamb. Dice the truffles, reserving the liquid, and mix with the sausage meat. Crumble the bread, soak in milk, and add to the sausage meat. Stuff the roasts with this mixture, then reshape the lamb, and tie securely. In a large deep roasting pan (or several smaller pans), melt the butter and brown the four roasts with the onions, carrots, and garlic, turning the meat to brown on all sides. Add the white wine and the Port. Cook until the sauce is reduced a little and season to taste. Add enough bouillon to come halfway up the meat. Braise in a medium oven (350°) for about 1½ hours, or more for well-done lamb.

Remove the roasts, slice, and arrange on serving platters. Strain the sauce and remove as much fat as possible. Add reserved truffle juice and thicken with arrowroot or cornstarch to complete the sauce. Serve the sauce separately.

MENU 80   Tarte à l'Orange *(for 24)*

½ recipe for puff pastry (see p. 138)
18 large navel oranges
1½ cups sugar

1½ cups water
8 eggs, slightly beaten
3 cups heavy cream
⅓ cup Curaçao

Preheat the oven to hot (400°). Line three well-buttered pie plates, about 10 inches in diameter, with puff pastry. Place a large piece of wax paper inside the pastry and fill with rice or dried beans. Bake for about 10 minutes without browning the pastry, until just set. Remove from the oven, remove the rice or beans, and cool.

Remove the rind of the oranges, taking off as much of the white pith as possible, and cut the rind into julienne strips. Make a syrup of the sugar and water by simmering them together for 5 minutes. Add the orange rind and simmer for 20 minutes. If oranges are very large so that the syrup is not enough to cover all the rind, add more sugar and water in equal proportions. Carefully separate the peeled oranges into skinless sections. If any juice results from this separation of sections, pour it into the syrup with the rinds. Arrange the orange sections in the cooled tart shells. Beat the cream with the slightly beaten eggs, just enough to mix well. Add the cooked rinds, the syrup, and the Curaçao to the cream and egg mixture. Taste for sweetness, adding sugar if needed. Pour the mixture over the oranges in the pastry shells. Reduce oven heat to medium (375°) and bake the tarts for 40 minutes, or until a knife comes out clean when inserted in the side of the tart. If the oven is too small for all three tarts, do not fill the pastry shells until ready to bake, or the pastry will get soggy.

3 *Holiday Dinners*

HOLIDAY dinners are the best of the year; all ages mix happily; the old friends, close friends, sort themselves out; and the parties have a supra-party reason: to mark a wonderful day, or to follow a family custom. And for these brief seasons, at Thanksgiving and at Christmas, even the most tradition-spurning among us turn, in our own way, to the ageless traditions based on love and faith and hope.

The best of the holiday parties have something visibly traditional in them—in the way the house looks, in the food, the drinks, in the games we play, the music we listen to. At Thanksgiving we are a little chauvinistic, with remembrance of those early new Americans and their harvest feasts with the native Americans. But at Christmas we are akin to all Christendom; we feel the whiff of magic, the faint far-off distillation of hundreds of years of roving carollers, of wassail drinking, mysterious stars, triumphant singing.

All over America there is a look of Christmas in the cities and towns. The wonderful cross of lights on the great building at the end of New York's Park Avenue, with the Christmas trees lighted all the way down the avenue, is a stirring sight. And in New York's Gramercy Park there are lights too, but of a quite different order—all of the houses bordering the park have Christmas trees in their windows or outside the houses so that the whole effect is of a small-town family celebration. It is something like that in Washington's Georgetown, too, where all through the Christmas season the houses, eighteenth and nineteenth century, are brilliantly lighted, the windows and doors decorated.

In Provence, there is an old custom to represent the twelve days of Christmas, and the thirty days and thirty nights of December, in the Christmas Day feast. Turkey and goose are the traditional birds, to be surrounded by twelve partridges (or, in 1964, by twelve small rock hens) or twelve stuffed cabbage leaves. For the thirty days of December, thirty eggs encircle these, with thirty truffles for the thirty December nights.

Here is a gargantuan Provençal Christmas Day menu. We do not suggest it be used in entirety, but it might give ideas.

The feast begins with pâté, toast, and Champagne in the living room. Then, into the dining room where, on one huge platter or tray, are spread turkey Provençal stuffed with bread, chestnuts, and apricots; twelve cabbage leaves stuffed with rice and ground beef, in tomato sauce; thirty eggs stuffed with ham and mushrooms in Mornay sauce; thirty truffles in Madeira sauce; braised celery; purée of turnips; hot rolls. The wine is a red Burgundy. At the end, the *Bûche de Noël* is brought in— a cake shaped like a Yule log with four egg shells baked in the surface of the cake. When the cake is served, shells are filled with brandy, then lighted, and the log is carried flaming to the table.

The reverse of this Provençal accent on tradition is found in some households who prefer non-traditional food. Among the choices are. roast pheasant, roast prime ribs of beef, duck served with turnips, baked ham, roast pork with baked kidney beans. These can all be the backlog for holiday menus; and holiday decorations form an ambience for these dinners as well as for the four classic menus that follow, each based on a meat traditional for either holiday.

MENU 84 (for ten)

Oysters on a Bed of Ice

Roast Suckling Pig*

Applesauce

Chopped Beets Smitane*

Turnips Mousseline

Salad
of
Sliced Orange and Avocado

Zabaglione with Fruitcake

Ice Cream

Champagne

* Recipes on page 193.

MENU 85 (for ten)

Blini with Caviar*

Vodka

Thin Vegetable Soup

Roast Leg of Venison*
with
Sauce Poivrade*

Braised Chestnuts

Gratin
of
Brussels Sprouts

Tiny Croissants

Black Currant Jelly

Orange and Romaine Salad

Peaches Cardinal*
on
Pineapple Ice Mould

Champagne

* Recipes on pages 194-196.

MENU 86 (for twelve)

*Black Bean Soup
with
Diced Ham and Lemon**

*Roast Turkey
with Port Wine Sauce
and Chestnut Stuffing**

*Sweet Potato Croquettes
with Shredded Almonds*

*Green Beans with
Fried Onion Rings*

Bibb Lettuce Salad

Stilton Cheese in Port

*Plum Pudding with
Mocha Brandy Foaming
Sauce*

Coffee   Liqueurs

Miniature Almond Tarts

Champagne

* Recipes on pages 196-197.

MENU 87 (for twelve)

Baked Oysters in Shells

*Braised Goose**

Red Cabbage and Apples

Purée of Chestnuts

Crescent Rolls

Currant Jelly

Hearts of Palm Salad

*Flaming Baba au Rhum
with
Hot Nectarines*

Champagne

* Recipe on page 198.

HOLIDAY DRINKS

During the Christmas holidays, traditional drinks that one might not think of serving at other times of the year are a pleasant variation on the usual cocktail. Beginning on this page are recipes for twenty holiday drinks, some with very ancient lineage—English, Scandinavian, Dutch, and very early American.

"Lordlings, Christmas loves good drinking," sang out an Anglo-Norman carol of the early thirteenth century. Here, for lordlings and ladies, is a vocabulary of Christmas drinks that reaches back in time—some, way, way back. The recipes have been adapted for 1964 and may, for all we know, have what an 1888 bartender's guide insists most Christmas drinks do have: "A wonderful effect on healing an old cold."

Bishop

A drink involving oranges, cloves, and dry Port that Dutch sailors taught to English sailors, who spread it around the world.

Stick 2 oranges full of cloves and roast in the oven, then quarter the oranges and put them in a saucepan. Rub 12 lumps of sugar on a lemon half to imbue with lemon flavour. Add the sugar to the oranges with the juice of 1 lemon. Pour in 3 bottles of Port, heat to boiling, and simmer gently a few minutes. Dust with nutmeg and serve immediately in a mug. Makes 12 drinks.

Blue Blazer

The spectacular drink conceived by the late Jerry Thomas, "Michelangelo of all Bartenders," as he was known in the last century. Here is the recipe bartenders used in the old Waldorf, where the Empire State Building now stands.

In one silver mug dissolve a lump of sugar in ½ jigger boiling water. Into another silver mug pour 1 jigger Scotch. Ignite the Scotch and mix by pouring the ingredients back and forth, blazing, to resemble a continuous stream of liquid fire. Serve in a highball glass in which a silver teaspoon has been placed.

Carol Punch

To keep the carollers in voice, there have been special punches ever since there have been carollers. This one is a Christmas tradition in Philadelphia.

Combine 2 quarts tea, 1 quart light rum, 2 cups lemon juice, 1 cup sugar, 3 dashes Angostura bitters. Correct sweetness to taste, add 3 pints soda water, and pour over ice in a punch bowl. Makes 42 cups.

Celery Cup

The German *Selleriebowle* has a crisp flavour and holiday colour.

Clean a bunch of celery well and scrape any rough stalks. Slice into a bowl. Sprinkle with sugar, stir in ½ cup each of rum and water. Cover the bowl and refrigerate until needed. Strain, add 1 bottle chilled Moselle, and adjust sweetness to taste. Mix well, decorate with celery leaves, and serve at once from a pitcher. Makes 15 drinks.

Clover Club

This pink froth, first shaken up in Philadelphia some forty years ago in the bar of the old Bellevue-Stratford where members of the Clover Club met, has a special affinity for crystal and silver and candlelight and, in general, the look of Christmas.

Combine 1 tablespoon lemon juice, 1 teaspoon granulated sugar, 1 tablespoon Framberry liqueur, ⅓ slightly beaten egg white, 2 ounces gin. Shake with cracked ice. Strain into a 5-ounce cocktail glass.

Fish House Punch

The celebrated American drink, born in 1732 at the Fish House of the Philadelphia club known as State in Schuylkill.

Bring 4 cups water and ½ pound brown sugar to a boil. Extract the juice from 6 lemons, reserving the rinds. Pour the hot sugar syrup over the rinds and let them stand until the syrup is cool. Discard the rinds and strain the syrup. Add the lemon juice, 2 cups pineapple juice, 1 quart Jamaica rum, 1 pint Cognac, and 1 cup peach brandy. Pour the mixture over a large block of ice in a punch bowl. Keep mixing by ladling the liquid over the ice. Makes about 30 cups of punch.

Glögg

Usually made in quantity by Scandinavians and bottled for the holiday season.

Heat these ingredients over a low fire: ½ bottle Cognac, 1 bottle red Bordeaux wine, 1 bottle Port or sweet Sherry; 18 cloves, 2 cinnamon sticks, 1 cup sugar, 1 cup seeded white raisins, 1 cup blanched almonds. Stir until the sugar is melted. Do not boil. Cook, simmering, over the lowest heat for 10 to 15 minutes. Ignite, and serve immediately from a heated silver bowl. Ladle into punch cups, spooning raisins and almonds into each portion. Cinnamon sticks may be used to swizzle. Makes 12 drinks.

Hot Buttered Rum

The outdoor man's bracer from Colonial days. Here is the recipe of Revolutionary Colonel Ethan Allen. "Butter the size of a black walnut. Maple sugar the size of a large hickory nut. Puddle the butter and sugar in the bottom of a tall porcelain cup or a protected glass, with boiling water. Add 1 gill [5 fl. oz.] rum. Fill with boiling water. Dash nutmeg for the ladies."

Le Brulo

Often after coffee at New Orleans holiday dinners, all lights were extinguished and Le Brulo was brought in—a flaming brandy punch.

Cut a large, thick-skinned orange in half, remove all pulp, put 2 lumps of sugar in each half. Fill each with brandy and set a match to it. Provide each guest with a wineglass; pour a little brandy from orange into each glass. *Santé!* Makes about 4 small drinks.

Milk Punch

Soothing descendants of the syllabub and the posset are milk punches and eggnogs. Called in Scotland "Auld Man's Milk," they crop up somewhere in many American Christmases, especially in the morning. Here is a hot milk punch, refreshingly mild and flavourful.

Beat 12 eggs till very frothy. Combine with 1 pint Madeira, ¾ cup sugar, ½ tablespoon grated nutmeg. Keep beating. Meanwhile, heat 1 quart milk with the rind of a lemon. When the milk is scalding, pour from a great height into the eggs and wine, whisking the eggs with the left hand to keep the whole bubbly. Drink immediately. Makes about 16 drinks.

Mulled Cider

Mulling—the heating, sweetening, and spicing of drinks—has been going on since the time of Queen Elizabeth I. Here is a wassail to the apple tree.

Tie 1 teaspoon whole cloves, 1 teaspoon whole allspice, and 4 sticks cinnamon in cheesecloth. Add to 2 quarts hard cider and 1 fifth of apple brandy in a large pot, along with 1 cup light brown sugar. Bring to a boil, stirring gently to help sugar dissolve. Simmer for 10 to 15 minutes. Serve immediately in heated mugs from a heated pitcher. Makes 16 drinks.

Mulled Wine

Queen Victoria's recipe was simply "boil some spice in a little water till the flavour is gained. Then add an equal quantity of good Port wine, some sugar and nutmeg. Boil, and serve with crisp unsweetened biscuits." You may prefer this even simpler one for 4 drinks.

Heat 1 bottle red Burgundy with 10 cloves and ¼ teaspoon pepper. Pour 1 jigger Kirsch into each of 4 tall glasses. Pour the hot wine over the Kirsch. Glasses to be held with napkins.

Posset

This old English drink means in Old English: "Drink good for cold in the head." Originally milk, curdled with ale or with sack (that dry white wine imported from the south into England in the seventeenth and eighteenth centuries), old-time possets often included crumbled biscuits or white bread. This modern posset forgoes such starch.

Heat 4 ounces white wine, 1 tablespoon sugar, nutmeg, 1 pint milk, and the rind of a lemon together. As soon as the milk simmers, it is ready for serving. Makes 2 drinks.

Punch

The word punch probably stems from the same place the punch idea did, India. *Panch* in Hindustani means five, and five ingredients are what those Hindu punches supposedly had—toddy, lemon or lime, tea, sugar, water. Some things to remember about making punch: if there is a sparkling ingredient —wine or carbonated beverage—add it last. In the cold punch bowl, use blocks of ice rather than cubes, which dilute the bowl too quickly. A frozen block of sherbet can replace both fruit and ice. Hot punches are most charmingly kept warm on the hearth, with a hot poker nearby to thrust into the punch for a fast reheat. Where there is no fireplace, a chafing dish will do nicely.

Rumfustian

One of the oldest mixed drinks in America, Rumfustian, along with Rumbullions, Rumbustions, and Rum Flips, reflects the enthusiasm with which the early colonists found names for rum punches.

Heat the contents of 1 bottle sweet Sherry with 2 sticks of cinnamon, 1 teaspoon grated nutmeg, 12 lumps of sugar, and the zest of 1 lemon. Beat the yolks of 12 eggs until foamy, add 1 quart beer and 8 ounces dark rum to them. When the wine boils, strain into the eggs in a thin stream, beating the while to prevent curdling. Serve hot and at once. Makes 12 drinks.

Syllabub

Anne Boleyn called it silly bubbles, and the way these bubbles were formed was by milking a cow directly into spiced and sweetened wine or ale until all frothed. Until some 150 years ago, obliging cows were led into London parks for just this purpose. An 1834 Bucks County recipe called for "sillabubs" whipped with a wire. A new formula leaves it all to an electric blender.

Pour the following into a blender in two batches: 1 quart light cream, the juice and grated peel of 2 oranges, ½ cup fine granulated sugar, 1 teaspoon orange water, 4 wineglasses semidry Sherry, 2 ounces brandy. Blend at low speed till very foamy. Makes 6 drinks.

Tom & Jerry

Said to be invented by "Professor" Jerry Thomas, author of *The Bar-Tender's Guide*, 1862. Or possibly the product of two fictional English rakes, Jerry Hawthorne and his Elegant Friend Corinthian Tom, 1821. In any event, the Tom & Jerry Bowl was a holiday adornment of turn-of-the-century New York bars. Recipe:

Separate the yolk and white of 1 egg, and beat the yolk. Beat the white until fairly stiff, add 1 teaspoon sugar, then beat to a stiff froth. Combine yolk and white and add a pinch of allspice. Put the mixture into a scalded mug. Add 1½ ounces Jamaica rum, then fill with boiling water. Stir, then top with a dash of brandy.

Wassail Bowl

The well-loved English Christmas drink that was ceremoniously brought in to the guests every day of the twelve days of the season. Toast used to float in it, and to this fact we owe the "toast" in "a toast to your health, sir." Now, beaten egg whites usually replace the toasted bread.

Pour 3 quarts ale, 1 bottle cream Sherry, 1 ginger root cut up, 1 teaspoon nutmeg, 8 whole cloves, and 2 cups brown sugar into a cooking pot and heat gently. Let simmer for a few minutes to blend the spices and melt the sugar. Separate 6 eggs and beat the yolks well and the whites stiff. Fold the whites into the yolks and pour the hot liquid into the eggs in a thin stream, heating the while. Pour quickly into a heated punch bowl. Add hot baked apples or crab apples and 3 jiggers heated brandy and serve immediately. Makes 18 drinks.

White Christmas Punch

For those to whom the holidays are not official without Champagne, here is a vodka-Champagne bowl, all white with a touch of greenery, that will make it clear The Season's here.

Combine 1 pint 100-proof vodka with $\frac{1}{2}$ cup Kirsch and $\frac{1}{2}$ cup Cointreau, and pour over a large block of ice in a punch bowl. Add 3 bottles iced dry Champagne at serving time and float 30 small strips of cucumber peel.

Sazarac

"The drink that made New Orleans famous." The recipe of the old Waldorf bar called for a dash of absinthe in its construction; Pernod now stands in for the absinthe. The Peychaud Bitters that always characterized the flavour are still to be had, a memory of Antoine Peychaud, a late eighteenth-century New Orleaner, one of the innumerable people to whom the invention of the cocktail is attributed.

In an old-fashioned glass muddle 1 lump of sugar, 1 teaspoon water, 2 dashes Peychaud bitters, $1\frac{1}{2}$ ounces Bourbon, 4 drops of Pernod. Add a lump of ice and serve with twist of lemon peel.

MENU 84   Roast Suckling Pig *(for 10)*

10- to 12-pound suckling pig	1 potato
1 tablespoon coarse salt	2 cups light beef bouillon
2 garlic cloves	2 cranberries
¾ teaspoon sage	1 small red apple
Salt and black pepper	Parsley

Preheat oven to hot (400°). Wash the pig thoroughly with warm water, inside and out. Dry well with paper towels. Crush the coarse salt, garlic, and sage together to make a paste. Rub the pig well with this paste. Season the inside with salt and pepper, and pepper the outside well. Arrange the pig on a rack in a roasting pan with the hind legs tucked forward under it. Place the potato in its mouth to keep the jaws open. Roast for 30 minutes and then reduce the heat to medium (350°). Cover the ear tips with foil. Continue roasting for 3 hours, basting with the fat. Turn the heat up again to hot (400°) and bake for 30 minutes longer, until the pig is crusty. Remove to a platter. Remove the rack from the roasting pan, and pour off the fat. Add the beef bouillon and deglaze, scraping up all the brown bits, and simmer for 6 to 8 minutes on top of the stove. Strain into a sauceboat and keep warm until serving time. Place the cranberries in the pig's eyes and the apple in its mouth and surround with parsley.

To carve, slit the skin down the centre of the back with a very sharp knife; then slip the skin off—it should fall off readily. Pull away the surface fat; then begin with the ham and cut thin slices, along the grain of the meat. When ready to carve the ribs, separate them from the backbone with knife and fork, and remove individually. Carve the shoulder last.

MENU 84   Chopped Beets Smitane *(for 10)*

24 medium beets	Salt and black pepper
2 cups thick sour cream	

Put the beets into 8 cups cold water in a saucepan. Bring them to a boil and continue boiling briskly until the beets can be pierced with a fork. Drain, reserving the cooking water for future beet soup; put the beets in cold water for 10 minutes or so, drain again, and slip off the skins. Chop the beets quite fine.

About 15 minutes before serving, add the sour cream, salt, and a generous sprinkling of freshly ground black pepper, and reheat. The dish should not be mushy, but the beets should hold their shape and the cream be evenly spread through.

MENU 85   Blini with Caviar *(for 10)*

1 package dry yeast	2 cups sifted flour
1 teaspoon sugar	½ cup heavy cream
¾ teaspoon salt	2 cups butter
½ cup hot water	1 pound pressed black caviar
4 eggs	2 cups thick sour cream
2 cups milk	

Four hours before blini are to be served, dissolve the yeast with the sugar and salt in the hot water in a large warm bowl. Warm the eggs to room temperature and separate. Scald the milk and cool; when lukewarm, add gradually to the flour. Add the flour and milk to the yeast and blend until the mixture is smooth. Add the well-beaten egg yolks to the yeast mixture and set the dough, covered with a clean tea towel, in a warm place to rise for at least 3 hours, or until tripled in bulk. When the dough has risen, beat the egg whites very stiff and fold them into the batter. Whip the cream and fold it into the batter along with 3 tablespoons melted, cooled butter. Let the batter rest again for a good 30 minutes.

Clarify the remaining butter by heating it in a pan as slowly as possible so the oil separates from the water and whey. Strain very carefully through the finest strainer into a clean saucepan, discarding the foamy milky residue.

Heat a 5-inch pancake pan or preferably a Norwegian pan—a flat iron pancake pan with seven 3-inch depressions—until a drop of water sizzles when dropped on it. If using the Norwegian pan, pour ½ teaspoon butter into each pancake hollow, spoon in about 1 tablespoon of the batter, and fry until puffy and golden, about 1 minute, taking care that it does not burn. Add more butter as needed. Turn the pancakes with a narrow spatula or knife and brown for about 30 seconds on the other side. If you have no Norwegian pan, use the smallest pancake pan obtainable. For a 5-inch pan, use 1 teaspoon clarified butter, spoon in a scant ¼ cup of the batter, and proceed. Keep the finished pancakes hot in a low oven (300°) in an uncovered serving dish. Make about half of the pancakes and serve those while cooking the remaining pancakes. Serve clarified butter, caviar, and sour cream with the blini.

MENU 85   Roast Leg of Venison with
Sauce Poivrade *(for 10)*

6- to 7-pound leg of venison
Salt and black pepper
3 celery stalks, chopped
2 carrots, sliced thin
2 onions, sliced thin
2 shallots, chopped
3 parsley sprigs, chopped
2 garlic cloves, crushed
6 peppercorns, crushed
6 juniper berries, crushed

1 teaspoon dried rosemary (optional)
½ teaspoon dried thyme
1 large bay leaf, crumbled
3 cups dry white or red wine
1 cup wine vinegar
½ cup olive oil
Sauce poivrade for venison (see below)

Season the venison with salt and pepper. Mix the vegetables, herbs, and spices, and place half the mixture at the bottom of a deep, narrow pan. Place the venison on the mixture and spread the rest over the meat. Mix the wine, vinegar, and olive oil, and pour the liquid over all. Marinate in a cool place for two days, if possible, or at least overnight. Turn the meat several times each day so that it is well seasoned all over. Drain the meat, reserving the marinade, and dry it with paper towels. Roast the vension in a medium oven (375°) as you would beef, allowing about 12 minutes per pound for rare venison. Serve with sauce poivrade.

SAUCE POIVRADE FOR VENISON

Marinade from venison
3 tablespoons olive oil
¼ cup vinegar, scant
2 tablespoons tomato paste
½ cup Madeira or tawney Port

4 cups prepared brown sauce
8 peppercorns, crushed
¼ cup dry white wine
2 tablespoons butter

Strain the marinade used for the venison, reserving 1 cup of the liquid. Drain the vegetables thoroughly and brown them in the olive oil. Drain the oil and add the vinegar and ½ cup of the marinade. Reduce the mixture by simmering to one third. Add the tomato paste, the Madeira or Port, and the brown sauce. Bring to a boil, reduce the heat, and simmer for 35 minutes, stirring occasionally and skimming the surface. Add the crushed peppercorns and cook for 10 minutes longer. Strain into a clean saucepan. Add the remaining ½ cup reserved marinade liquid. Simmer for 30 minutes, skimming it carefully. Deglaze the pan in which the venison was roasted with the white wine. Add the white wine to the sauce and cook for 5 minutes more. Strain again and stir in the butter to make the sauce shiny.

MENU 85   Peaches Cardinal on Pineapple
Ice Mould *(for 10)*

3 pints pineapple ice
Two 1-pound, 13-ounce cans fine white peaches
½-inch piece of vanilla bean, or
2 teaspoons vanilla extract

3 packages frozen raspberries
¼ cup Kirsch, or more
½ cup sliced blanched almonds

Pack the pineapple ice into a ring-shaped or melon mould and store in the freezer until ready for use. Remove the peaches from the syrup and reserve them. Place the peach syrup and the vanilla bean in a saucepan over low heat and reduce the syrup by half. Cool. Defrost the raspberries and force through a sieve to remove the seeds. Add the Kirsch and the cooled peach syrup to the puréed berries. If you are using vanilla extract instead of the bean, add it now. Pour syrup over the reserved peaches and chill. Just before serving, unmould the pineapple ice and, if the mould is dome-shaped, surround with the peaches; or put them in the centre of a ring-shaped mould. Pour the red syrup over the fruit and ice and sprinkle the top with the sliced almonds.

MENU 86   Black Bean Soup with Diced
Ham and Lemon *(for 12)*

Four 8-ounce cans black bean soup
7 cups beef bouillon
1 cup diced cooked ham

8 peppercorns
¾ cup Sherry
2 lemons

Mix the bean soup and the bouillon thoroughly, bring to a boil, and add the ham, stirring until well mixed. Crush the peppercorns to fine particles and add to the soup. Add the Sherry. Slice the lemons into very thin slices. Serve the hot soup in cups with a slice of lemon floating on top of each cup.

This is a very hearty soup, here used as the introduction to a dinner. It can be served with bread and butter, salad and fruit, as a "meal in itself" for late suppers, or as a country lunch.

MENU 86   Roast Turkey with Port Wine Sauce and Chestnut Stuffing *(for 12)*

14-pound turkey
4 cups fresh bread cubes
1 cup butter
2 medium onions, chopped
2 celery stalks, diced
3 cups beef bouillon
2 cups chopped boiled chestnuts

½ teaspoon each of sage, marjoram, and thyme
¼ cup chopped parsley
Salt and freshly ground black pepper
1 cup tawney Port

Be sure to have butcher give you the turkey liver. Remove pinfeathers and singe the turkey. Carefully wipe it dry inside and out.

Prepare the chestnut stuffing. Dry the bread cubes in a wide pan in a very low oven (250°), until the bread is golden. Melt half the butter, and sauté the onion, celery, and turkey liver until the vegetables are brown and soft. Chop the liver and add it to the dried bread cubes. Add 1 cup bouillon, the chestnuts, and the herbs, and a lavish amount of freshly ground pepper. Season the inside of the turkey with salt and pepper. Raise the oven heat to very hot (425°). Fill the turkey loosely with the stuffing. Also fill the breast cavity through the neck opening, folding over the skin and skewering into place. Close the larger opening by sewing it, or with foil, or with a piece of buttered thread. Tie the legs, and tuck wings under. Butter a large roasting pan with 2 tablespoons of the remaining butter. Use the rest to butter the outside of the turkey generously. Place the bird in the roasting pan on its side. Season with additional salt and pepper and roast for 20 minutes. Turn the turkey over on the other side, season, and roast for 20 minutes longer. Turn the turkey on its back, and lower the heat to medium (350°). Add the Port wine. Cook for 2 hours, basting frequently with the butter and Port. Now cover the breast with foil, and loosely overlap the legs. Watch the turkey for the next hour, making sure it does not stick to the pan. Wiggle the legs to see if the turkey is done; if so, they will move freely.

When the turkey is done, remove the foil and place the bird on a platter. Take out the skewers and stitching. Deglaze the pan with the remaining bouillon, scraping up all the brown particles. Strain the sauce into a sauceboat. Remove some stuffing to the platter, then carve the turkey. Arrange the carved pieces over and around the stuffing and serve the Port wine sauce separately.

MENU 87   Braised Goose *(for 12)*

Two 8-pound geese
Salt and black pepper
4 onions, chopped
1 carrot, chopped

½ cup Port
3 cups prepared brown gravy
2 cups dry white wine
2 cups beef bouillon

Be sure the butcher includes the livers, gizzards, and hearts of the geese, as these will be needed to make the sauce.

Preheat oven to very hot (450°). Wipe the geese carefully inside and out. Season inside with salt and pepper, and truss. Place the birds, breast down, in a roasting pan with a cover and prick all over with a fork. Roast for 30 minutes, uncovered, turning them to colour evenly. Then turn the birds breast up and season with salt and pepper. Remove the fat from the pan, reserving about 3 to 4 tablespoons. Save the rest for some other cooking purpose. Lower the heat to medium (350°). Heat the reserved goose fat in a skillet and brown the onions, carrot, gizzards, and hearts. Place them around the geese in the roasting pan. In the same skillet sauté the goose livers until they are thoroughly cooked but not dried out. Remove from the pan and reserve. Deglaze the frying pan with Port and pour the Port over the geese. Mix the brown gravy, white wine, and bouillon and bring to a boil. Pour over geese. Cover and braise, lowering the heat to low (325°) so that the sauce just simmers. Braise for 2 hours, or until the legs move freely when tested. Uncover and roast for 20 to 30 minutes more. Place the birds on a platter, and put the roasting pan over medium heat on top of the stove. Reduce the sauce and correct the seasoning. Remove any fat from the surface and strain the sauce. Dice the reserved sautéed livers and add them to the sauce. Carve the geese, pour some sauce over them, and serve. Serve the remainder of the sauce in a sauceboat.

PART THREE

Luncheons,

Cocktails,

Eleven-Thirty

Suppers

To do with style whatever she does is a natural habit with a certain kind of woman. Even her comparatively less important parties have the mark of planning, of imagining in advance what will make the party flow, the guests comfortable. The cocktail party for six or sixty, the country terrace luncheon for any number, and the eleven-thirty supper for twenty—all of them need to use logistics, concealed, but there.

In the country, quantity is more important than variety; at a gala little midnight supper the accent is on the impromptu, on light but satisfying food. At cocktails, drinks pleasantly easy to find, canapés available but not pressured, are points she watches. And at luncheons the subtle difference between a menu for a "ladies' lunch" and a luncheon party with gentlemen present is carefully observed.

The menus and recipes in this section are for several kinds of more or less casual entertaining. They do not represent casual planning.

1

"She Specializes in Sunday Luncheons"

FOR EIGHT TO FOURTEEN

MRS. JAMESON'S LUNCHEONS IN TOWN

JANE JAMESON (Mrs. Nathan Hale Jameson) is a happy woman for several reasons. She has an amusing and literate husband; three children she likes and who like her; a city apartment sunny, airy, and gay—bought years ago, now trebled in value, maintenance low; and a little white and grey seashore house the children can spill out of all summer long—not too far from the city for Nathan Jameson to make it out most summer nights, unfailingly on weekends.

The Jamesons have the hospitable inclination to do their entertaining of friends at home; but their supper parties, cocktail parties, small dinners, for some reason or another, never gave Mrs. Jameson quite the feeling of satisfaction a good hostess deserves. Now the Jamesons have developed a specialty for the winter months in town—the Sunday luncheon party. They discovered this satisfaction one November about two years ago, almost by accident, and that first Sunday luncheon set the pattern for others that have given Mrs. Jameson a gratifying little niche in the local Hall of Fame for hostesses. It has become not only the Jamesons' own favourite party, but invitations to it have a certain pleasant special meaning in their city.

It happened that friends of friends were in the Jamesons' city for a few days only—not long enough to plan a dinner for them, with the specially desired guests and the free-lance waitress and manservant who were part of Mrs. Jameson's living plan. But miraculously, also as it happened, several of the local guest prizes proved to be free for Sunday luncheon; so were Margaret and Roger, a husband-and-wife serving team who enjoyed Mrs. Jameson's parties as much as she did. By Friday morning, the eighth guest had accepted; then Nathan's nephew, Alex, telephoned that he was coming down from Yale; and the prettiest girl in town was not too proud to be a fill-in for the luncheon. Fourteen instead of twelve; well—two tables instead of one. But what was a little reshuffling compared with the addition of a handsome nephew and an enchanting girl?

Mrs. Jameson planned to cook most of the luncheon herself, leaving the finishing details and the serving to Margaret and Roger. On Friday the food was ordered, the wine and liquors checked. On Saturday the cleaning woman came, and a thorough cleaning and silver polishing went on; flowers were ordered, put in vases, then into the cool laundry room to stay fresh for the next day. Any possible advance food preparations, any possible pre-cooking was done.

This is the menu for that first Sunday luncheon, dictated both by the wish to have food that could be partly prepared in advance, and by a present of pheasants from huntsmen friends.

MENU 88 (for fourteen)

Clams Southside*

Pheasants
baked with
Apples and Oranges

Steamed Whole
Green Beans
with
Dill and Butter

Bright Green Salad

Hot Fruit Compote*
with
Marrons Glacés

The Wine:

A Chablis with the clams and a
red Burgundy, a Volnay, with
the pheasant.

* Recipes on page 216.

On Saturday the clams, which had been ordered Friday, were cooked and put into a bowl and into the refrigerator, ready to be reheated, with cream added the next day. The pheasants were made ready for the next day's oven; however, the apples could not be peeled in advance—this had to be at the last minute. But the orange sections were cut up; the salad greens were washed and wrapped in wax paper and put into the vegetable box in the refrigerator. The fresh vegetables to eat with the cocktails were prepared, immersed in cold water, put in bowls, and back into the refrigerator. The fruit compote, with the exception of the *marrons glacés*, was cooked and ready to have the chestnuts added and to be reheated at the last minute before lunch the next day.

The guests were invited for a quarter past one; by half past everyone had come and was drinking either a Martini or a Bloody Mary, except two of the men who wanted Scotch, and Dulcie the debutante who had asked for Sherry. Nathan usually made the cocktails, but young Alex took over masterfully, and Dulcie passed the tray of big black olives and cucumber sticks once. Then these were put on the coffee table near the big bowl of fresh vegetables—the *crudités*—to be eaten when anyone felt inclined. There were cocktail napkins on this table, but no plates. The only other canapé served was a tray of tiny cheese biscuits brought in piping hot by Margaret. This cheese biscuit mixture was kept on hand in the refrigerator; Mrs. Jameson made up a sizable batch every two weeks or so. To roll out this dough, cut out the biscuits, and put them in the oven for about 20 minutes was Margaret's only canapé duty.

Luncheon was to be served at quarter of two, and at twenty of two Mrs. Jameson slipped into the dining room for a last critical glance. Place cards were in place—Mrs. Jameson's cards with guests' names written on them. She believes firmly in place cards for everything beyond a family dinner. "I have to," she says. "At our first two dinners after we were married I made two ghastly failures trying to seat guests from a chart. I learned." She reassessed the tables—heavy green linen mats on the dining table for eight, with her old French ceramic cauliflower as centrepiece, and the black and white Creil place plates; heavy, deep pink, linen cloth on the table for six, with a covered white ironstone bowl in the center, and the black and white ironstone place plates. "They do look pretty," she thought. Mrs. Jameson rarely uses flowers for her tables; instead, some one of her ceramics or a handsome black and white Lowestoft bowl, or a silver bowl of fruit. Once, when she felt rather daring, she put on the table, between two green quartz slabs, a small white marble head of the Empress Caroline, a "recent acquisition" in the Jamesons' modest collection.

The guests who were the reason for this Sunday luncheon party were even nicer than their advance notices. The banker husband was chairman of the board of an excellent municipal art gallery in his native small Midwest city. The wife was a "pretty, talking young woman" and easy to like. To meet them, the Jamesons asked one of the curators of their own city museum, with his wife; one of Jane's two really rich friends, a widow who, with her husband, had assembled one of the world's famous modern art collections, a handsome woman, unimpressed either with herself or anyone else; for odd man, an up-and-coming politician, formidably ambitious, exciting, and a charmer. The other four guests were diverse—a surprising high-school English teacher, about forty, chic, aware of new literary currents, non-routine in her opinions, a respected minor poet; the family lawyer, Jane's and Nathan's great friend—disillusioned, faintly cranky, acidly witty—a guarantee against dullness; and a serious young couple, the husband an electronics future blue chip, the wife a biologist in the Children's Hospital.

This mixing of people with all sorts of interests became part of the fame of the Sunday luncheons. And perhaps another element in their success was the feeling that the guests were important to the Jamesons. The house had a welcoming air, with big vases of loosely sprawled flowers in the rooms, and an open fire in the living room and the library. The liquor was of the best, the glasses were fine and shining; cigarette boxes were full, cigarette lighters were conveniently near (and filled), ashtrays were big and plentiful; there were French and English magazines about, sometimes two or three new jigsaw puzzles, and a variegated collection of records, usually in use in the library. It never seemed "just another luncheon party," but an occasion, the guests obviously chosen with considered care for their interest in and to each other. And the food was good.

The successful menus in Jane's Sunday luncheons are all planned on a basic scheme that Jane finds workable. Canapés are simple, often only nuts and olives plus the bowl of uncooked vegetables—carrots, radishes, celery, cauliflower, fennel. Martinis, Bloody Marys, Bourbon or Scotch, plus Sherry, are usually the limits of the cocktail table. One wine only is served with luncheon, usually a light red wine. If the menu begins with fish, the wine is not poured until the main course. If the main course is fish, a Chablis or other dry white wine is served.

Sometimes a green vegetable is substituted for the salad, or the other way round. Soup is not often used as a first course, unless it is one of a substantial meal-in-itself soups—crab gumbo or clam chowder, for example—which, plus salad and dessert, occasionally makes up the whole menu. There is always one quite hearty dish out of respect for the men in the party, and always a dessert. Coffee is served in the living room. With the two trained visiting aides entirely familiar with the ways of the house, service is agreeably quick and deft. And since Mrs. Jameson is something of a cook herself, she has a small, forgivable pride in the fact that she does much of the cooking. The first lunch of fourteen was as large a number as Mrs. Jameson attempts. When the table is for eight or ten, Roger or Margaret alone can serve.

On the following pages are twelve other menus that might be served for Sunday luncheon in town.

MENU 89 (for eight)

Hot Onion Tart*

*Thin Slices
of
Cold Corned Beef
with
Mustard Sauce*

Vegetable Salad

Spoon Bread*

Vanilla Soufflé
with
Rum Sauce**

The Wine:

*A mountain Zinfandel from
California.*

* Recipes on page 217.

MENU 90 (for eight)

*Mushrooms Filled
with
Mushroom Soufflé**

Guinea Hen in Casserole*

*Salad
of
Endive, Beets, Watercress*

*Port-Salut Cheese
Crackers*

Apple Tart*

The Wine:

*A red Bordeaux goes well with
the guinea hen, and also with the
cheese.*

* Recipes on pages 218-219.

MENU 91 (for eight)

Terrine of Pâté

French Bread
Sweet Butter

Roast Leg of Lamb

Potatoes Dauphine*

Sautéed Whole Zucchinis

Salad
of
Watercress and Celery

Lemon Pudding*

The Wine:

A light red wine from the Loire,
such as Bourgueil or Chinon,
would be interesting here.

* Recipes on pages 220-221.

MENU 92 (for eight)

Gnocchi à la Parisienne*

Shad and Roe Normande*

Salad
of
Romaine and Boston Lettuce

Prune Soufflé*
with
Lemon Custard Sauce*

Cookies

The Wine:

A white Loire such as a Vouvray,
or a Pouilly-Fumé.

* Recipes on pages 222-223.

MENU 93 (for ten)

Hot Watercress Soup*

Seafood Risotto*

Salad
of
Romaine and Chicory

Italian Bread

Pineapple Ice
with
Fresh Black Raspberries

The Wine:

A white Rioja from Spain.

* Recipes on page 224.

MENU 94 (for ten)

Crown of Asparagus
Soufflé*

Roast Partridges
with
Watercress Salad

Brie Cheese

Fresh Strawberries
with
Sour Cream

The Wine:

*A light claret from the Médoc,
or a Beaujolais.*

* Recipes on page 225.

MENU 95 (for ten)

Tomato Mushroom Purée*

*Toast Strips
with
Grated Parmesan Cheese*

Boned Ham in Pastry*

Cauliflower Salad

Baked Oranges

The Wine:

A claret or a rosé would be acceptable here.

* Recipes on page 226-227.

MENU 96 (for ten)

Cold Cucumber Soup

Vitello Tonnato*

Cold Rice

*Sliced Tomatoes
Herb Dressing*

Peach Ice Cream

Hot Macaroons

The Wine:

Either white or red with the veal—claret or California Zinfandel for the red; Pouilly-Fumé for the white.

* Recipe on page 228.

MENU 97 (for ten)

MENU 98 (for twelve)

Individual Cheese Soufflés

Fried Chicken Breasts

Green Rice*

Cucumber Sticks

Orange Layer Cake

Gratin of Fresh Asparagus

Italian Whole-Wheat Bread

Cold Boiled Beef en Gelée*

Hot Potato Salad*

Marrons Café Bombe*

The Wine:

An Alsatian Riesling.

The Wine:

A claret such as Château Palmer from the township of Margaux.

* Recipe on page 228.

*Recipes on pages 229-230.

MENU 99 *(for twelve)*

Petites Quiches Lorraines*

Boiled Kennebec Salmon

Parsleyed Potato Balls

Thin Slices
of
Tomato and Cucumber
with
French Dressing

Apricot Trifle*

The Wine:

A Chablis or a California Pinot Blanc.

* Recipes on page 231.

MENU 100 *(for twelve)*

Sausage in Pastry*

Ragout of Lamb
with
Baby Onions, Baby Carrots

Buttered Green Peas

Small Whole-Wheat Rolls

Macédoine of Fresh Fruit
with
Kirsch and Almonds

The Wine:

A robust red wine from the Rhone such as Châteauneuf-du-Pape, or a full-bodied St. Émilion.

* Recipe on page 232.

MRS. JAMESON'S COUNTRY LUNCHEONS

In the country, in the summer, in the little grey and white house, Sunday luncheons are quite different affairs. The cooking, the serving, and clearing away the débris are all a family matter. The kitchen opens directly to a terrace, and it is there that the Sunday guests eat, at a long outdoor trestle table under the awning—there are rarely fewer than twelve or fourteen at the table. The food is served directly from the kitchen, often directly from the stove. The luncheons consist, often, of one main dish, with a green salad served at the same time; the dessert is always hearty. Nathan Jameson specializes in pancakes, which are transported immediately from stove to guests, with the proud chef standing ready for new orders. He is also an accomplished omelet maker, preferring to make them in a series, for two guests at a time. Sometimes, if the Jamesons are feeling a little extravagant, luncheon can be half a dozen lobsters—boiled, split in half, and chilled—for twelve guests.

Here are six menus for country luncheons at the Jamesons'.

MENU 101 (for twelve)

*Brunswick Stew**

Cornmeal Muffins

Lettuce, Spinach and Romaine Salad

Applesauce with Cream

Cookies

The Wine:

No wine here, but ice-cold beer.

* Recipe on page 232.

MENU 102 (for twelve)

*Boiled Half Lobsters with Mayonnaise**

Whole Green Beans, Hot, with Fresh Dill

Fresh Peaches with Ice Cream Topping

The Wine:

With this delicious luncheon, a chilled fresh Muscadet.

* Recipe on page 233.

MENU 103 (for twelve)

*Cheese Soufflé**

Vegetable Salad

*Cold Rice Pudding
with
Rum-Flavoured Cream*

The Wine:

A claret would be a good choice with the cheese soufflé and the salad.

* Recipe on page 234.

MENU 104 (for twelve)

*Meat Loaf with Pâté
en Croûte**

*Baked Zucchini Casserole**

*Hot Fruit Compote
with
Thick Cream*

The Wine:

A light red wine is suggested here; a Beaujolais would be nice.

* Recipes on pages 234-235.

MENU 105 (for fourteen)

*Kasha with Meatballs**

*Sliced Cucumbers
with
Sour Cream Dill Dressing*

Watermelon Slices

The Wine:

Carafes of red Italian wine would be excellent with this menu.

* Recipe on page 236.

MENU 106 (for fourteen)

*Cornmeal Pancakes
with Strawberry Jam*

*Baked Corned Beef Hash**

*Green Salad
with Sliced Beets*

Cheeses and Crackers

The Wine:

A well-chilled vin rosé would be a nice accompaniment for this luncheon.

* Recipe on page 236.

MENU 88   Clams Southside *(for 14)*

6 dozen cherrystone clams
1 cup butter
2 medium onions, chopped
¼ cup sifted flour
1 tablespoon chopped parsley

1½ cups chicken broth, or more
   Cayenne pepper and salt to
   taste
2 cups heavy cream

Cut away the muscles from the clams, and discard or reserve to make clam broth for another time. Cut the clams with kitchen scissors into medium pieces. Melt the butter in a large heavy pan and sauté the chopped onions. Slowly add the flour and cook, stirring, until the mixture is golden brown. Then add the parsley and enough chicken broth to make a smooth sauce. Stir and cook until the sauce is thick and smooth. Add the clams and the rest of the chicken broth, stirring in slowly; simmer for just 13 minutes. Season to taste with cayenne pepper and salt. Add the cream and place over low heat just long enough for the mixture to become hot, but do not allow it to come to a boil. Serve immediately with toasted bread triangles.

MENU 88   Hot Fruit Compote with
                Marrons Glacés *(for 14)*

1 pound dried pitted prunes
1 pound dried apricots
12 pieces each candied orange peel
   and grapefruit, diced

1 cup Cognac, or rum or Kirsch
4 cups *marrons glacés* in syrup
2 cups heavy cream
¼ cup sugar

In covered vessels, steam the prunes and apricots separately until tender, in just enough water to cover, about 4 cups. Put half of the orange peel and grapefruit peel in each vessel. There should be very little water left in the vessels when the fruit is done; the individual pieces should be separate and retain their shape. When the fruit is cooked, put it together in one large vessel and add Cognac or other liquor, then add the *marrons* with their syrup. Stir the mixture with a large spoon, taking care not to break the fruits. Return the vessel to the heat and bring the mixture to the boiling point. Serve hot with the very cold cream, whipped until stiff and sweetened with the sugar.

MENU 89   Hot Onion Tart *(for 8)*

1¼ cups butter	Salt and black pepper
3 cups chopped onions	Dash of nutmeg
6 eggs, separated	Two 9-inch flaky pastry shells (see
3 cups light cream	page 52)
½ cup white wine	

Melt the butter and sauté the onions in it very slowly, for 20 to 25 minutes. They should not be brown but a light caramel colour without any hard or burnt edges. Beat the egg yolks until light, mix in the cream and wine, and add salt and pepper to taste with a good dash of nutmeg. Add the slightly cooled onions, with any butter left in the pan in which they were sautéed. Beat the egg whites very stiff, but not dry, and fold them into the onion mixture. Pour into the partially baked flaky pastry shells. Bake in a preheated medium oven (350°) until puffed and golden, about 40 minutes. Serve hot.

MENU 89   Spoon Bread *(for 8)*

4 eggs	4 cups milk
6 tablespoons cooked rice	¾ cup water-ground cornmeal
½ teaspoon salt	

Preheat oven to medium (375°). Separate eggs; beat yolks well; add rice and salt. Bring milk to a boil, trickle in cornmeal, and stir over low heat until thickened. Off heat, add yolks and rice. Beat egg whites stiff; fold into the mixture. Pour into a well-buttered, fairly deep baking dish; bake 25 to 30 minutes. Serve hot, spooned out like corn pudding.

MENU 89 Vanilla Soufflé with Rum Sauce *(for 8)*

2 cups milk	6 egg yolks
⅓ cup flour	⅓ cup chopped citron
⅔ cup sugar, or more to taste	¼ cup chopped angelica
2-inch piece of vanilla bean, or	⅓ cup glacéed cherries, chopped
2 teaspoons vanilla extract	8 egg whites
¼ cup butter	Rum sauce (see below)

Preheat the oven to medium (350°). Butter and sugar two 6-cup soufflé dishes. Make a paste of ½ cup of the milk and the flour. Scald the rest of the milk with the sugar and vanilla bean. Add the hot strained milk to the flour paste. Return to the heat and cook very slowly, stirring, until thickened. Add the butter and the well-beaten egg yolks to the milk mixture, stirring briskly. Add the fruit. Transfer from the saucepan to a large bowl. Beat the egg whites and add one third of them to the mixture, folding in thoroughly. Fold in the remaining whites, gently, with a lifting motion, turning the bowl while folding. Pour into the prepared soufflé dishes and bake for 30 minutes for a soft soufflé, 35 to 40 minutes for a firm one. Serve immediately with rum sauce.

RUM SAUCE

1 cup sugar	½ cup dark rum
1½ cups apricot nectar	

Bring the sugar and apricot nectar to a boil and simmer for 5 minutes. Remove from the heat and add the rum. Serve warm or cold.

MENU 90   Mushrooms Filled with Mushroom Soufflé (for 8)

24 to 30 large mushrooms	½ teaspoon lemon juice
1 onion, chopped	3 parsley sprigs, chopped
¾ cup butter	Salt and black pepper
2 tablespoons flour	¼ cup grated Parmesan cheese, or
1 cup chicken broth	more
4 eggs, separated	

Choose mushrooms large enough so that two or three will make one serving. Wash, dry, and detach the stems, but do not peel the mushrooms. Chop the stems and six whole mushrooms, and sauté with the onion in 4 tablespoons of the butter. Make a white sauce of 2 tablespoons butter, the flour, and the chicken broth. Add the sautéed mushrooms and onions to this and cool. Beat the egg yolks and fold into the mixture with the lemon juice; add the chopped parsley. Season to taste with salt and pepper. Beat the egg whites very stiff and fold them into the mixture. Put the mushroom caps, hollow side up, on a buttered baking sheet. Brush with the remaining butter, fill high with the mushroom soufflé, and sprinkle with grated cheese. Bake in a medium oven (350°) until the tops are puffed and brown.

MENU 90   Guinea Hen in Casserole *(for 8)*

1½ tablespoons bacon fat
¾ cup butter
1 onion, coarsely chopped
2 garlic cloves, crushed
½ cup thinly sliced carrots
5 to 6 cups shredded red cabbage
Salt and black pepper
2 bay leaves, crumbled

6 whole cloves
¼ teaspoon nutmeg
1½ cups red wine
1½ cups chicken broth
3 guinea hens
1 teaspoon dried tarragon
4 bacon strips, blanched and diced
2 cups diced apples

Melt the bacon fat and 2 tablespoons of the butter in a heatproof 24-cup casserole. In this sauté lightly the onion, garlic, and carrots. Stir in the red cabbage, cover, and cook slowly for 10 to 15 minutes. Season to taste with salt and black pepper, and add the bay leaves, cloves, and nutmeg. Add 1 cup of the wine and 1 cup of the broth, cover, and cook for 20 minutes over medium heat.

Rub the hens inside and out with the tarragon and salt and pepper. Rub the outsides with 6 tablespoons butter. Put the hens in a heavy iron skillet with the remaining 4 tablespoons butter and the diced bacon and sear the birds lightly. Add the apples to the vegetables in the casserole, then put in the browned guinea hen. Deglaze the skillet with the remaining wine and broth, and add the liquid to the casserole. Cover with foil, then with the lid of the casserole, and cook in a medium oven (375°) for 50 minutes. Remove the cover and foil and cook for 15 minutes more in a hot oven to brown. Serve from the casserole, or on a fairly deep platter with the guinea hen arranged on top of the vegetables and apples.

MENU 90   Apple Tart *(for 8)*

2 cups applesauce
3 to 4 tablespoons Calvados or applejack
12-inch tart dish lined with almond tart pastry (see below)
6 to 8 large apples
¾ cup sugar

1 teaspoon cinnamon
1 tablespoon lemon juice
3 tablespoons butter
½ cup apricot preserves, heated and strained
⅓ cup chopped pistachio nuts

Mix the applesauce with the Calvados and spread it in the bottom of the pastry-lined tart dish. Peel and core the apples and slice into rings. Arrange the apple rings over the applesauce. Mix the sugar and cinnamon and sprinkle over the apples. Use more sugar if the apples are tart. Sprinkle with lemon juice and dot with butter. Preheat the oven to very hot (450°). Bake the tart in the very hot oven for 20 minutes, then lower the heat to medium (375°) and bake until the pastry is brown and the apples are tender. Glaze with the apricot preserves and sprinkle with chopped pistachios. Apple tart can be served cold or hot, with sweetened whipped cream if desired.

ALMOND TART PASTRY

2 cups sifted flour	3 egg yolks
⅓ cup sugar	½ cup sweet butter
Pinch of salt	3 tablespoons vegetable shortening
¼ cup ground almonds	1 egg white, slightly beaten

Resift the flour with the sugar, salt, and almonds. Make a well in the centre of the flour, on a board or in a bowl. Into the well put the egg yolks, the sweet butter, cut into small bits, and the vegetable shortening. Work the eggs, butter, and shortening together, incorporating the flour mixture gradually. Work quickly with the tips of the fingers until the pastry is firm enough to roll into a ball. Chill for 1 hour. Roll out between sheets of wax paper. This pastry is very delicate! Place carefully in a well-buttered 12-inch deep tart dish. Glaze with the egg white. Keep cold until ready to fill.

MENU 91   Potatoes Dauphine *(for 8)*

1 cup milk	4 eggs
¼ cup butter	2 cups mashed potatoes
½ teaspoon salt	3 to 4 cups fat for deep frying
1 cup sifted flour	

Scald the milk with the butter and salt. When boiling, dump in the flour at once, and stir briskly over the fire until the mixture forms a ball. Remove from the fire and add the eggs, one at a time, beating well each time. Then add the mashed potatoes. Heat the fat to 375° in a deep frying pan, and drop the mixture by teaspoonfuls into the hot fat to puff and brown. Do not make more than 8 or 10 at once, as it cools the fat too much. Drain on paper before serving. These can be made an hour or so ahead, and kept in a low oven (300°) until ready to serve. At serving time turn the oven heat to very hot (425°) for 3 minutes.

MENU 91   Lemon Pudding *(for 8)*

½ cup butter
½ cup sugar
½ cup sifted flour
 2 cups milk, scalded
 6 eggs, separated

1 lemon, juice and grated rind
¼ cup chopped candied lemon peel
¼ cup sweet Sherry
Sherry sauce (see below)

Cream 7 tablespoons of the butter in a saucepan. Add the sugar and the flour and mix until very smooth. Add the scalded milk. Place over low heat and bring to a boil, then keep cooking and stirring until it becomes a stiff paste. Remove from the heat and add the beaten egg yolks, little by little, working well into the paste. Add the lemon juice and grated rind, the candied lemon peel, and the Sherry. Cool. Beat the egg whites until very firm and fold in well. Butter a 6-cup pudding mould with the remaining 1 tablespoon butter. Fill it three fourths full with the mixture. Cover with a piece of buttered wax paper and tie with string. Put the mould in a pan with enough boiling water to come halfway up the sides of the mould and steam the pudding on top of the stove for about 1½ to 1¾ hours, replenishing the water as it evaporates. Unmould and serve with Sherry sauce.

This pudding is a basic one and may be flavoured with oranges or with highly flavoured liqueurs, such as Curaçao or anisette. It may also have 1 cup pitted chopped dates added to it instead of the lemon flavouring. A little *crème de cacao* might replace the Sherry in both pudding and sauce. Or the pudding could be flavoured with vanilla and served with a hot strawberry sauce made by heating frozen sliced strawberries, flavoured with Kirsch or brandy.

SHERRY SAUCE

½ cup sugar
1½ tablespoons cornstarch
Dash of salt
 2 cups water
 1 teaspoon lemon juice

2-inch cinnamon stick, or ¼ teaspoon cinnamon
3 egg yolks
¼ cup sweet Sherry
½ teaspoon grated lemon rind

Mix the sugar, cornstarch, and salt with 1½ cups of the water in the top of a double boiler. Add the lemon juice and the cinnamon stick and cook over direct heat until thick, about 5 minutes. Beat the egg yolks slightly with the remaining ½ cup water and stir them into the sauce. Put the double boiler over hot water and continue to cook, stirring constantly, until the sauce coats the spoon. Strain the sauce into a clean saucepan and stir in the Sherry and the grated lemon rind. Keep the sauce hot over hot water until serving time.

MENU 92   Gnocchi à la Parisienne (for 8)

1 cup water	4 eggs
½ cup butter	1½ cups grated Parmesan cheese
½ teaspoon salt	4 cups heavy cream
1 cup sifted flour	

Bring the water, butter, and salt to a boil, then add the flour all at once. Cook, stirring, until the paste comes away from the sides of pan, about 2 minutes. Remove from the heat and cool slightly, then add the eggs, one by one, stirring briskly each time. Add ½ cup of the cheese and stir in well. Put the paste in a pastry bag with a plain tube; press it out in 1½-inch lengths and drop the pieces as they are cut into a wide pan with 3 inches of salted, boiling water in it. Boil for 6 to 8 minutes, then drain in a colander and place on paper towels. Have ready a shallow 10-cup casserole, well buttered; put in 3 cups of the cream and ½ cup of the Parmesan. Add the *gnocchi* and the remaining cream and cheese. Bake in a preheated hot oven (400°) for 15 minutes; raise the heat to very hot (450°) and bake for 15 minutes more. Serve hot.

MENU 92   Shad and Roe Normande (for 8)

4 pounds boned shad with roes	½ small onion, minced
Salt and black pepper	3 tablespoons flour
½ cup dry white wine	⅓ cup heavy cream
1 cup water	10 cooked shrimps, cut fine
½ cup butter	1 to 2 tablespoons lemon juice
½ pound mushrooms, sliced	Parsley sprigs

Preheat the oven to hot (400°). Arrange the boned shad and roes in a well-buttered shallow roasting pan. Season with salt and pepper. Pour the wine and water over the fish and dot with 2 tablespoons of the butter. Bake for 20 minutes, or until the fish flakes easily and the roes are cooked. Keep the fish warm while making the sauce. Meanwhile, sauté the sliced mushrooms in 2 tablespoons of the butter and reserve. Sauté the onion without browning in the remaining 4 tablespoons butter; add the flour and cook over low heat, stirring, for about 2 minutes. Drain the liquid from the roasting pan and add to the flour mixture; stir over low heat until thickened. Correct the seasoning, add the sauteed mushrooms, the cream, and the cut-up shrimp; add lemon juice to taste. Arrange the fish on a platter, pour the sauce over it, and decorate the platter with parsley sprigs. Serve very hot.

MENU 92   Prune Soufflé with Lemon Custard Sauce (for 8)

Butter and sugar for the soufflé dishes	2 teaspoons lemon juice
2 pounds prunes	Grated rind of 1 lemon
½ cup sugar, or more to taste	10 egg whites, beaten stiff
	Lemon custard sauce (see below)

Butter and lightly sugar two 6-cup soufflé dishes. Soak the prunes if they are not tenderized. Cook the prunes in a very little water until very soft, and purée them. There should be about 2 cups purée. Add the sugar, lemon juice, and grated lemon rind. Preheat the oven to medium (350°). Beat the egg whites very stiff, and add one third of them to the purée, folding in thoroughly with a light lifting motion, turning the bowl while folding. Add the remaining whites and fold in gently. Pour into the prepared soufflé dishes. Bake for 35 to 40 minutes. Serve with lemon custard sauce.

The egg yolks which remain after making this soufflé may be beaten with cream and used for thickening soups and sauces; or they may be used in mayonnaise, or hollandaise sauce, or in custards of all kinds. Egg yolks keep well if they are covered tightly with heavy foil.

LEMON CUSTARD SAUCE

4 egg yolks	1 tablespoon lemon juice, or more to taste
3 tablespoons sugar	
2 cups milk	1 teaspoon grated lemon rind

Beat the egg yolks, add the sugar and milk, and cook in a double boiler over barely simmering water, until the mixture coats a spoon. Flavour with lemon juice and lemon rind; cool before serving. This sauce may be made ahead of serving time; do not chill, but serve at room temperature.

MENU 93   Hot Watercress Soup *(for 10)*

2 medium potatoes
1 large leek
1 medium onion
8 cups chicken broth
1 large bunch watercress

Salt and white pepper
Dash of nutmeg
3 egg yolks
¾ cup light cream

Peel and wash the potatoes and the leek. Slice the potatoes, the onion, and the white part only of the leek. Place them in a saucepan and cover with chicken broth. Simmer, covered, for about 25 minutes, or until vegetables are very soft. Meanwhile, wash the watercress and remove all the tough stems, leaving only tender leaves and sprigs. Save enough of the sprigs to garnish the soup. Blanch the watercress in a little boiling salted water for about 5 minutes. Purée the vegetables and watercress in the liquids through a fine strainer or in a blender. Return to a saucepan and add the remaining chicken broth. Season with salt, pepper, and a dash of nutmeg. Beat the egg yolks into the cream and pour a little soup into this mixture, stirring briskly, then combine with the rest of the soup and reheat without boiling. Garnish each soup plate with a sprig of the reserved watercress.

MENU 93   Seafood Risotto *(for 10)*

1 pound bay scallops or cut-up sea scallops
1 cup dry white wine
2½ cups chicken broth
2½ cups clam broth
½ teaspoon saffron
½ cup butter
2 medium onions, chopped

3 cups raw long-grain rice
Salt, white pepper, and cayenne pepper
2 large tomatoes, skinned, seeded, and diced
1 pound cooked lobster meat
6 tablespoons browned butter
2 tablespoons chopped parsley

Simmer the scallops in the white wine for about 4 minutes. Drain them and add the liquid to the combined chicken and clam broths in a saucepan. Add the saffron, bring to a boil, and keep simmering gently. Meanwhile, melt the butter in a large heavy saucepan and slowly sauté the onions without browning; add the rice and cook gently, stirring with a fork to prevent sticking or scorching, and to mix with the onion. When the rice is slightly golden, add the hot broths, seasoned to taste with salt, white pepper, and cayenne pepper. Add the diced tomatoes, stir well with a fork, and bring to a boil. Lower the heat to keep the mixture just simmering and cook, uncovered, for 15 to 20 minutes. The rice should have absorbed the liquid, but if it is still wet, cook, uncovered, for a few minutes longer; if the rice is too dry, add a few spoonfuls of broth, just enough to moisten the rice. Add the cooked lobster and the prepared scallops to the rice and cover the saucepan. Heat for 5 minutes, or until the shellfish is heated through. Toss the rice and fish together, and transfer to a heated serving dish. Pour on the browned butter and sprinkle with the chopped parsley.

MENU 94   Crown of Asparagus Soufflé (for 10)

½ cup butter	2 cups ground cooked ham
1 medium onion, minced	40 asparagus tips, blanched
6 tablespoons flour	8 egg yolks
2 cups chicken broth	10 egg whites
¾ cup light cream	Grated Parmesan cheese
⅓ teaspoon black pepper	

Preheat the oven to medium (350°). Melt 6 tablespoons of the butter in a heavy-bottomed saucepan, add the onion, and sauté gently for 3 minutes. Sprinkle with the flour, stir constantly, and cook for 5 minutes longer. Remove from the heat and gradually add the chicken broth. Return to the heat and cook gently until the mixture has the thickness of very heavy cream. Add the light cream and cook gently for 5 minutes more, stirring occasionally. Add the pepper. Strain the sauce and let it cool for 10 minutes. Add the ground ham and 10 of the asparagus tips, chopped; beat well to mix. Beat the egg yolks until light and fold them into the mixture. Beat the egg whites stiff and fold them in. Pour into two 6-cup soufflé dishes that have been buttered with the remaining butter and then well dusted with grated Parmesan cheese. Arrange the remaining asparagus tips on top of the soufflé to form a circle, tipping the tips up gently to form a crown. Bake for 35 to 40 minutes, until golden brown and well puffed. Serve at once.

MENU 95   Tomato Mushroom Purée (for 10)

Three 6-ounce cans Italian tomato purée
6½ cups light beef bouillon
1 medium onion, minced
¼ cup butter
1 cup minced raw mushrooms

Salt and black pepper
½ cup boiled rice
1 cup light cream
3 tablespoons fresh chopped dill
1½ cups croutons, sautéed in butter

Dilute the tomato purée with the bouillon and simmer gently. Cook the onion in the butter, then add the mushrooms and simmer until they render their juice, adding more butter if needed. Season with salt and pepper. Add this mixture, with the rice, to the tomato soup. Simmer for 10 minutes. Purée through a fine strainer. Add the cream and reheat. Taste and add more salt and pepper if needed. Sprinkle with dill and croutons.

MENU 95   Boned Ham in Pastry (for 10)

Brioche dough, made 24 hours
ahead (see below)
10-pound canned boned cooked
ham
2 egg yolks, beaten

1 tablespoon water
2½ cups white-wine aspic (see below)
Watercress

Roll out brioche dough into a large thin oval ⅓ inch thick. Trim the ham if necessary and pat dry. Wrap the ham loosely with the brioche dough, overlapping the dough slightly, and place it in a roasting pan with the seam under the ham. Let the dough rise for 1 hour. Preheat the oven to hot (400°). Paint the dough with the egg yolks slightly mixed with the water. Make a hole or two in the pastry large enough to insert 2 buttered metal pastry tubes. Bake in the oven for 30 minutes, or until the pastry is golden brown. Cool. Pour cool aspic that is nearly on the point of setting through the pastry tubes, using as much of the aspic as possible. Carefully remove the pastry tubes. Chill the ham to set the aspic. Pour the remaining aspic into a flat pan. Chill to set, and scramble lightly with a fork. At serving time, place the ham on a large platter and surround it with the scrambled aspic. Decorate with watercress.

BRIOCHE DOUGH

½ cup milk
1 package yeast
1 tablespoon sugar
1 teaspoon salt

4 eggs
1 cup butter
3½ cups sifted flour

Scald the milk and cool it slightly. Dissolve the yeast with the sugar and salt in the warm milk in a large bowl. Beat the eggs and add them to the yeast mixture. Melt the butter, cool it slightly, and add. Then add the flour, working it in well. Knead the dough on a floured board, as you would knead bread dough, until it is smooth and satiny. Put the ball of dough into a warm buttered bowl, rolling it around so it is buttered all over. This prevents formation of a crust. Put the bowl in a warm place, cover it with a cloth, and let the dough rise for 1 hour or a little more. Punch down the dough and place the bowl in the refrigerator for overnight. In the morning remove the dough from the refrigerator in time to bring it to room temperature before using it.

WHITE-WINE ASPIC

3 cups chicken broth
2 whole cloves
1 egg white, slightly beaten, and crushed shell

⅔ cup dry white wine
2 tablespoons unflavoured gelatine
⅓ cup cold water

Put the cold broth in a large saucepan with the cloves, egg white, and shell. Add the white wine; bring to a boil, stirring constantly. Simmer for 15 minutes and pour through a fine strainer lined with dampened cloth. Soften the gelatine in the cold water and dissolve it in the clarified hot broth. Correct the seasoning and cool the aspic until it is just beginning to set.

MENU 96 Vitello Tonnato *(for 10)*

4-pound boneless veal roast, from the leg	1 carrot, chopped
7 flat anchovy fillets	4 cups white wine
2 garlic cloves, chopped	2 tablespoons lemon juice
3 parsley sprigs	Two 7-ounce cans tuna fish, packed in oil
¼ cup olive oil	2 tablespoons mayonnaise
1 onion, chopped	5 tablespoons capers

Have the butcher trim, roll, and tie the roast. Make little slits in the outside surface of the meat and insert 4 of the anchovies, each cut into three pieces. Put the meat in a 16-cup baking dish with the garlic, parsley, olive oil, onion, carrot, and the white wine. Cover and roast for about 2 hours in a medium oven (350°), or until the meat thermometer reads 175°. Let the meat cool in the baking dish, then remove it to a platter and slice it. Strain the juices from the baking dish. Beat in the lemon juice, tuna fish and oil, the remaining anchovies, mashed, and the mayonnaise. Continue to beat the sauce until it is well mixed and very smooth. Pour the tuna fish sauce over the veal and sprinkle all with the capers. If you wish, you may garnish the platter with hard-boiled egg halves, tiny pickles, and watercress. Serve cold, with a dish of cold boiled rice.

MENU 97 Green Rice *(for 10)*

6½ cups well-seasoned chicken broth	3 tablespoons butter, or more
2½ cups raw rice	½ cup chopped parsley
	Black pepper

Bring the broth to a boil. Trickle in the rice and stir well once. Bring to a boil again and then lower the heat to medium; simmer for 15 minutes. Taste for doneness; the broth should be absorbed and the rice firm but not starchy. If the broth is absorbed but the rice is not as done as you would like it, cook for about 3 minutes more, adding a very small amount of hot broth. Drain the rice, then steam it in a colander for 5 minutes. Place the rice in a foil-lined dish, stir in the butter, cover over with foil, and keep warm until serving time in a low oven (300°). The rice can be kept hot for 30 minutes without drying out. At serving time, toss the grains with parsley, sprinkle with pepper, and add more butter if desired.

MENU 98   Cold Boiled Beef en Gelée *(for 12)*

8 cups beef bouillon
2 cups dry white wine
1 cup chopped carrots
1½ cups chopped onion
Leaves from 6 celery stalks
Bouquet garni composed of 2 garlic cloves, 1 bay leaf, 8 peppercorns, and 2 thyme sprigs

6-pound sirloin tip, rolled and tied
Aspic for beef (see below)
2 carrots, cooked and sliced
Fresh tarragon leaves
2 hard-boiled eggs, sliced
Parsley sprigs

Make this a day ahead. Pour the bouillon into a 24-cup soup pot and add the wine, vegetables, and *bouquet garni*. Bring to a boil and simmer for 15 minutes. Put a meat thermometer in the meat. Plunge the meat into the boiling broth and simmer until the thermometer registers 140°, about 1½ hours. Strain off the broth and reserve to make aspic (see below). Wrap the meat in foil so it does not discolour, and cool. Make the aspic. Remove the strings from the roast. Spoon liquid aspic, just on the point of setting, over the roast. Dip slices of cooked carrots, blanched tarragon leaves, and sliced hard-boiled eggs in liquid aspic and arrange them on the meat. When the decorations and the first layer of aspic are firm, spoon more aspic over the meat and chill until set. Do this a third time; by this time the aspic should be about ¼ inch thick. Pour the remaining aspic into a flat pan. Scramble with a fork and arrange around the meat at serving time.

If the meat is to be sliced before serving, do not decorate the top, but put the carrots and egg slices around the meat. Surround with the aspic diamonds and garnish with the parsley sprigs.

ASPIC FOR BEEF

6 cups beef bouillon
3 egg whites, slightly beaten, and crushed shells

3 tablespoons unflavoured gelatine
½ cup cold water
⅔ cup dry Madeira wine

Put the cold bouillon in a large saucepan and add the egg whites and shells. Bring to a boil, stirring constantly. Simmer for 15 minutes and pour through a fine strainer lined with dampened cloth. Soften the gelatine in the cold water and dissolve it in the clarified hot bouillon. Add the Madeira. Correct the seasoning. Cool the aspic until it is just beginning to set.

MENU 98   Hot Potato Salad (for 12)

12 large potatoes
 1 bunch scallions with some of the green tops, minced, or 2 medium onions, minced
½ cup chopped parsley
½ teaspoon fresh or dried tarragon
½ teaspoon dried chervil

 1 cup warm olive oil
⅓ cup tarragon wine vinegar
 2 teaspoons salt
⅔ teaspoon freshly ground black pepper
1½ teaspoons Dijon mustard

Choose firm potatoes without blemishes, but do not use new potatoes for this. Boil the potatoes in their jackets until tender but not mushy. While the potatoes cook, make a dressing of all the remaining ingredients, stirring briskly for 2 to 3 minutes. Peel the potatoes while still hot, slice them, and pour the dressing over. Mix gently with wooden spoons to distribute the dressing, and serve immediately.

MENU 98   Marrons Café Bombe (for 12)

2 quarts coffee ice cream
2 cups canned purée of marrons glacés

Two 9-ounce jars marrons glacés in syrup, in pieces
½ cup Cognac

Soften the ice cream a little and pack it into a melon mould, filling it to the top. Cover the mould and place it in the freezing part of the refrigerator until the ice cream is fairly firm again, about 30 minutes. Take the mould out of the freezer and scoop enough ice cream out of the center to make a space big enough to hold 2 cups puréed marrons. Put the purée into this hollow and cover completely with the ice cream just removed. Smooth over the surface, cover again, and return to the freezer for 2 hours.

Make a sauce from the pieces of marrons glacés, the syrup, and the Cognac.

Mix thoroughly. Unmould the ice cream on a platter and pour the sauce over it. Slice and serve, spooning some sauce over each slice as it is served.

MENU 99   Petites Quiches Lorraines *(for 12)*

Pastry for 12 tart pans
24 slices Gruyère cheese
12 small slices boiled ham
4 eggs
2 cups light cream

½ teaspoon salt
Dash of cayenne pepper
Grated nutmeg
Butter

Preheat the oven to very hot (450°). Use regulation tart pans slightly larger than muffin tins. Butter 12 tart pans and line them with tart pastry (see page 136), or puff pastry (see page 138), or flaky pastry (see page 161). Line the pastry with wax paper filled with raw rice or dried beans. Bake the tarts without browning for 10 minutes. Remove from the oven and discard the rice or beans and the wax paper. Reduce the oven heat to medium (350°).

Cut the cheese and ham into rounds which will fit exactly the inside diameter of the tart shells. Place at the bottom of each shell a slice of Gruyère cheese, then a slice of ham, then another slice of Gruyère. Beat the eggs with the cream and add the salt and cayenne and nutmeg to taste. Fill the tarts with this mixture. Scatter bits of butter on top. Return to the oven and bake for about 20 minutes until a nice golden brown. Quickly remove the tarts from the moulds and serve hot. These can also be served cold, but they are more delicious when hot.

MENU 99   Apricot Trifle *(for 12)*

2 pounds dried apricots
1½ cups sugar
½ lemon
25 macaroons
1 cup sweet Sherry
1 tablespoon unflavoured gelatine

¼ cup cold water
2 cups light cream
2-inch piece of vanilla bean
4 egg yolks
1½ cups heavy cream
1½ teaspoons vanilla extract

Cook the apricots in just enough water to cover with ⅔ cup sugar and the lemon, unpeeled, until the apricots are very tender. Remove the lemon and purée the apricots. Meantime, soak the macaroons in the Sherry in a large serving bowl. Make a custard: Soften the gelatine in the cold water. In the top of a double boiler scald the light cream with the vanilla bean and ½ cup sugar. Beat the egg yolks very well, pour in a little hot cream, stirring constantly, and then add the warmed egg yolks to the rest of the cream. Place over hot water and cook, stirring, until the mixture coats the spoon. Remove from the heat, add the gelatine, and stir until dissolved. Strain the custard. Open the vanilla bean, scrape the seeds into the custard, and stir. Put the custard into the refrigerator to cool for 30 minutes. Pour the apricot purée over the soaked macaroons and the cooled custard over the apricots. Now whip the heavy cream with the remaining ⅓ cup sugar and the vanilla extract. Arrange the whipped cream like little floating islands on the custard. Chill well before serving.

MENU 100   Sausage in Pastry *(for 12)*

2 Polish-type sausages, about 3 inches thick and 15 inches long, cooked

Puff pastry (see page 138)

Plunge the sausages into boiling water for 5 minutes. Cool a little and remove the outer casing. Cut them in half crosswise. When they are completely cooled, wrap them in puff pastry rolled out to ⅓-inch thickness. Put the rolls on a cookie sheet with the pastry seam underneath. Prick all over with a fork. Preheat the oven to very hot (425°) while chilling the pastries for 30 minutes. Bake the rolls until the pastry is puffed and golden, about 20 minutes. This is very rich; a 2-inch serving is a good portion. Serve hot. The sausage rolls may be made ahead and baked at the last moment, or they may be baked ahead and reheated just before serving.

MENU 101   Brunswick Stew *(for 12 to 14)*

Two 5- to 6-pound chickens
½ cup tomato purée
2 cans whole tomatoes, or 10 ripe fresh tomatoes, quartered
2 large Bermuda onions, diced
2½ cups raw green lima beans

6 small okra pods, cut in pieces
2 small, dried hot red pepper pods
Salt and black pepper to taste
1 cup butter
2 cups fresh corn, cut from the cob, or 2 cups frozen or canned corn

Stew the fowls until the meat can easily be taken from the bones. Drain the meat, reserving the broth, and cool. Remove the meat from the bones and dice it. Put the chicken and all the vegetables except the corn into a large kettle. Add 2 cups of the reserved broth and half the butter. Simmer very gently until the beans are tender. Remove the red pepper pods and add the corn and the remaining butter. Continue cooking for about 15 minutes. The stew should be thick in con- sistency and should be very highly seasoned with pepper. If the red peppers are too hot for your taste, cut down on the quantity, or omit them, but Brunswick stew is a peppery dish. If the mixture is too dry before the corn is added, put in more broth. Serve in soup plates, with squares of buttered cornbread or corn- meal muffins.

This Brunswick stew can be made with other meats as well—with beef, veal, or rabbit.

MENU 102   Mayonnaise *(for 12)*

1 whole egg	5 to 6 dashes cayenne pepper
3 egg yolks	2½ cups olive oil
1½ teaspoons salt	¼ cup white-wine vinegar, or
1½ teaspoons dry mustard	lemon juice, or half and half

Have the eggs at room temperature. Put the whole egg and the egg yolks, salt, mustard, and cayenne pepper into a large bowl. Beat with a wire whisk, or with an electric hand-beater, until well mixed and slightly thickened. Trickle in the oil while continuing to beat steadily until half the oil has been absorbed. Add the vinegar or lemon juice, beating constantly. Pour in the remaining oil slowly, but not as slowly as at the start, until all the oil is absorbed. Store the mayonnaise in a cool place.

When making mayonnaise in a blender, put the whole egg, the egg yolks, and the seasoning into the glass container and blend for a few seconds to mix. Turn off the motor and push the eggs down with a rubber spatula. Turn on the motor again and pour in half the oil in a thin stream while blending at medium speed. After 2 minutes, add the vinegar, then the remaining oil.

For a green mayonnaise, blanch a few parsley sprigs, 6 or 7 spinach leaves, and a little watercress in boiling water for 2 minutes. Press out the water and add the leaves to the blender with the eggs.

MENU 103   Cheese Soufflé *(for 10 to 12)*

⅓ cup grated Parmesan cheese, approximately
½ cup butter
⅓ cup flour
2 cups milk
2 cups grated Gruyère cheese

8 egg yolks
1 teaspoon dry mustard
Black pepper
Cayenne pepper
Salt
12 egg whites

Preheat the oven to medium (350°). Butter two 6-cup soufflé dishes. Sprinkle the dishes with the Parmesan cheese, rolling them around until they are well covered, and tapping out any excess. Melt the ½ cup butter in a large saucepan, add the flour, and cook it slowly, stirring until smooth, for 3 minutes. Do not let it brown. Add the milk and bring to the boiling point over low heat, stirring until thickened and smooth. Add the Gruyère cheese and stir in. Remove from the heat and cool the mixture a little. Beat the egg yolks and add them to the mixture. Add the mustard, black pepper to taste, and several dashes of cayenne pepper. Add salt to taste, depending on the saltiness of the cheese. Whip the egg whites with a dash of salt only until you can turn the bowl over without the eggs sliding out. Stir a third of the whites quickly but gently into the cheese mixture, then pour this mixture over the remaining whites, and fold in, turning the bowl all the time until well incorporated. Pour into the prepared soufflé dishes and bake without peeking for 25 minutes, preferably on the lower shelf of the oven. After 25 minutes shake one of the soufflé dishes very gently; if the mixture is very loose, bake for another 5 minutes for a soft soufflé. For a firm soufflé bake for 35 minutes in all. Serve immediately. Be sure to have ready very hot plates.

For a soufflé that will wait a little, place the dishes in pans of water and bake for 45 minutes.

MENU 104   Meat Loaf with Pâté en Croûte *(for 12)*

4 pounds top round of beef, ground
1 tablespoon salt
1 teaspoon freshly ground black pepper
1 pound liver pâté

6 bacon strips
Flaky pastry (see page 161)
1 egg yolk
Parsley
Mushroom sauce (see below)

Season the ground beef with the salt and pepper and shape the meat into two loaves. Have the liver pâté very cold and cut it into 8 slices. With a very sharp knife slice each meat loaf four times from the top almost to the bottom, but not deep enough to make the loaf fall apart. Into each of these cuts put one slice of the pâté. Press each loaf firmly together so that it looks once more like a solid loaf. Put 3 bacon strips across the top of each loaf. Bake the loaves in a medium oven (350°) for 35 minutes. Remove from the oven, discard the bacon, and cool. Wrap the partially cooked meat in aluminum foil and store it in the refrigerator. Store the flaky pastry in the refrigerator until ready to use. The meat loaves and the flaky pastry may be prepared ahead of time.

About 40 minutes before you are ready to serve, roll out the pastry into 2 thin sheets large enough to wrap the loaves. Remove the loaves from the refrigerator and wrap each in a pastry envelope. Lap the dough over on the bottom and seal the edges with cold water. Brush the surface of the pastry with cold water and prick well with a fork. Put the loaves into a roasting pan in a hot oven (400°) and bake for 35 minutes. If the pastry becomes brown before the time is up, cover with foil and continue baking. About 10 minutes before the finish, brush the crusts with the beaten egg yolk. Transfer the finished loaves to serving platters and garnish with parsley. Serve mushroom sauce separately.

Mushroom Sauce

Two 10½-ounce cans cream of mushroom soup	1 cup light cream
	4 tablespoons catsup

Heat the mushroom soup with the cream, stirring constantly. When it is very hot and smooth, add the catsup and mix well. Serve very hot.

MENU 104   Baked Zucchini Casserole (for 12)

6 tablespoons butter, or more	3 sweet Italian onions, sliced
3 tablespoons olive oil, or more	Salt and black pepper
12 medium zucchini, sliced	½ cup cracker crumbs
4 large firm tomatoes, sliced	½ cup Parmesan cheese, grated

Heat butter and oil as needed and sauté the zucchini for a few minutes on each side. Butter an 8-cup casserole. Arrange layers of zucchini, tomatoes, and onions, seasoning each layer with salt and pepper and dots of butter, ending with zucchini. Sprinkle the top with cracker crumbs and Parmesan cheese. Bake the casserole in a medium oven (375°) for about 40 minutes, or until the vegetables are tender and the top browned and crisp.

MENU 105   Kasha with Meatballs (for 14)

3 cups buckwheat or kasha	1½ teaspoons salt
1 cup butter	¼ teaspoon black pepper
4 cups water	½ teaspoon orégano
2 eggs	½ teaspoon dried chives
4 pounds round steak, ground	¾ cup vegetable shortening

Shake the kasha in a colander to remove any particles of husks. Melt ½ cup of the butter in a large frying pan; add the kasha and cook over low heat, stirring constantly, until the kasha is browned, about 20 minutes. Add about 4 cups water to the browned kasha; the liquid should be about an inch above the grain. Cover and steam for about 20 minutes, or until the water has been absorbed. Stir in the remaining butter. Transfer the kasha to a warmed deep platter and keep it hot until the meatballs are ready.

Beat the eggs slightly and add them to the ground beef with the salt, pepper, orégano, and dried chives. Mix thoroughly. Form the meat into small round balls and cook them in very hot vegetable shortening, being careful in turning them to keep the shape of the meatballs, as it makes a more attractive platter. Arrange the cooked meatballs on top of the kasha and serve the dish piping hot.

MENU 106   Baked Corned Beef Hash
(for 14)

12 medium potatoes	½ cup chopped parsley
2 onions, chopped fine	Freshly ground black pepper
1 cup butter	1 cup beef bouillon, or more
6 pounds cooked corned beef, ground	

Preheat the oven to hot (400°). Boil the potatoes in their jackets in salted water, keeping them firm. Cool, peel, and dice them into ¾-inch cubes. Sauté the onions in half the butter until they are tender and golden. Mix the ground corned beef, the onions, potatoes, chopped parsley, and lots of freshly ground black pepper. Butter two oven-to-table casseroles or baking dishes. Put half the hash in each dish and add a little bouillon to each. Add more bouillon during the baking, just enough to keep the meat moist. Dot with the remaining butter and bake until golden and crusty, about 25 minutes. Baked hash can be made ahead and reheated just before serving.

2

Committee Food:
Luncheons and Teas

LUNCHEON WITH THE COMMITTEE

As ANY committee member knows ("committee member" includes practically every woman living), the luncheon committee
meeting is a very special kind of luncheon if the members are all
women. Any hostess worth her name shies away from the idea of
something called "lady food," but nevertheless there are certain
menus that one can offer to women with the expectation of
pleased acceptance, but which would probably be varied if men
were to be present. The suggested menus here are, without exception, light; for one thing, people cannot think well or work
well after a rich, heavy meal; and, for another, most women,
even if not strict dieters, are calorie conscious today. If the
hostess is an omelet maker, menu planning is fairly simple,
for omelets can be varied interminably and are an excellent
basis for an attractive, unrich luncheon menu. One hostess we
know, Spartan in her own diet, offers her women guests at
luncheon what some of them call meagre fare, but adds to the
menu an "off limits" dessert which the slim or the nonweight-
watchers can eat after the rigors of a sensible lunch.

The following menus are planned for pleasant light luncheons, but for a more gala luncheon these could be supplemented
by additional dishes or more voluptuous desserts.

The only wine offered is Sherry, before lunch.

MENU 107 (for eight)

Asparagus Soup*

Fish Pudding*

Green Salad

Melon with
Small Scoops of Sherbet

* Recipes on page 242.

MENU 108 (for eight)

Beef Chinois*

Endive Salad

Fruit Soufflé*

* Recipes on page 243.

MENU 109 (for eight)

Smoked Salmon
with Black Pepper

Vegetable Casserole of
Eggplant, Okra, Mushrooms

Oranges Dulcinea*

* Recipe on page 243.

MENU 110 (for eight)

Hot Turkey Hash*

Baked White Potatoes

Green Bean Salad*

Fresh Pineapple
with a Dash of Kirsch
or
Lemon Layer Cake

* Recipes on page 244.

TEA WITH THE COMMITTEE

Afternoon tea seems casual, but even for four or six it deserves special care and "tea with the committee" can combine business at hand with a graceful, hospitable gesture. When the number of guests is definite and the dining table can accommodate them, it is pleasant to follow the European custom and serve tea in the dining room, with the hostess behind the tea service and with a special kind of delicate tea food on the table. Practically, it is easier to discuss committee matters when there is some sort of focus for the speakers and when the guests are not trying to balance a tea plate, a tea cup, and perhaps even a cigarette at the same time.

Tea tastes being variable, it is probably impossible to please every guest in the matter of blend. However, if at all workable, it is considerate to offer a choice of China black or Lapsong Souchong, and either Darjeeling or English Breakfast tea.

With tea, it is well to serve both sweet and nonsweet food. For example, hot orange biscuits, toasted English muffins with fruit jelly, and toasted brioche loaf are not sweet enough to be unsuitable for late afternoon, and they do please many people, with tea. Others will prefer nonsweet offerings such as thin slices of buttered white bread spread with chutney; rye bread sliced thin, rolled and filled with chopped chives and parsley; caraway wafers, heated and buttered.

Many of these could be offered also when the tea party is not seated at one table. But, hopefully, there will be little tables near at hand, on which the guests can put their plates and cups and saucers.

As for the tea itself, plenty of hot water is advisable, as not everyone likes "tea as it comes"; a teaspoon of rum in the tea may furnish a pleasant variation for some of the guests. Very small lumps of sugar, both cream and milk, and thin slices of oranges, as well as lemon, should be on the tea table.

Here are some other suggestions for sweet food to serve with tea:

Small hot croissants with strawberry jam
Squares of hot gingerbread
Tiny fruit turnovers
Fresh angel-food cake
Hot macaroons
Toasted poundcake
Small squares of fruitcake
Tiny cream puffs

Or these nonsweet foods may be served:

Tiny crabmeat turnovers
Toasted bite-size chicken sandwiches
Finger sandwiches of smoked turkey on whole-wheat bread
Rolled sandwiches of buttered white bread with chopped chives and parsley
Thin toast spread with mixed Roquefort and cream cheese
Hot buttered beaten biscuits
Smallest possible finger rolls with slivers of prosciutto or smoked ham

MENU 107   Asparagus Soup *(for 8)*

2 small cans asparagus, or 12 to 16   2 peppercorns
  stalks cooked fresh asparagus   2 canned pimientos, chopped very
6 cups beef bouillon   fine
½ teaspoon celery salt

Drain the asparagus, if canned, and cut it into thin slices. Heat the bouillon, add the seasonings, then the asparagus and pimientos. Simmer gently for 15 minutes. Discard the peppercorns. Serve hot, with thin caraway wafers.

MENU 107   Fish Pudding *(for 8)*

3 pounds boned fish, haddock   2 teaspoons salt
  or cod   4 eggs, separated
2 cups white wine   2 cups skim milk
Bouquet garni composed of   Two 8-ounce packages protein spa-
  1 bay leaf, 1 garlic clove,   ghettini
  1 teaspoon dried thyme, and   ¼ cup butter
  8 peppercorns   ¾ cup grated Parmesan cheese

In a heavy frying pan, poach the fish over very low heat in the wine and *bouquet garni* for about 12 to 15 minutes. The fish should be tender but not flaky. Remove the fish and strain and salt the broth. Beat the egg yolks well and combine them with the fish broth and the milk. Break the raw spaghettini into 2-inch pieces and cook it for just 15 minutes in boiling salted water. Drain well and add it to the prepared liquid. Mix thoroughly, then fold in the well-beaten egg whites. Butter a 12-cup oven-to-table baking dish with half the butter. Place the mixture in the bottom of the baking dish and arrange the poached fish on top of the pasta. Bake for 30 minutes in a medium oven (350°). Sprinkle the top thinly with Parmesan cheese, dot with the remaining 2 tablespoons butter, and bake for 10 minutes more. When ready for the table, this pudding should be moist, but not runny, and well-browned on top. Serve hot, with the rest of the grated Parmesan cheese in a separate bowl.

MENU 108   Beef Chinois *(for 8)*

1½ cups finely sliced green peppers	⅛ teaspoon black pepper
¾ cup finely chopped onions	2 cups canned bean sprouts,
¾ cup beef bouillon	drained
2 pounds beef steak, 1½ inches	3 tablespoons soy sauce
thick	½ cup Port wine

Simmer the green peppers and onions in the bouillon until tender but still firm. Slice the steak across the grain into slivers 2 inches long and 1½ inches wide. Put the steak slices, the green peppers, and the onions in a heavy frying pan and sprinkle with the black pepper. Cook over high heat for about 6 minutes. Add the bean sprouts, soy sauce, and wine. Mix thoroughly and simmer for 5 minutes longer. If the mixture seems too dry, add a little more wine. Serve piping hot.

MENU 108   Fruit Soufflé *(for 8)*

3 tablespoons unflavoured gelatine	½ teaspoon vanilla extract
4 cups skim milk	⅛ teaspoon nutmeg
3 eggs, separated	1 cup canned peaches, pears or
2 tablespoons sugar	apricots, puréed
Dash of salt	

Soften the gelatine in ½ cup of the milk. Heat the remaining milk. Beat the egg yolks lightly and stir into the milk with the sugar and salt. Cook in a double boiler over simmering water, stirring, until the mixture coats the spoon. Add the gelatine and stir until it dissolves. Remove from the heat and blend in the vanilla and nutmeg. Cool the custard until it begins to thicken. Beat the egg whites until stiff. Fold them into the custard with the puréed fruit. Chill until the gelatine has set.

MENU 109   Oranges Dulcinea *(for 8)*

8 large navel oranges	2⅔ cups dark brown sugar
2⅔ cups skim milk	3 tablespoons sifted flour
8 eggs, separated	½ teaspoon vanilla

Peel the oranges carefully, removing the white pith, but leaving the inner skin intact. Cut out the centres from stem end with a sharp knife or sharp corer, removing *only* white core and leaving meat intact. Sharp scissors may be needed to cut some of the skin to avoid tearing the oranges. Cut a thin slice off bottom of orange so it will rest firmly in pan. Scald the milk. Beat the egg yolks and sugar together and slowly add the flour, stirring to make smooth. Add the vanilla. Slowly add the mixture to the scalded milk and cook the custard in a double boiler over low heat until the mixture coats a spoon, 6 to 7 minutes. Remove from the heat and set aside to cool. Beat the egg whites very stiff and fold thoroughly into the cooled custard. Spoon this into and on top of the prepared oranges, piling high. Put oranges into baking pan; bake in a hot oven (400°) for about 10 minutes, but watch carefully to keep from scorching. Serve hot or cold.

MENU 110   Hot Turkey Hash *(for 8)*

2 medium Bermuda onions, sliced thinly
6 inside celery ribs, cut in tiny pieces
6 tablespoons butter
4 cups diced white meat and 1 cup diced dark meat of cooked turkey
3 cups chicken broth
1 tablespoon burnt sugar
Salt and black pepper
1 tablespoon cornstarch

Cook the onions and celery in very little water with 4 tablespoons of the butter. Let the liquid cook down, but do not brown the vegetables. Put the cut-up turkey in a heavy saucepan, about 8-cup size, add the broth, and mix well. Cover the saucepan and simmer gently for 20 minutes. Then add the cooked onions and celery, also the burnt sugar to give a good colour. Add salt and black pepper to taste. Thicken slightly with the cornstarch dissolved in a little cold water. Stir in the remaining 2 tablespoons butter and serve very hot.

MENU 110   Green Bean Salad *(for 8)*

2 packages frozen whole green beans
1 cup beef bouillon
½ teaspoon powdered dill
2 tablespoons finely chopped onions
¼ cup French dressing
1 tablespoon Roquefort or blue cheese (optional)

After defrosting the beans, put them in a saucepan with the bouillon, dill, and onions. When the liquid comes to a boil, lower the heat. Simmer for about 15 minutes, uncovered, by which time all the liquid should be absorbed. Watch carefully to avoid scorching. Remove the beans from the heat, add the dressing and the crumbled Roquefort or blue cheese, if desired. Mix well and marinate for 15 minutes. Serve without chilling further.

3

Cocktails:
Small and Cozy,
or for Fifty Plus

COCKTAILS FOR FIFTY OR MORE

NO ONE knows just when the big afternoon tea developed (many think, degenerated) into the cocktail party. Too big cocktail parties with too much to drink and too many people are unhappily prevalent. They are, indeed, so prevalent that there is a question in many hostesses' minds as to whether they should try to give a big cocktail party ever again. But it can be attractive; it can be a friendly gesture toward a wide group of acquaintances whom one would like to see but who cannot all be invited to dinner at once.

A successful cocktail party is always slightly crowded; the emphasis here is on *slightly*. If there are too, too many people, not only is there an unattractive physical discomfort, but the fact of being one of too many guests is not very flattering to any of them. If the cocktail party is to be a compliment to the guests, they should be comfortable, offered enough to drink but not plied, and presented with pleasantly varied canapés.

An R.S.V.P. on written cocktail invitations is desirable. The response is a courtesy often honoured in the breach rather than in the observance; but an experienced hostess can make a point of expecting an answer. If you feel that you cannot make, say, one hundred cocktail guests comfortable at one time in your house, you might try having parties of fifty on two successive afternoons.

The flow of traffic through your rooms is an important part of the arrangements. The most agreeable scheme has a room for the women guests which permits them to shed their coats and wraps and repair their faces before they meet the eyes of the guests already arrived. If the women guests are to remove their coats in the outer hall without going to a dressing room or a bedroom, it is important that a mirror be available for them.

Many successful hostesses arrange that someone, either a member of the family or a waiter, offers the arriving guest something to drink even before she or he has reached the hostess's side. This can be done by presenting a tray of varied drinks, or by an immediate question as to what drink is preferred. The canapés can wait; any guest is content to sip a cocktail for a few moments before being offered food.

It is not usual at most attractive cocktail parties to offer an extremely wide variety of drinks. Nor is it the most elegant arrangement to have an imitation bar, with a uniformed waiter trying to look like a bartender in service. The custom of having drinks mixed in the pantry or the kitchen or some other room, and brought in either by a waiter or waitress or a member of the family, is more hospitable and makes the cocktail party a more personal form of entertainment than any imitation of restaurant or hotel service can be. At a Washington embassy, where as many as three hundred guests might be invited for cocktails, the drinks were mixed in the pantry, and served on trays by the waiters. Canapés and appetizers were never passed to the guests, but were placed on tables about the rooms, so that people might serve themselves when ready; the danger of being interrupted in the middle of a good conversation by the sudden imperious appearance of a platter was thus avoided.

At cocktail parties large and small, the usual drinks are Scotch, Bourbon, rye whiskey, or vodka—all in the form of a straight drink with ice, or with soda, or ginger ale or water; gin and lemon or gin-and-tonic; gin or vodka Martini; Manhattan cocktails or Bloody Marys (vodka and tomato juice). Vodka is frequently served in a small glass like a liqueur glass, and drunk without any addition. Anything more elaborate than these drinks is unnecessary; if a guest is so unobservant as to request something other than these, the waiter or waitress can be instructed to say, "I'm sorry, but we are not serving those today."

It is rather chancy to try to estimate the exact amount of each liquor needed for any given number of people, as drinks vary in popularity, from section to section. For example, on the eastern seaboard, as far down as Washington, D.C., Scotch is the preferred whiskey; in Washington and points south, Bourbon is likely to be first choice; in certain communities there is a rise in the preference for vodka, both as a straight drink and as a substitute for gin in Martinis. But these are all individual preferences, and the hostess will surely have some idea as to the popularity of the various drinks among her own friends.

It is usually estimated that a fifth of whiskey should make twelve to fourteen moderate drinks—whiskey on ice, or whiskey and water, or a whiskey and soda. Quite probably, half the guests will be drinking whiskey (Scotch or Bourbon, depending on the custom of the community) and, assuming that the whiskey-drinking guests will have at least two drinks each, one bottle of whiskey for every six or seven people seems ample.

Ready-mixed Martinis or Manhattans are one solution for quick serving and for estimating the number of cocktails available, as the bottles state the amount of the contents. If you have a prejudice against ready-made cocktails, estimate the approximate number of Martini drinkers and allow one quart of gin for sixteen to eighteen Martinis (depending on how dry the Martinis are). Three bottles of vodka for vodka Martinis and Bloody Marys should be enough for a cocktail party of fifty, if whiskeys and gin are in ample supply.

A good general rule is to have a reserve of liquor amounting to about one quarter of the estimated need. Most liquor dealers will take back the extra bottles or will store them for you if you do not wish to keep the unused liquors in your own house.

The canapé range is so wide that no list can present everything that is desirable, but there are certain things a canapé should *not* be, and these might be well to keep in mind, particularly for a big cocktail party.

Canapés should not be hard to eat or too big (two or three bites is about the limit). They should not be elaborate or look contrived. And, if possible, no canapé should have any appendage that requires disposal (even stuffed olives are preferable to whole ones, delicious as big black ripe olives are).

The over-decorated, fussy-looking canapés that, unfortunately, are often served in restaurants and hotels have no place in a private cocktail party. The late Frank Lloyd Wright is credited with saying, when a tray of these over-elaborate, colourful things was presented to him, "It is bad enough to have to look at modern art without having to eat it."

For a smaller party, one or two delicious spreads in a crock or bowl, served with Melba rounds or crackers, could be offered for the guests to serve to themselves. The Roquefort cheese spread (page 262) is one; minced clams with mayonnaise; avocado paste and a crock of pâté are among the possibilities. However, such spreads are only for a small party—they can be rather messy even so. For more than ten or twelve, the self-service spread is to be avoided.

As a general rule, experienced caterers judge that four canapés per person will be enough. This need not mean that, for a party of fifty, fifty of each kind of canapé be prepared. It seems a little more interesting to have five or six different kinds of canapés (one or two of them hot), and to make varying quantities of each, so that the total number of pieces prepared is a little over 200.

Here are suggestions for combinations of canapés from which choices can be made for any number of cocktail parties; it is not necessary to vary them from party to party. People seldom remember what they have been served, and if they do, no matter.

Naturally, various other combinations can be made of these thirty ideas; none is too difficult to make or have made at home. Add to these a big bowl of fresh, crisp vegetables on ice. The bowl might include peeled cucumbers, sliced into sticks; carrot sticks; raw cauliflower flowerets; cherry tomatoes; slices of fennel; whole cooked baby beets.

MENU 111 (for fifty)

Eggs Stuffed
with
Red Caviar*

Roquefort Pecans*

Finger Sandwiches
of
Smoked Turkey
on
White Bread

Cucumber Boats
filled with
Crabmeat and Mayonnaise

Tiny Hot Finger Rolls
filled with
Bacon Crumbles

*Recipes on page 259.

MENU 112 (for fifty)

Watercress Sandwiches
on
Black Bread and Butter

Avocado Spread
on
Caraway Wafers

Eggs Stuffed
with
Chopped Olives*

Hors-d'oeuvre Puffs
with
Smoked Salmon*

Hot Finger Rolls
with
Slivers of Ham

*Recipes on page 259.

MENU 113 (for fifty)

Small Raw Mushrooms
Stuffed with Avocado

Cream Cheese and
Nut Balls*

Hot Beaten Biscuits
Buttered
with
Anchovy Paste

Thin-Sliced Pumpernickel
with
Sweet Butter

Cheese Wafers with
Pecans*

MENU 114 (for fifty)

Smoked Herring Fillets
en Croûtes

Small Hot Turnovers
Filled with Ground Ham*

Artichoke Toast
with
Sweet Butter

Thin Sandwiches
of
Whole-Wheat Bread
with
Roquefort Spread*

Minced Truffles in Pastry*

* Recipes on page 260.

* Recipes on pages 261-262.

MENU 115 *(for fifty)*

*Sandwiches
of
Nut Bread and Butter*

*Cheese Thimble Biscuits**

*White Bread Sandwiches
of
Chicken
Chopped Walnuts
and
Mayonnaise*

*Small Hot Turnovers
with
Minced Clams**

*Spicy Pecans**

MENU 116 *(for fifty)*

*Hot Sesame Shortbread**

*Sandwiches
of
Cucumber and
Chopped Dill
on
Buttered White Bread*

*Stuffed Cherry Tomatoes
with
Cream Cheese and Chives*

*Chopped Hard-Boiled Eggs
in
Curry Mayonnaise
on
Round Crackers*

*Hot Parmesan Greenery**

* Recipes on pages 262-263.   * Recipes on page 264.

COCKTAILS AND AFTER

There is a growing and pleasant custom of prolonging the cocktail party into a buffet dinner party, or supper party, for some of the guests. The invitations may read "Cocktails 6 to 10," and the later guests then, quite reasonably, expect something more substantial than canapés with their drinks. Or the hostess may ask a certain number to stay on for supper. This is especially pleasant on Sunday nights when guests, driving in from country weekends, are happy to find a flexible dinner hour, and a reasonably early home-going.

Here are suggested combinations for an after-cocktail buffet.

MENU 117 (for twenty)

*Veal Spezzatino**

Avocado and Crab Salad

*Bowl
of
Scoops of Lime Sherbet*

Cookies

The Wine:
A light claret from the Médoc.

* Recipe on page 98.

MENU 118 (for twenty)

*Beef
and
Kidney Pie**

*Salade Schiaparelli**

Cheesecake

The Wine:
A Burgundy from the Côte de Beaune.

* Recipes on pages 87 and 96.

MENU 119 (for twenty-four)   *MENU 120 (for twenty-four)*

*Jellied Parsleyed Ham**	*Fish Tetrazzini**
*Peas and Lima Beans au Gratin**	*Curried Chicken**
Fresh Slices of Orange and Pineapple Sprinkled with Cognac	*Salad of Lettuce and Water Chestnuts*
	*Lady Baltimore Cake**

The Wine:

Champagne.

The Wine:

Chablis with the fish; a full-bodied red Rhone with the curry.

* Recipes on pages 74 and 89.   * Recipes on pages 101, 98, and 70.

SHE SPECIALIZES IN SMALL COCKTAIL PARTIES

Caroline Cazenovia is a young woman, not too young, who lives alone in her small apartment in a big city. She knows a good many people; some she has met professionally (she is a reader for a publishing firm), some are old-school-tie friends; and some she has met through distant relatives in the city, whose kindness is based partly on their pride in her looks and general manner. There is always an adequate number of young men around, some suitors, some merely interesting companions.

Since her space and means are both on the narrow side, and since Caroline is not only hospitable by nature but independent enough to wish to return courtesies shown to her, she has needed to devise a way of entertaining friends who have entertained her. She makes no effort to "return in kind" since a weekend in a big country place, for example, cannot well be returned by a young woman in her circumstances. But she *has* made an effort and has found it worth while to imagine what some of her hosts and hostesses might really like, without any attempt on her part to impress them. She decided that for her a dinner party, even a small one, was out of the question; she is no Cordon Bleu cook, and frankly feels that she is not in a position to ask some of the people who entertain her to come to her limited quarters for dinner. Her real talent is for people, and around her fondness for people, her interest in them and, fortunately, their returned interest in her, she has built her entertainment plans—small cocktail parties are her specialty. She never has more than eight guests, as she says she can't seat more, comfortably. Some of her parties are so small that they can hardly be called parties; but each of them is planned from the first guest to the last canapé as meticulously as if she were really giving a dinner party. Her guests are her *pièces de résistance,* and when Caroline invites someone to come for a cocktail at six o'clock on Thursday, the invited one knows that he is more than likely to be amused, entertained, or sometimes dazzled by his fellow guests. Caroline has no household help except a twice-a-week cleaning woman who comes for a half day in the mornings. Since she is working through the day, all of Caroline's preparation and planning must be done before the day of the party. She lives near her office so that between the end of her working day and the arrival of her guests, she has time to (1) change her clothes; (2) put into thermos containers the ice which she ordered the day before, to be delivered at six (her baby refrigerator does not have enough cubes for more than two drinks); and (3) finish the canapé preparations. Cocktail plates, forks, small knives, napkins, and the glasses and liquor were put out the night before, on a corner table in the living room. The liquor: Scotch, Bourbon, gin, vermouth, vodka, Sherry. Addenda: bitter lemon, soda, ginger ale, lemon peel, tonic water, plain water. She does not, in her own house, like the idea of portable bars or anything even resembling them.

Caroline argues with herself quite sensibly that no one really comes to cocktails for canapés—they come for interesting company, a drink or two; the canapés are incidental. But whatever the canapés are, they are pristine in their looks, they are presented on handsome plates, and, having been presented once, they are left, visible, available for the guests.

Caroline had experimented with pastry mix, found it easy to use and excellent when cooked. So she bought some tiny tart tins in which she baked the tart shells of the ready-mixed pastry and frequently had these as canapés, hot, filled with various mixtures such as minced clams or curried shrimps, or sautéed mushrooms, or chopped chicken with sour cream and dill. These are made the day before (filling mixed, and tart shells baked) and are put together as the first guest arrives, popped in the small oven for just long enough to heat through. There is always a bowl of crisp, fresh, iced vegetables with whatever canapés are served.

One special cocktail party that Caroline has two or three times during the winter season is for six or eight people, who are invited to come to her before going on to a big dance or charity dinner or museum opening. The dinners at these enormous affairs are always late, and it has proved very pleasant to be able to have cocktails comfortably and to be served something a little more substantial than the casual canapé, something to assuage hunger until the late, late dinner. Hot *quiche lorraine* in not-too-small slices has proven successful; so have hot pizza squares, or even fake pizzas. And once, when some admirer had sent her caviar instead of flowers, she made a caviar tart to serve with the cocktails.

The guests usually linger long after the cocktail hour, and Caroline gives them small cups of black coffee before they all set out for the big party of the evening.

Here are four menus for small cocktail parties; the last two are slightly more substantial than the usual.

MENU 121 (for six to eight)   *MENU 122 (for six to eight)*

Miniature *Curried Shrimp Tarts**
Cucumber Sandwiches *on* *Small Triangles* *of* *Thin White Bread*
Olives
Spicy Pecans*
Bowl of *Fresh Vegetables*

Thin Rounds *of* *Black Bread with* *Prosciutto* *and* *Mustard Butter*
Hot Turnovers *with* *Ground Chicken* *and* *Chopped Parsley**
Olives
Bowl of *Fresh Vegetables*

* Recipes on pages 264 and 263.   * Recipe on page 265.

MENU 123 (for eight)

MENU 124 (for eight)

Crock of Pâté
with
Water Biscuits
Caraway Wafers
Artichoke Toast

Hot Bite-Size Tarts
with
Ground Ham*

or

Water Chestnuts
Wrapped in Bacon*

Finger Sandwiches
of
Nut Bread and Butter

Olives

Bowl of
Fresh Vegetables

Caviar Tart*

Smoked Turkey
Thin Slices
of
White Bread

Macadamia Nuts
Pistachios and Hazelnuts

Bowl of Fresh Vegetables

Bowl of Hard-Boiled Eggs
with
Small Tray of Seasonings

* Recipes on 265 and 266.

* Recipe on page 266.

MENU 111   Eggs Stuffed with Red Caviar

10 eggs
  Juice of ½ lemon

¼ cup mayonnaise
3 tablespoons red caviar

Hard boil the eggs. Cover them with cold water, bring to a boil, and boil for 10 minutes. Crack the boiled eggs and put them in cold water for 10 minutes to loosen the shells, then shell and peel them. Slice the shelled eggs in quarters lengthwise. Remove the yolks and then mash them with the lemon juice and mayonnaise. Add a little more of each if the yolks seem too stiff. Add the red caviar and mix well. Fill the egg whites with the mixture, shaping smoothly over the tops. Makes 40 pieces.

MENU 111   Roquefort Pecans

100 pecan halves

Roquefort spread (see page 262)

Select only perfect pecan halves. Spread the Roquefort mixture carefully across the tops of half the pecans, thick enough to make the rest stick when firmly pressed down. The appearance is that of chubby whole pecans and the taste is delightful. Makes 50 pieces.

MENU 112   Eggs Stuffed with Chopped Olives

Follow the directions for Eggs Stuffed with Red Caviar on this page. Omit the caviar and the lemon juice. Use ½ cup stuffed olives, chopped very fine, to mix with the egg yolks and mayonnaise. Fill the egg whites and smooth the tops. Makes 40 pieces.

MENU 112   Hors-d'oeuvre Puffs with Smoked Salmon

8 slices smoked salmon
½ cup heavy cream, whipped
 1 tablespoon finely cut fresh dill

Dash of cayenne pepper
36 hors-d'oeuvre puffs
 (see below)

Purée the smoked salmon in an electric blender. Fold in the whipped cream, dill, and cayenne pepper, and mix until well blended. Split the prepared puffs, put 1 teaspoon of the salmon mixture into each, and replace the tops. Makes 36 pieces.

Hors-d'oeuvre Puffs

1 cup water	1 cup sifted flour
⅛ teaspoon salt	4 eggs
½ cup butter, cut into pieces	

Preheat the oven to medium (375°). Bring the water, salt, and butter to a boil. When the butter is melted, pour in the flour all at once. Stir vigorously with a wooden spoon over low heat until the mixture forms a ball in the pan. Continue cooking and stirring for about 4 minutes. Remove from the heat and beat in the eggs, one at a time, continuing to stir until the mixture is smooth. Use 2 teaspoons to drop the batter onto an ungreased cookie sheet in amounts about the size of a hazelnut. Leave at least a 2-inch space between the mounds as the pastry swells and puffs in cooking. Bake until golden and no moisture shows, about 20 minutes. Do not underbake or the puffs will collapse. It is a good idea to test one by opening it. Cool the puffs and store them in a tin box or in foil. Makes about 36 puffs.

MENU 113   Cream Cheese and Nut Balls

8 ounces salted almonds	½ cup grated Parmesan cheese
8 ounces cream cheese	2 dashes Tabasco

Wrap the almonds in a heavy cloth and crush them with a rolling pin until they are crumbs. Mix the nut crumbs with the cheeses and Tabasco until all is smoothly mixed. Chill thoroughly, then mould into balls about ½ inch in diameter. Chill again before serving. If the mixture is very cold, it will not stick to the fingers while it is being shaped. Makes 36 to 40 pieces.

MENU 113   Cheese Wafers with Pecans

Cheese biscuit dough (see below)	1 egg
Pecan or walnut halves	

Preheat the oven to medium (375°). Roll out cheese biscuit dough to the desired thickness—about ⅛ inch is ideal. Cut the dough with a small round cookie cutter into rounds, about 1½ inches across. Arrange the rounds on cookie sheets with ample space between. Place half a walnut or pecan on each cookie. Beat the egg slightly and use to brush the cookie tops to form a glaze. Bake for 10 to 15 minutes, until golden brown. When cooled, these wafers can be stored in tins until ready to use. They can be warmed again before serving. Makes about 8 dozen pieces.

CHEESE BISCUIT DOUGH

1 pound sharp Cheddar cheese   Pinch of salt
4 cups flour, not sifted   2 cups margarine

Grate the cheese into a large bowl, then mix well with the unsifted flour and the salt. Add the margarine, working it in until the ingredients are well blended, forming a pliable dough. This can be stored in refrigerator for four or five days. Bring it back to room temperature before rolling out.

MENU 114   Small Hot Turnovers Filled with Ground Ham

Tart pastry (see page 136)   2 cups ground cooked ham
½ cup butter

Double the recipe for tart pastry and make the pastry a day ahead, if possible. Chill it thoroughly in the refrigerator before rolling. Preheat the oven to very hot (450°). Roll out the pastry to about ⅛-inch thickness and cut out rounds with a fluted 2½- or 3-inch cookie cutter.

Soften the butter and cream it until very smooth. Add the ground ham, and mix thoroughly until the filling is almost smooth. Spread one half of each round with about 1 tablespoon of filling. Turn the other half over the filling and seal with a fork, pinching along the edges. Place the turnovers on cookie sheets and bake them for about 20 minutes, or until the pastry is brown.

These turnovers may be completely baked a day ahead and reheated briefly just before serving. Makes 30 to 36 pieces.

MENU 114   Roquefort Spread

8 ounces Roquefort cheese   Paprika
4 ounces cream cheese   ¼ cup butter
1 tablespoon Worcestershire sauce   3 tablespoons brandy
    Dash of Tabasco

Break the Roquefort into small pieces and blend in an electric blender at high speed until smooth. Add the cream cheese, broken up, and blend at low speed. Add Worcestershire, Tabasco, paprika, and the butter, cut into pieces. Stop the blender and push the ingredients down into the blades with a rubber spatula. Add the brandy, and blend.

   If the spread is not made in a blender, mash the cheeses and sieve them, then blend with the softened butter and seasonings. The consistency will be slightly less smooth. Makes enough spread for 36 to 40 hors-d'oeuvre sandwiches.

MENU 114   Minced Truffles in Pastry

Tart pastry (see page 136)   8-ounce can liver pâté
7-ounce can truffles

Double the recipe for tart pastry and chill thoroughly. Preheat the oven to very hot (450°). Roll the pastry to about ⅛-inch thickness, and cut it into 4-inch squares. Cut the squares into triangles.

   Mince the truffles finely, then add them to the liver pâté, blending thoroughly. Put 1 heaping teaspoon of filling on each triangle, fold the pastry over on itself into a smaller triangle, and seal the edges with a little cold water. Prick the tops with a fork and arrange on cookie sheets. Bake for about 20 minutes, until the pastry is brown. Makes about 30 pieces.

MENU 115   Cheese Thimble Biscuits

Make cheese biscuit dough (see page 261). Preheat the oven to medium (375°). Roll out the dough to ¼-inch thickness, and cut it into rounds the size of a thimble, about ¾ inch across. Bake the tiny biscuits for 15 minutes and serve them very hot.

This dough can be made ahead and stored in the refrigerator until ready to bake; it should be taken out of the refrigerator about ten minutes before rolling out. Also, the biscuits can be served cold. Or the biscuits may be baked, cooled, and reheated later just before serving. Store cooled baked biscuits in tins. Makes about 16 dozen pieces.

MENU 115   Small Hot Turnovers with Minced Clams

Tart pastry (see page 136)   ¼ cup heavy cream
Two 7-ounce cans minced clams   Salt and black pepper

Double the recipe for tart pastry and chill thoroughly. Preheat the oven to very hot (450°). Roll out the pastry to ⅛-inch thickness and cut out rounds with a 3-inch cookie cutter.

Drain the clams, reserving the liquid for some other use. Mix the clams with the cream, season to taste, and stir until smooth. Put about 2 teaspoons of filling in each turnover. Fold the pastry over the filling and seal the edges. Prick the tops with a fork and place the turnovers on cookie sheets. Bake for about 20 minutes, or until the pastry is brown. Serve hot. Makes 30 to 36 pieces.

MENU 115   Spicy Pecans

3 tablespoons butter   ¼ teaspoon cayenne pepper
2 teaspoons salt   ½ teaspoon ground cinnamon
1 pound pecan halves   Tabasco
3 tablespoons Worcestershire sauce

Melt the butter in a large saucepan. Stir in the salt and add the pecan halves, stirring well so that the nuts are thoroughly coated. Add the Worcestershire sauce, cayenne pepper, cinnamon, and a good dash of Tabasco. Stir again. Put the whole mixture in a baking pan and roast in a low oven (300°) for 30 minutes, turning frequently, until the nuts are slightly browned and very crisp.

MENU 116   Hot Sesame Shortbread

1 cup butter
8 ounces cream cheese

2 cups whole-wheat flour, not sifted
½ cup sesame seeds

Preheat the oven to hot (400°). Cream the butter and cream cheese together until well mixed and soft. Work in thoroughly the unsifted whole-wheat flour and, lastly, the sesame seeds. If the mixture is too stiff, add a little more creamed butter to make a firm dough. Roll out to about ¼-inch thickness, and cut into rounds the size of a half dollar. Put the rounds on cookie sheets, not too close together, and bake until brown, about 10 to 12 minutes. Serve hot. Makes about 50 pieces.

MENU 116   Hot Parmesan Greenery

Thinly sliced white bread
8 ounces Parmesan cheese, grated

4 to 6 tablespoons mayonnaise
¼ cup chopped parsley

Preheat the oven to very hot (425°). Cut the thin slices of white bread into rounds about 1½ inches across. Toast the bread rounds on one side. Blend together the Parmesan cheese, the mayonnaise, and the parsley to make a thick paste. If the mixture is too stiff, add a little more mayonnaise. Pile the cheese mixture in a high mound on the untoasted sides of bread rounds. Place the canapés on a baking sheet and heat them in the oven just until the cheese begins to melt. Serve immediately. Makes about 36 pieces.

MENU 121   Miniature Curried Shrimp Tarts

16 tiny tart shells
1 teaspoon flour
½ teaspoon curry powder

½ cup hot milk
1 cup minced cooked shrimp
Dash of Tabasco

Make the tart shells in 1½-inch tart pans from tart pastry (see page 136) or from one 10-ounce package piecrust mix, fully bake them, and cool.

Preheat the oven to very hot (450°). Mix the flour and curry powder; then slowly add the hot milk, stirring to keep smooth. Stir in the minced shrimp and cook over low heat for 2 to 3 minutes. Add a dash of Tabasco. Fill the tart shells with the mixture and heat them in the oven for 5 to 6 minutes. Miniature curried crab tarts may be made in the same way by using 1 cup cooked crabmeat in place of the minced shrimps.

The filling and the tart shells can be made a day or so ahead, and put together just before the final heating. Makes 16 pieces.

MENU 122   Hot Turnovers with Ground Chicken and Chopped Parsley

Tart pastry (see page 136)
8 ounces boned cooked white meat
  of chicken
2 tablespoons soft butter
2 tablespoons heavy cream
Salt and black pepper
1 tablespoon chopped parsley

Preheat the oven to very hot (450°). Make tart pastry, or use one 10-ounce package piecrust mix, and roll it out to ⅛-inch thickness. Cut out 16 rounds with a 3-inch cookie cutter.

Grind the chicken fine; add the butter, cream, and salt and pepper to taste, stirring until quite smooth. Heat over low heat for 5 minutes, stirring. Remove from the heat and add the parsley. Spoon 1 tablespoon of filling onto each round of dough, fold over, and seal the edges. Place on cookie sheets and bake for about 20 minutes, or until the pastry is brown. Makes 16 pieces.

Miniature turnovers can be made by cutting the rounds with a 2-inch cookie cutter and filling them with 1 teaspoon of filling. There will be 32 to 40 miniature turnovers.

MENU 123   Hot Bite-Size Tarts with Ground Ham

16 tiny tart shells
¼ cup butter
½ teaspoon prepared mustard
1 cup ground cooked ham
¼ green pepper, finely chopped

Make the tart shells in 1½-inch tart pans from tart pastry (see page 136) or from one 10-ounce package piecrust mix, fully bake them, and cool.

Preheat the oven to very hot (450°). Soften the butter and mix it well with the mustard. Stir in the ground ham and minced green pepper and blend all together smoothly. Fill the tart shells, using about 1 tablespoon of filling in each. Heat the tarts in the oven for 5 to 6 minutes, to be heated through.

The filling and the tart shells can be made a day or so ahead and put together just before the final heating. Makes 16 pieces.

MENU 123　Water Chestnuts Wrapped in Bacon

Four 5-ounce cans water chestnuts　　15 strips of lean bacon

Drain the water chestnuts and dry them with paper towelling. Cut the bacon strips in half. Wrap each chestnut in bacon and fasten with a toothpick. Brown them in a hot skillet, adding a little butter if the bacon does not release enough fat. Or brown them in a hot oven (400°). Put the cooked pieces on paper towelling to absorb excess fat. Reheat them in the oven just before serving. Makes about 30 pieces.

MENU 124　　　　Caviar Tart (for 8)

Two 6-inch tart shells　　　　　1 cup thick sour cream
1 pound caviar, fresh or pressed

Make the tart shells with tart pastry (see page 136) or with flaky pastry (see page 161) or with one 10-ounce package piecrust mix. Bake them fully and fill them as soon as they come out of the oven. Or bake the tart shells a day ahead and reheat just before filling.

Put the caviar into a cold bowl and mix it gently with the sour cream. Spread it—cold as cold—over the two hot tart shells. Serve—and eat—immediately. The combination of crisp hot pastry and very cold caviar and cream makes a new taste, and a delicious one.

4

Suppers
At Eleven-Thirty

FOR TWELVE TO TWENTY

THERE'S something rather festive in the very idea of a little supper late in the evening—"Cold bird and a bottle" sort of thing. And "Come home with us after the theatre" is a cheerful invitation heard often and often in the cities of the U.S.A. The need for an early and sometimes hasty dinner before the theatre makes a small supper afterwards especially welcome; and this holds true not only after the theatre but after skating parties, early lectures, museum openings, concerts, or card games. They have a special character, these "eleven-thirty" parties, and so has the food that seems most successful. It naturally should not be too heavy but it should be interesting, varied, and substantial enough so that it is more than a casual snack. In the very few households that still maintain staffs, even fewer are asking them to "wait up" for special late service and these hosts and hostesses, like the unstaffed majority, plan food that can seem spontaneous, and almost impromptu. But what is required is a particular system of planning—nothing (almost nothing) to be done after the party arrives, except to assemble or to heat already prepared food. Here are ten menus planned with exactly that system in mind.

MENU 125 (for ten)

Crabmeat Mousse*

Finger Sandwiches
of
White Bread,
Mustard Butter

Salad
of
Lettuce and Raw
Mushrooms

Hot Stewed Pears
and
Black Cherries with Cognac

Cookies

The Wine:

A white wine: Pouilly-Fumé.

* Recipe on page 273.

MENU 126 (for twelve)

Chicken Liver Pâté*
Sea Toast

Lobster Salad

Caraway Wafers

Little Cakes

The Wine:

Chablis or Champagne.

* Recipe on page 273.

MENU 127 (for twelve)

Hot Crabmeat Creole*

Cold Beaten Biscuits

Baked Fruit Compote*

The Wine:

Sancerre, from the Loire Valley.

* Recipes on pages 274.

MENU 128 (for twelve)

Split Baked Potatoes
with
Caviar and Sour Cream

Platter
of
Prosciutto
or
Yorkshire Ham
with
Crescents of Melon

Small Apple Turnovers*

The Wine:

Champagne or a vin rosé; or a
claret, Château Gruaud-Larose.

* Recipe on page 275.

MENU 129 (for twelve)　　*MENU 130 (for twelve)*

Chicken with Noodles*

*Lemon Sherbet Mould
with
Fresh Orange Sections*

*Old-Fashioned
Spongecake*

*Casserole
of
Chicken and Oysters**

*Salad
of
Whole Baby Beets,
Romaine
with
French Dressing*

*Kumquats and Mandarins
with
Cointreau*

Cookies

The Wine:

*Champagne, or California Pinot
Chardonnay or Johannisberg
Riesling.*

The Wine:

A Muscadet or a Chablis.

* Recipe on page 276.　　　* Recipe on page 276.

MENU 131 (for fourteen)   *MENU 132 (for fourteen)*

Petite Marmite*
with
Sliced, Toasted
French Bread

Cold Cheese Soufflé*

Sizzling Little Sausages
Cooked at the Table

Chocolate Mousse*

Cookies

Sandwiches
of
Brown Bread
and Watercress

The Wine:

A red Bordeaux.

The Wine:

A light red Bordeaux or beer.

* Recipes on pages 277-278.   * Recipe on page 278.

HOLIDAY SUPPERS

Sometimes, on the night before Christmas, friends gather to see the tree or trim the tree, and often some of them slip away to go to midnight church services. When they come back, it might be nice to find one of these suppers waiting. And some of the best New Year's Eve parties are small parties for twenty or more guests who may arrive from other dinners to see the Old Year out, to welcome the New with near and dear. One of these suggested menus would be pleasant also for a New Year's Eve supper to serve from eleven-thirty until next year.

MENU 133 (for twenty)

Hot Strained Onion Soup
with
Brandy and Cheese Straws

Turkey Tetrazzini*

White and Green
Asparagus
with
Vinaigrette Dressing

Macédoine of Fruits

Hot Macaroons

The Wine:

Champagne.

* Recipe on page 279.

MENU 134 (for twenty)

Cold Smoked Pheasant

Hot Rice Pilaff

Onion and Bacon Tarts*

Cold Broccoli Vinaigrette
with
Mushrooms
and
Stuffed Tomatoes

New Year's Cake
Baked with Lucky Pieces

Mont Blanc*

The Wine:

Champagne.

* Recipes on page 280.

MENU 125   Crabmeat Mousse *(for 10)*

2 pounds cooked crabmeat	2 tablespoons unflavoured
1 tablespoon dried chives	gelatine
1 tablespoon finely chopped fresh	6 tablespoons cold water
parsley	½ cup mayonnaise
2 scallions or 1 mild onion, chopped	1½ cups heavy cream
very fine	2 egg whites
1 tablespoon lemon juice	6 or 8 parsley sprigs
	6 or 8 watercress sprigs

This recipe may be prepared a day in advance. Pick over the crabmeat carefully, being sure that every piece is flaked and all the hard bits removed. Add the chives, parsley, scallions, and the lemon juice. Soften the gelatine in the cold water, then dissolve it over boiling water. Stir until completely dissolved, then add to the crabmeat mixture. Mix thoroughly, cool for 10 minutes, and then stir in the mayonnaise. Whip the cream until it is stiff. In a separate bowl whip the egg whites until they form peaks. Fold the egg whites into the crabmeat and last, gently fold in the whipped cream. Spoon the mixture into a 10-cup mould and cut through the mixture with a knife to eliminate any air space at the bottom. Refrigerate, but not in the freezer compartment, until set, about 3 hours at least. When ready to serve, wrap the mould in a cloth wrung out in hot water, invert the mould over a large round serving platter, and tap gently so the mousse comes out intact. Garnish with parsley and watercress sprigs.

MENU 126   Chicken Liver Pâté *(for 12)*

1 cup butter	¼ teaspoon mace
2 small onions, chopped	¼ teaspoon cloves
1 pound chicken livers	Salt and black pepper
½ tablespoon unflavoured gelatine	Several dashes of cayenne
2 tablespoons cold water	pepper
1 cup chicken broth	¼ cup Cognac
½ teaspoon dry mustard	¼ cup chopped parsley

Melt ½ cup of the butter in a frying pan and sauté the onions for 2 minutes. Add the chicken livers and sauté them for 5 minutes or so, turning them to cook evenly. Meanwhile soften the gelatine in the cold water and dissolve it in the chicken broth. Add the broth and gelatine to the livers and simmer for another 5 minutes. Add the remaining ½ cup butter, the seasonings, and the Cognac, and pour all into a blender. Blend at high speed until smooth, for about 1 minute. Pour the mixture into a 4-cup crock, or into a serving bowl, and put the pâté in the refrigerator to set for 24 hours before serving. The pâté may be served from the crock or bowl. Or unmould it onto a serving dish. Sprinkle the pâté with the chopped parsley and serve with sea toast.

MENU 127   Hot Crabmeat Creole *(for 12)*

2 onions, chopped	½ teaspoon salt
¼ cup butter	½ teaspoon black pepper
¼ cup flour	Pinch of dried thyme
6 tablespoons catsup	1 green pepper, chopped fine
1 tablespoon Worcestershire sauce	4 cups lump crab
1 cup clam juice	3 cups heavy cream

Brown the onions in the butter, but watch against scorching. Add the flour slowly, stirring to combine smoothly, then blend in the catsup, the Worcestershire sauce, and the clam juice. Add the salt and pepper, a generous pinch of thyme, then the chopped green pepper and last, the crabmeat. Simmer slowly for 15 minutes over low heat. Cool and refrigerate. At serving time stir in the cream and reheat, but do not let the mixture come to a boil.

MENU 127   Baked Fruit Compote *(for 12)*

1-pound, 13-ounce can pitted black cherries	Juice of 1 orange
1-pound, 13-ounce can sliced peaches	1½ cups rum
1-pound, 13-ounce can apricot halves	1 cup heavy cream
Juice of 1 lemon	3 tablespoons sugar

Drain the fruit, reserving the syrup, and arrange it in a low 10-cup heatproof glass dish. Sprinkle with the lemon and orange juice. Mix 1 cup of the reserved fruit syrup with 1 cup of the rum. (Reserve rest of syrup for future use.)

Pour this over the fruit. Cover the dish and bake in a medium oven (350°) for 20 minutes. Remove from the oven and put aside, but do not refrigerate. At serving time reheat the compote for 10 minutes. While reheating, whip the cream with the sugar until stiff, then add the remaining ½ cup rum. Serve the compote hot, in the baking dish, with the whipped cream in a separate bowl to be put on the individual servings.

MENU 128   Small Apple Turnovers *(for 12)*

12 cooking apples	Sweet tart pastry (see below)
¾ cup sugar	¼ cup Calvados or applejack
1 orange, juice and grated rind	2 teaspoons vanilla extract
½ cup butter	1 egg yolk

Peel and core the apples and cut them into eighths. Put them in a saucepan with the sugar, orange juice, grated orange rind, and butter. Cook until the apples are tender and nearly all the juice has evaporated, about 30 minutes. Meanwhile make the pastry. When the apples are done, add the Calvados and vanilla and cool completely.

Preheat the oven to hot (400°). Roll out the pastry into a thin sheet and cut it into 3-inch rounds. Place 1 tablespoon of the cooled apple mixture on one side of each pastry round. Fold over the pastry and press with the tines of a fork to seal the edges. Chill again. Beat the egg yolk with 2 tablespoons water and paint the pastry with this. Bake for 20 to 25 minutes, or until golden. Serve warm or cold. Serve plain, to be eaten with the fingers, or fancy, to be eaten with a fork—that is, with sweetened whipped cream flavoured with Calvados or applejack.

SWEET TART PASTRY

3½ cups sifted flour	2 tablespoons sugar
1 cup butter	¼ teaspoon salt
3 egg yolks	

Put the flour in a large bowl and make a well in the centre. Into the well put the butter, cut into pieces, the egg yolks, sugar, and salt. Mix the ingredients in the well and slowly incorporate the flour. Roll the dough into a ball, wrap it in wax paper, and keep it cold until ready to use.

MENU 129   Chicken with Noodles *(for 12)*

1½ pounds noodles	3 cups diced poached chicken
3 quarts boiling salted water	4 egg yolks
½ teaspoon salt	1 cup heavy cream
½ teaspoon black pepper	2 cups chicken broth
6 tablespoons butter	½ cup Swiss cheese, grated
½ cup grated Swiss and Parmesan cheese, mixed	

Put the noodles into boiling salted water and boil for 8 minutes. Drain, and add the salt, pepper, 4 tablespoons of the butter, and the mixed grated cheeses. Butter a round baking dish, about 8-cup size, with the remaining butter and fill to three fourths of its depth with the noodles. Spread the diced chicken on top of the noodles. Beat the egg yolks and cream together and add the chicken broth. Cook slowly, stirring, in a double boiler over simmering water until the mixture is thick and coats a spoon. Continue to cook, stirring constantly, for 7 to 8 minutes longer. Pour this sauce over the chicken and noodles, and sprinkle the grated Swiss cheese over the top. At serving time, put the baking dish in a very hot oven (450°) for 10 minutes to brown. Serve hot.

MENU 130   Casserole of Chicken and Oysters *(for 12)*

6 double chicken breasts	2 teaspoons salt
½ cup flour	½ teaspoon black pepper
6 tablespoons butter	3 dozen oysters
2 cups chicken broth	

Have the breasts cut from small chickens, such as fryers, and split them. Dredge the chicken breasts with the flour and brown them quickly in the butter in a large saucepan. Take care not to burn the flour. When the chicken is browned, place it in a 12-cup casserole with any butter remaining in the saucepan. Add just enough broth to reach the top of chicken without "drowning it"; add the salt and pepper. Bake in a medium oven (350°) for about 30 minutes; the chicken should be tender and the gravy quite thick; if not, cook for 5 to 10 minutes longer. If the colour of the gravy is not brown enough, add a little burnt sugar for a darker colour. Drain the oysters, reserving the liquor. Set everything aside.

About 20 minutes before serving time, add the oyster liquor to the casserole, turning the chicken pieces so the liquor is mixed well with the gravy. Bring to a boil in the oven. If the gravy seems too thin after adding the oyster liquor, thicken with 1 teaspoon flour, smoothly mixed with a little liquid from the casserole. Turn the oven to very low (275°). Prepare the oysters by draining them to remove any remaining liquor; then poach them in a saucepan over low heat for 5 minutes. Now add the oysters to the chicken casserole and turn gently to mix well. Raise the oven heat to medium (350°) for 2 minutes. Then turn off the heat, remove the casserole, and serve immediately.

MENU 131   Petite Marmite *(for 14)*

4-pound chicken	3 white turnips, diced
4 to 5 tablespoons vegetable oil	4 celery stalks, sliced
4 pounds beef and veal bones	6 quarts light beef bouillon
3 pounds rump of beef	1 cup julienne-cut carrots
Salt and black pepper	1 cup julienne-cut celery
2 large onions, each stuck with	1 cup julienne-cut white turnips
2 cloves	1 loaf French bread
3 large carrots, sliced	¼ cup chopped parsley
3 large leeks, sliced	1½ cups grated Parmesan cheese

This soup is best made 24 hours ahead. Preheat the oven to very hot (450°). Wipe the chicken and truss it. Rub it well with 2 tablespoons of the oil. Spread another tablespoon of oil in a roasting pan and put in the chicken and all the bones. Roast in the oven until the chicken is golden, about 30 minutes. Meanwhile, wipe the rump of beef and tie it. Brown the beef in the remaining oil in a large frying pan, season with salt and pepper, and place it in an 8- to 10-quart soup kettle. Add the roasted beef and veal bones, the whole onions, the sliced and diced vegetables, and the beef bouillon. Bring to a boil and skim carefully of any scum until nothing but a white froth appears. Wipe the sides of the kettle to remove any scum. Simmer gently; violent boiling makes the broth cloudy. Cover the kettle, leaving a little vent for steam, and cook for 2 hours. Add the browned chicken, still trussed, and continue simmering for 1 more hour.

Remove the beef and chicken and reserve them; strain the soup, discarding the bones and the cooked vegetables. Cool the strained broth and chill overnight.

In the morning remove any fat from the surface of the broth, return the broth to a kettle, and add the julienne-cut vegetables. Remove and discard the strings from the beef and chicken and slice the meat into small pieces. Add the meat to the broth and simmer gently for 30 minutes, adding salt and pepper to taste.

Preheat the oven to very low (250°). Cut the French bread into thick slices and place on cookie sheets. Oven dry in the low oven until golden, about 1 hour, turning the bread once. At serving time, reheat the soup, and transfer to a crockery bowl or tureen; sprinkle with the parsley. Arrange the toast slices on a serving dish and have the grated cheese in a bowl. Ladle *petite marmite* into heated soup plates with pieces of meat and vegetables in each plate. Add to each serving 2 slices of toast and a generous sprinkling of cheese.

MENU 131   Chocolate Mousse *(for 14)*

1 pound semisweet chocolate	½ cup softened butter
¼ cup hot coffee	2½ cups heavy cream
14 eggs, separated	1 teaspoon vanilla extract

Melt the chocolate with the coffee in the top of a double boiler over barely simmering water. Beat the egg yolks until lemon-coloured. When the chocolate is soft, remove from the heat and combine with the egg yolks and the butter. Whip 1 cup of the cream and beat the egg whites very stiff. Fold both into the chocolate, gently but thoroughly. Pour into a 14-cup serving dish. Chill overnight if possible, but at least for 8 hours. Sweeten the remaining 1½ cups heavy cream to taste and flavour with the vanilla extract. Serve the cream, unwhipped, as a sauce for the mousse.

If a sweeter mousse is preferred, add ¾ cup sugar to the egg yolks and beat together thoroughly before adding to the chocolate.

MENU 132   Cold Cheese Soufflé *(for 14)*

1 pound Roquefort, Stilton,	½ cup cold water
Gorgonzola, or blue cheese	8 eggs, separated
4 tablespoons unflavoured gelatine	2 cups heavy cream

Put the cheese through a fine sieve. Soften the gelatine in the cold water and dissolve in a small saucepan over hot water. Beat the egg yolks slightly and stir them into 1 cup of the cream in a double boiler over hot water. Cook, stirring constantly, until the custard coats the spoon. Remove from the heat. Add the sieved cheese and the dissolved gelatine to the mixture, stirring thoroughly; cool. Beat the egg whites stiff and whip the remaining 1 cup cream until firm. Fold the cream and egg whites into the cheese mixture. Pour the mixture into a large mould and place it in the refrigerator to set for at least 24 hours. Serve unmoulded, garnished with watercress or parsley.

MENU 133   Turkey Tetrazzini *(for 20)*

2 pounds spaghetti
1 pound mushrooms, sliced
8 tablespoons butter
2 cups diced smoked turkey
2 cups diced roast turkey
2 cups diced ham
4 egg yolks
1 cup heavy cream

10 cups white sauce (double the recipe on page 20)
½ teaspoon nutmeg
Salt and black pepper
Two 1-ounce cans truffles, minced
6 tablespoons Sherry
½ cup grated Parmesan cheese

Cook the spaghetti according to the directions on the package. Sauté the mushrooms in 6 tablespoons of the butter. Combine the diced meats and add the sautéed mushrooms. Beat the egg yolks with the cream and add to the prepared white sauce. Heat, stirring constantly, to the boiling point. Add the nutmeg and correct the seasoning. Add the truffles and Sherry. Combine about 3 cups of the sauce with the meats. Combine the cooked spaghetti with 1 cup of the sauce. Line the sides of a large oven dish with the spaghetti. Fill the centre with the meat mixture and cover with the remainder of the sauce. If the sauce seems too thick, add a little cream or rich milk. Sprinkle the top of the sauce with the cheese and dot with the remaining 2 tablespoons butter. Store in the refrigerator until 1 hour before serving time. At serving time put the dish in a medium oven (350°) for 20 minutes, then place under the broiler for 5 minutes or more to brown the top.

MENU 134   Onion and Bacon Tarts *(for 20)*

12 large onions, sliced
 4 large leeks, sliced
 1 cup plus 1 tablespoon butter
 6 tablespoons flour
 3 cups milk
   Salt and black pepper
 ¼ teaspoon nutmeg, or more to
   taste

4 egg yolks
1 cup light cream
8 slices Canadian bacon, diced
  Two 11-inch flaky pastry shells
  (see page 52)

Press the onions in a towel to remove some of the juice. Simmer the onions and leeks in ½ cup of the butter. Cook them until they are transparent, but do not let them brown. Make a white sauce with ½ cup of the butter, the flour, and the milk. Cook over low heat, stirring, until the sauce is smooth and thickened. Season with salt, pepper, and nutmeg. Beat the egg yolks with the cream. Cook the sauce for a few minutes longer, then add the egg yolks and cream, stirring constantly, and continue to cook until the sauce comes to a boil. Reserve a few spoonfuls of the sauce. Add the onions and leeks to the larger part of the white sauce and keep the mixture over hot water. Sauté the bacon quickly in the remaining tablespoon of butter and add to the onions and sauce. Divide the mixture between two 11-inch pastry shells, which have been baked for 10 minutes until firm, but not brown. Spoon the reserved sauce over the onions so that the top of the tarts is smooth. A little chopped chives and parsley may be added to the masking sauce. Bake the tarts in a hot oven (400°) for about 25 minutes, or until bubbling and golden.

The tarts may be prepared ahead, refrigerated, and reheated before serving. Tarts may also be frozen before baking. In this case, they should be defrosted for at least 1 hour before baking. Heat the defrosted tarts in a medium oven (375°) until golden and bubbly, about 45 minutes.

MENU 134   Mont Blanc *(for 20)*

6 pounds chestnuts in shells
6 cups milk
2½ cups sugar
   Two 2-inch pieces of vanilla
   bean

⅓ cup brandy
¼ cup *crème de cacao*
4 cups heavy cream
1 tablespoon vanilla extract

Slit the chestnut shells on one side and roast in a hot oven (400°) for 10 minutes. Remove the shells. Put the chestnuts in a large pot of cold water and slowly bring them to a boil. Let them boil for 1 minute and then cool them in the water. As soon as they are cool enough to handle, but while they are still warm and wet, remove the skins. It does not matter if the chestnuts break.

Simmer the chestnuts in the milk with 2 cups of the sugar and the vanilla bean until the nuts are very soft. Lift out the vanilla bean and scrape the seeds into the mixture. Drain the nuts and reserve any remaining cooking liquid. Add the brandy and the liqueur to the chestnuts, mash the nuts, and whip into a purée with a wooden spoon. Add a little of the cooking liquid if the purée is too stiff. Brush a large cake pan with bland oil. Put the purée into a pastry bag with a perforated tube and press out the purée into the oiled pan, loosely, so that it looks like spaghetti. Or force the purée through a coarse strainer into the oiled pan. Chill well.

At serving time turn the purée out onto a round platter. Whip the heavy cream, sweeten it with the remaining sugar, and flavour it with the vanilla extract. Pile the whipped cream over the chestnut purée, making a mound which is higher in the centre. Serve chilled, but not frozen.

PART FOUR

Friday-to-Sunday Guests

A WEEKEND

WITH SIX GUESTS

AND A HOSTESS-COOK

THE PROGNOSIS was a fairly complicated sort of October weekend for Mrs. Xavier. Both boys would be down from college, each with a crony. And four other guests—two couples—would bring the household up to ten. To help in the care and feeding of this weekend party, there was a general helper for Friday and Saturday mornings, and a fill-in, free-lance waitress who could be snared for the Saturday night dinner party that was part of the weekend plan. Other than that, Mrs. Xavier was on her own, but not frightened. She had the fault occasionally of trying to do too much, but her family was experienced and willing when she needed their help. She was not only a good cook, but also an organizer. She had shopped, ordered, and begun her cooking on Wednesday, storing much of it in the big freezer that was primary in her kitchen plans.

Who was to meet whom where; what they would eat when they arrived at the house on Friday night; whether to ask the boys to her Saturday night dinner or let them go their own way at the club; whether to have Sunday lunch late and substantial because of late Sunday sleepers, or early and casual with a "high tea" to follow in the late afternoon for the departing ones —these were questions that Mrs. Xavier's IBM mind took in, sorted, examined, rearranged. The four boys would probably be the last to arrive on Friday night and would be hungry, say, anywhere from six to eight o'clock; one of the married couples, the Perrys, would come by airplane, arriving at the local airport at seven; the others, the Connaughts, were driving out from town and hoping to be there by five o'clock. Mr. Xavier would have the family car in town, and probably could not reach home before half past six. (Actually, he got there at about half past seven.)

FRIDAY NIGHT SUPPER

The first urgent question was how and when to give Friday night supper to the unpredictable arrivals without resorting to cold cuts and safe dullness. This meant food that could be kept hot for an hour, or an hour and a half, without impairing its quality. The dessert should be hearty, possibly hot, substantial and not easily spoilable. This is what Mrs. X planned for Friday night supper.

MENU 135 (for ten)

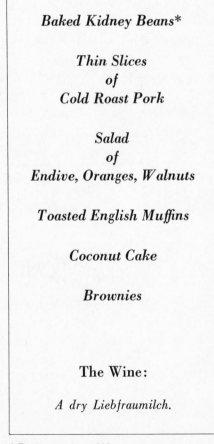

Baked Kidney Beans*

*Thin Slices
of
Cold Roast Pork*

*Salad
of
Endive, Oranges, Walnuts*

Toasted English Muffins

Coconut Cake

Brownies

The Wine:

A dry Liebfraumilch.

* Recipe on page 303.

The baked beans had been started on Wednesday night. They were taken from the oven for the last time at half past six on Friday night and put on a hotplate to remain until the last straggler had come in and eaten. The pork had been cooked for Thursday dinner and Mrs. X had bought a roast large enough for Friday night, too. The salad was prepared Friday morning and put into the refrigerator, ready for the last minute addition of French dressing. The coconut cake was made on Thursday and was large enough, hopefully, for at least sixteen slices.

Here are four more menus Mrs. Xavier might have used for Friday night.

FRIDAY NIGHT SUPPER

MENU 136 (for ten)	*MENU 137 (for ten)*
Onion Soup*	*Shepherd's Pie**
Cold Chicken Mousse*	*Tomato Aspic Ring* *with* *Cooked Vegetables*
Beet Salad	
Sour Cherry Pie	*Apples and Pears* *with* *Cheeses*
The Wine:	**The Wine:**
A Pouilly-Fuissé is an excellent *white wine choice.*	*A California claret or a Beau-* *jolais.*

* Recipes on pages 303-304.   * Recipe on page 305.

FRIDAY NIGHT SUPPER

MENU 138 (for ten)   *MENU 139 (for ten)*

*Quick Shrimp Jambalaya**   *Pot-au-Feu**

Rice   *Buttered Beaten Biscuits*

Green Salad   *Lime and Lemon Sherbet*

Hot Fruit Turnovers
with
Several Kinds of Fruit

The Wine: The Wine:

Pouilly-Fuissé, an agreeable   *A robust Nuits-Saint-Georges.*
white wine with the shrimp.

* Recipe on page 306.   * Recipe on page 306.

SATURDAY BREAKFAST AND LUNCH

The Saturday morning breakfast question settled itself in various ways. The Connaughts were non-breakfasters, or almost. Black coffee and fruit was their unfailing breakfast diet, and they liked, so they said, to have coffee the minute they awoke; so two thermoses of boiling hot coffee and two cups and saucers went upstairs at bedtime with them. There were already a bowl of fruit, two plates, and two fruit knives on the bedroom table. On the other hand, the Perrys are congenital early risers; they like to sit at a breakfast table and have a fairly substantial meal around half past eight. So it was planned that the Perrys and the heads of the house could breakfast together. As for the four boys—the two sons in the house were responsible for their guests' breakfasts. The refrigerator was stocked with fruit, jams, eggs and bacon, and Mrs. Xavier had mixed a pitcher of pancake batter, just in case. So, about half past nine, after Mr. Xavier and Mr. Perry had gone off to look at a piece of property about ten miles away, and while the Connaughts were still sleeping, Mrs. Xavier heard boy food-noises in the kitchen. As it turned out, they did want the pancakes, and Roger, the older son, presided at the pancaking. The Xavier boys had been trained from early days to wash their own dishes when they ate at offbeat times, and they left the kitchen very tidy. They also left a note saying they would not be in again until six o'clock, when the two sons were engaged to help with dinner preparation.

That left six for lunch. They played bridge for an hour or so; at a little before one o'clock Mrs. Xavier rose from her chair and went into the kitchen. At half past one she invited the card players in to luncheon. A bowl of consommé was at each guest's place. Sour cream was in a small silver bowl. After the consommé, Mrs. Xavier brought in the gratin of turkey, piping hot. The pie had been made two days earlier and kept refrigerated, not frozen. As the guests sat down at the luncheon table, the pie was put in the oven (set down to 350°) and was ready to eat after the main course. After the peach pie, they all went back to the living room for coffee, and to finish the rubber of bridge.

MENU 140 (for six)

Jellied Tomato Consommé
with
Sour Cream

Gratin of Smoked Turkey*

Hot Peach Pie

The Wine:

Chassagne-Montrachet.

* Recipe on page 307.

The consommé and the sour cream were ready and waiting in the refrigerator. The gratin of turkey took about half an hour to make, since Mrs. Xavier feels that béchamel is best when freshly made. All the ingredients were at hand, the turkey sliced, the beans cooked. And the pie only needed to be heated. Here are some other menus for a simple Saturday luncheon which Mrs. Xavier might have used.

SATURDAY LUNCH

MENU 141 (for six)

Scaloppini of Veal
with Tarragon*

Fresh Asparagus
with Browned Butter

Field Salad

Fresh Cold Apples
with Cheese

The Wine:

A Bardolino, slightly chilled if
desired.

* Recipe on page 308.

MENU 142 (for six)

Baked Shrimp
and Mushrooms*

Buttered Beaten Biscuits

Crisp Romaine Salad

Camembert
with Raspberry Jam

The Wine:

A white California Riesling.

* Recipe on page 308.

SATURDAY LUNCH

MENU 143 (for six)

Chicken and Ham Paella*

Italian Bread

Crème de Marrons*

The Wine:

A red Rioja from the Marqués de Riscal.

* Recipes on page 309.

MENU 144 (for six)

Broccoli with Prosciutto and Almonds*

Salad of Endive, Beets, Romaine

Italian Bread

Stewed Rhubarb

The Wine:

A white Graves—Château Olivier —or a vin rosé.

* Recipe on page 310.

SATURDAY NIGHT DINNER PARTY

The dinner Saturday night was for twelve people—the household of six (the boys had elected to go to the club) and six guests. Mrs. X decided to have two tables of six in the dining room rather than one long table. On each of the pale pink tablecloths were two little low bowls, tightly packed with red and pink geraniums, with a fat low candle in the centre of each. A carafe of red wine was on each table, and on the sideboard were two ice buckets with bottles of Champagne, electric hot plates, artichoke toast, and plates for the main course, the salad and dessert. The guests were invited for eight o'clock, and dinner was planned for a quarter to nine, allowing enough time for guest-lateness and for leisurely cocktails. With the cocktails, a big beautiful bowl of raw vegetables, and the *specialité* of the house—tiny hot tarts, some filled with minced clams and some with minced chicken. These had been started on Friday morning—the shells baked and the fillings mixed—and were ready to be put in the oven for 10 minutes at eight o'clock Saturday night.

Here is the menu, and this is how it was served without the maid seeming breathless. The soup was already on the table when the guests came in. After the soup plates were removed to the sideboard, the dinner plates were put down and the lamb and zucchini were served. While these were being eaten, the soup plates were quietly removed to the kitchen and the two aspic rings brought in to the sideboard. When it was time to remove the dinner plates, these were put on the sideboard and the salad plates and artichoke toast were put on the tables. The waitress put six plates and one aspic ring in front of Mrs. X, who served it family-style to the guests at her table; the waitress served the other table in the conventional way. While the aspic was being eaten, the dinner plates were removed to the kitchen. There was a measurable pause between the salad and dessert; the salad plates were taken directly to the kitchen and before the dessert plates were put down there was time for a cigarette, and two or three of the guests changed tables. The dessert was served and eaten unhurriedly while the Champagne was being poured.

MENU 145 (for twelve)

*Bombay Soup**

*Braised Leg of Lamb**
with Carrots and Onions

Baked Zucchini

Aspic Ring
of Tomato and Cucumber

Artichoke Toast

Frozen Rum Raisin
*Custard**

The Wine:

A St. Estèphe, Château Calon-
Ségur.

* Recipes on pages 310-312.

The Bombay soup was made on Thursday, to be reheated. The cream was whipped on Saturday after Mrs. X had dressed. The two tomato and cucumber aspic rings were made on Friday as was the rum raisin custard. So, on Saturday afternoon the only serious preparation for dinner that remained was the braised lamb and the zucchini casserole. After dinner, the waitress brought the coffee tray into the living room, and Mr. X took charge of the liqueur tray, which was already arranged on a side table. Other manageable menus for a Saturday night dinner party are on the following pages.

SATURDAY DINNER

MENU 146 (for twelve)

Oyster Soufflé*
with
Pilot Crackers

Jellied Cold Duck
with
Black Cherries*

Baby Okra
with
Butter and Lemon

Fruit Meringue*

The Wine:

Pouilly-Fuissé with the oyster soufflé, a light red Burgundy with the duck.

---

* Recipes on pages 312-314.

MENU 147 (for twelve)

Oxtail Soup Amontillado*

Pork à l'Orange*

Baked Acorn Squash

French Bread

Baked Apple and Raisin
Dumplings*

The Wine:

A full-bodied Steinberger from the Rhine.

---

* Recipes on pages 314-316.

SATURDAY DINNER

MENU 148 (for twelve)

MENU 149 (for twelve)

Smoked Trout Amandine

Roast Beef*
with
Yorkshire Pudding*

Broccoli
with
Lemon and Butter Sauce

Mousse Diplomate*

Liver Pâté with Hot Toast

Braised Tongue*

Braised Endive

Raw Spinach Salad
with
Crumbled Bacon Dressing

Caraway Wafers

Peach Ice Cream Mould

Ladyfingers

The Wine:

A Pouilly-Fumé with the trout;
Beaune Clos-des-Mouches with the
beef.

The Wine:

A red wine; a Corton if possible.

* Recipes on pages 317-318.

* Recipe on page 318.

SUNDAY BREAKFAST

Sunday morning breakfast was served from half past ten to eleven. An electric hotplate with a covered ovenproof dish was on the sideboard waiting, ready, for the one-by-one arrivals. Places were set at the dining table so that everyone could serve himself, seat himself, and absorb the Sunday papers, or talk, as he wished. There was a pitcher of cold orange juice. Sausages with apple quarters were in the hot dish, and a toaster was on the table with protein, white, and whole-wheat breads ready to be toasted by the guests. Small Danish pastries, English muffins toasted and buttered, marmalade and fruit jam were on the sideboard; and the big coffee urn was replenished freely from the kitchen.

For other weekends, when Sunday lunch was to be eaten at the club, Mrs. X might plan one of these more ambitious breakfasts.

SUNDAY BREAKFAST

MENU 150

*Peaches and Raspberries
in Orange Juice*

*Eggs Baked in Cream
with Slivers of Ham*

Corn Muffins and Honey

Coffee or Tea

MENU 151

Orange Juice

*Chipped Beef
with Scrambled Eggs*

*Protein Bread Toast
with Apricot Jam*

Coffee or Tea

SUNDAY BREAKFAST

MENU 152

Baked Apples

Canadian Bacon

*Hot Kasha with Butter or
Hominy Grits with Butter*

Crescent Rolls

Coffee or Tea

MENU 153

Applesauce

Roast Beef Hash

Poached Eggs

Baking Powder Biscuits

Whipped Honey

Coffee or Tea

MENU 154

*Orange and Grapefruit
Juice*

*Blueberry Pancakes
with Heated Honey*

Frizzled Ham

Coffee or Tea

MENU 155

*Melon Quarters
with Mint and Lemon*

Coddled Eggs

Bacon

Brown-and-Serve Brioches

Blueberry Jam

Coffee or Tea

SUNDAY LUNCHEON

Sunday lunch after the late breakfast was planned for half
past two. It was primarily a party for the young. The Xaviers'
sons invited six of their friends—five girls and one young man;
with the Xaviers and their friends and the two visiting college
men there were sixteen in all. Sixteen guests seemed to indicate a
buffet luncheon, but in Mrs. X's mind that did not necessarily
mean a stand-around, sit-around party—not for as few as sixteen in any case. Mrs. X likes a certain semblance of order even
for the very young parties, so she decided to put the food on the
dining table, and set up four card tables for the sixteen; much
more comfortable for everyone and less trouble in the end. And
even for as casual a young party as this, Mrs. Xavier had place
cards on the tables. It was one more step in avoiding confusion at
the beginning of the luncheon.

Much of the food had been prepared in advance, and at half
past two all was on the long table except the dessert. The Xavier
boys and their two visitors had set the tables and were charming
waiters after the guests had served themselves—removing plates,
supplying fresh ones, filling glasses when needed, putting the
desserts on the serving tables, and the candies and nuts on the
four tables after the main course was eaten. There was a carafe
of red wine on each table; in the dining room there were milk
and soft drinks for those who were not drinking wine, and a
coffee urn on the buffet. It was all leisurely and pleasantly re-
laxed even for the Xavier boys, who took their duties as a matter
of course and performed with style but in slow motion, when it
suited their ideas. Then, after the luncheon, two boys put the
dishes in the dishwasher, two others cleared up, took the table
linens away, and folded the card tables, and the house was in
order again. It was almost five o'clock when luncheon was over;
the young wandered away, and the Connaughts and Perrys drove
off about half past six with corned-beef sandwiches, a thermos of
coffee to sustain them on the drive home. This is what they had
for luncheon:

MENU 156 (for sixteen)

---

*Risotto with
Chicken Livers**

*Thin Slices of
Cold Corned Beef with
Mustard Cream*

*Green Salad with
Whole Baby Beets*

Water Biscuits

*Orange and Lemon Sherbet
with White Layer Cake*

The Wine:

Carafes of California Zinfandel.

The *risotto* was made in the morning before most of the house guests were out of bed. It was reheated at quarter past two and put into two casseroles on two electric hot plates, to stay heated for the next hour or so. The corned beef had been cooked on Thursday, wrapped in foil, and put into the lower part of the refrigerator. It was taken out and sliced very thin at two o'clock —it should be eaten soon after it has been sliced. The baby beets for the salad were canned. The romaine lettuce and escarole for the salad were washed and dried early in the morning—wrapped first in a linen cloth and then in wax paper to be ready for mixing just before serving time. The orange and lemon sherbets were ordered the day before from the regular ice-cream dealer and were put into moulds to be unmoulded just as the last mouthful of salad was being eaten. The white layer cake was Mrs. X's one concession to "time and circumstance." She did not make it, although she could have, but bought it from a neighbour friend who was an accomplished cook. Here are other manageable luncheon menus which Mrs. X had prepared before, and without being absent too long from her guests or becoming too tired to be attractive.

SUNDAY LUNCHEON

MENU 157 (for sixteen)	*MENU 158 (for sixteen)*
*Sweet Ham Loaf**	*Prosciutto with Melon*
*Délices du Jardin**	*Spaghetti with Red Clam Sauce**
French Bread	*Green Salad*
Applesauce with Sour Cream	*Camembert Cheese Roquefort Cheese and Crusty Bread*
Cookies	
The Wine:	**The Wine:**
Vin rosé *or a claret—perhaps* Château Léoville-Poyferré.	*Carafes of Italian Chianti and Italian Soave.*

* Recipes on pages 320-321.   * Recipe on page 321.

SUNDAY LUNCHEON

MENU 159 (for sixteen) | *MENU 160 (for sixteen)*

Curried Crab and Turtle
Soup*

Cold Roast Veal

Green Salad

Buttered Small Rolls

Bowl of Cut Fruit
with
Champagne or Kirsch

The Wine:

*A white wine with the veal,
Pouilly-Fumé perhaps.*

Beef and Noodle
Casserole*

Sesame Bread Sticks

Lettuce and Tomato
and
Water Chestnut Salad

Hot Mince Pie

The Wine:

A Savigny-lès-Beaune.

* Recipe on page 322.   * Recipe on page 323.

MENU 135   Baked Kidney Beans *(for 10)*

3 pounds dried kidney beans	6 slices lean bacon
6 to 8 cups beef bouillon	8 peppercorns
12 to 14 thin slices prosciutto or baked or boiled Virginia ham	2 tablespoons dried parsley
	1 cup dark brown sugar

These beans should be prepared one or two days in advance. Wash the kidney beans thoroughly and soak them, preferably overnight, in the beef bouillon. The beans should be well covered with the liquid.

Next morning sauté the slices of prosciutto or Virginia ham and the bacon slices until they are browned and crisp. Crush the peppercorns to fine crumbs. Drain the soaked kidney beans, reserving any beef bouillon which was not absorbed. Line the bottom of a deep 24-cup earthenware casserole with some slices of fried ham and bacon. Next put in a 1½- to 2-inch layer of the soaked kidney beans. Sprinkle with some of the pepper and parsley and lightly cover with brown sugar. Put in another layer of fried ham and bacon, then another layer of beans and sugar and seasonings. Repeat until casserole is three fourths full. Pour the reserved beef bouillon over all. If there is not enough liquid to cover the beans, add more beef bouillon. Cover the casserole and bake in the slowest possible oven (250°) for 8 hours straight. If possible, cook the beans for 4 more hours on a second day. The beans will actually be done enough to eat at the end of 8 hours, but the added 4 hours makes them even better. Keep the beans moist at all times with beef bouillon, adding some as it cooks away. During the last hour the liquid can be absorbed. Remove the cover from the casserole for browning. Serve the beans hot in the casserole in which they are baked.

MENU 136   Onion Soup *(for 10)*

2 dozen medium Spanish onions	6 egg yolks, lightly beaten
1 cup butter	Black pepper
12 cups beef bouillon, or 8 cups milk and 4 cups beef bouillon	French bread slices
1 teaspoon salt	1 cup grated Parmesan cheese

Slice the onions medium thick. Sauté them slowly in the butter until they are soft and golden, but do not let them get too dark. Put the sautéed onions in a large saucepan with the bouillon and salt and simmer them for 20 minutes. After 20 minutes, beat the egg yolks into the hot broth. Season to taste with pepper and additional salt if necessary. At serving time, pour the soup over slices of French bread in individual bowls. Serve the Parmesan cheese separately to be sprinkled on the top of the soup according to taste.

If milk is used for part of the bouillon, simmer the onions, after sautéing, in the 4 cups beef bouillon. Then add the milk and bring the soup almost to a boil again before beating in the egg yolks.

MENU 136   Cold Chicken Mousse *(for 10)*

Two 5-pound chickens	2 tablespoons unflavoured gelatine
1 large carrot, sliced	6 egg yolks
3 white onions, sliced	2 teaspoons salt
2 celery stalks, sliced	½ teaspoon paprika
4 peppercorns	Pinch of cayenne pepper
2 whole cloves	2 cups heavy cream

Wash and truss the fowls, removing any accessible fat. Arrange them, breasts up, in a pot with enough water to cover three fourths of the birds. Add the vegetables, peppercorns, and cloves, and cover the pot. Bring to a boil, skim, and then simmer for about 2½ hours, or until the meat is very tender. Allow the chicken to cool in the stock. When the chicken is cool, remove it, wrap it in wax paper, and store it in the refrigerator.

Strain the stock and reduce it by boiling, uncovered, to about 2 cups. Pour the reduced stock into a bowl and let it cool. Soften the gelatine in 1 cup of the cooled stock. Put the remaining stock in the top of a double boiler over simmering water. Beat the egg yolks well with a fork and slowly add them to the stock with the salt, paprika, and cayenne pepper. Cook slowly, stirring, until the mixture starts to thicken, coats the spoon, and has the consistency of light cream; this may take about 10 minutes. As soon as the mixture is thick, remove the top of the double boiler from the heat; add the softened gelatine, stir until it is dissolved, and put the mixture aside to cool.

Put a 12-cup ring mould in the refrigerator to chill. Cut up the cooled chicken. Set aside the white meat and the meat from the second joints and reserve the rest

of the birds for other uses. Put the white meat and second-joint meat through a meat grinder twice, using the finest blade; there should be about 4 cups of ground chicken. Put the ground chicken in a bowl set in a pan of cracked ice. Add a pinch of salt to the heavy cream and whip the cream until stiff. Pour the cooled custard mixture over the ground chicken. Stir with a fork until the gelatine begins to set, then gently fold in the whipped cream. Spoon the chicken mixture into the chilled ring mould. Do this carefully to avoid any air spaces at the bottom. Smooth the top level. Put the mould in the refrigerator for 5 to 6 hours, or overnight. To serve, turn the mould upside down over a platter, wrap the mould with a cloth wrung out in hot water, and tap gently so that the mousse comes out smoothly.

MENU 137   Shepherd's Pie *(for 10)*

6 tablespoons butter	1½ cups gravy or beef bouillon
2 medium onions, minced	Salt and black pepper
2 garlic cloves, minced	6 cups mashed potatoes
8 cups ground cooked beef or lamb (about 3 pounds)	⅛ teaspoon nutmeg
2 tablespoons tomato paste	3 egg yolks
⅓ cup chopped parsley	½ cup grated Parmesan cheese

Melt 4 tablespoons of the butter in a large frying pan. Simmer the onions in the butter without browning for about 3 minutes; add the garlic and simmer for 1 minute longer. Add the meat, tomato paste, chopped parsley, and bouillon. Stir well and simmer gently for 15 minutes. Season with salt and pepper to taste.

Preheat the oven to hot (400°). Butter a 16-cup oven-to-table dish generously and spread half the mashed potatoes on the bottom. Spread the meat mixture over the potato layer. Season the remaining potatoes with nutmeg and salt and pepper, and add the slightly beaten egg yolks. Beat well and spread over the meat. With a fork make a decorative pattern on the top of the potatoes. Sprinkle with the grated Parmesan cheese and bake in the oven for 10 to 15 minutes, or until well browned. Serve very hot; keep hot for stragglers on an electric hot plate.

MENU 138   Quick Shrimp Jambalaya (for 10)

5 tablespoons butter
2 small garlic cloves, crushed
8 scallions (use white part only), chopped
2 celery stalks, sliced
1 green pepper, cleaned and cut into strips

1 pound, 13-ounce can of whole tomatoes
2 tablespoons tomato paste
1 teaspoon coarse salt, or more
Cayenne pepper to taste
1 teaspoon gumbo filé powder, or more
4 pounds cooked shelled shrimp

Heat the butter in a large heavy frying pan. When hot, add the garlic, scallion, celery, and pepper strips. Cook gently for 6 minutes; add the tomatoes. After a few minutes add the tomato paste, salt and cayenne pepper to taste, and 1 teaspoon or more of gumbo filé powder. When all is blended, add the shrimp and let the mixture simmer for 10 minutes or so. This dish may be made ahead, as it reheats very well.

MENU 139   Pot-au-Feu *(for 10)*

5 pounds good boiling beef, trimmed and tied
6½ quarts cold water
1 tablespoon coarse salt
2 pounds soup bones
12 leeks

10 carrots
8 white turnips
2 large onions
4 whole cloves
3 garlic cloves
2 tablespoons sugar

Use brisket, chuck, rump, or round to make this classic of the French country kitchen. Put the cold water and the coarse salt into an 8-quart soup pot. Add the meat and bones. Bring to a boil over moderate heat. Skim any scum off the surface until no more rises. Cover the pot but leave a tiny crack for the steam to escape. Keep the liquid at the slowest possible boil and let it cook gently for 2 hours.

Slit the leeks lengthwise and wash well; then tie them together in bundles so they can be lifted neatly out of the pot later. Cut the carrots and turnips into quarters. Peel the onions, and stick each with 2 cloves. Peel and crush the garlic. Add all these vegetables to the soup. When the liquid comes to a boil again, skim again and cover as before. Let it cook gently for at least 1½ hours. Then lift out the meat and vegetables and keep warm.

Strain the bouillon into a clean kettle. Make a caramel by slowly melting the the sugar in a small saucepan; when the sugar is brown, but not hardened, add a very little water. Remove from the heat, add 2 to 3 tablespoons bouillon or water, and stir rapidly. Add to the bouillon in the pot to deepen the colour. Reheat the soup. First serve the soup, in cups, with buttered beaten biscuits. Then serve the meat, surrounded by the vegetables. Serve separately two sauces, a cold mayonnaise and horseradish with sour cream.

MENU 140   Gratin of Smoked Turkey (for 6)

2 pounds green beans, cooked
Freshly ground black pepper, to taste
16 slices of smoked turkey breasts

6 cups béchamel sauce (see below)
¾ cup freshly grated Parmesan cheese

Arrange the beans in a layer in the bottom of a 12-cup casserole. Sprinkle the beans with the ground pepper and arrange slices of smoked turkey on top. Pour the sauce over the turkey and sprinkle the top with the Parmesan cheese. Place the casserole in a hot oven (400°) for about 15 minutes, until the sauce bubbles and the cheese browns.

This dish may be assembled ahead of time and stored in the refrigerator until needed. Instead of the beans, broccoli or asparagus may be used with the smoked turkey.

BÉCHAMEL SAUCE

½ cup butter
6 tablespoons flour
6 cups milk

6 chicken bouillon cubes
½ teaspoon nutmeg
Salt and black pepper

Melt the butter in a saucepan and blend in the flour. Warm the milk and dissolve the bouillon cubes in it. When the cubes have been dissolved, add the milk slowly to the butter and flour mixture in the saucepan, stirring to mix well. Cook over low heat, stirring constantly, until the sauce has thickened to the consistency of heavy cream. Add the nutmeg and salt and pepper to taste, stirring the sauce until the seasonings are thoroughly blended.

MENU 141   Scaloppini of Veal with Tarragon *(for 6)*

2 pounds veal cutlets
1 teaspoon salt
¼ teaspoon black pepper
½ cup flour
½ cup butter
Juice of 1 lemon

2 tablespoons chopped fresh tarragon, or 2 teaspoons dried
tarragon
¾ cup dry white wine
¾ cup beef bouillon

Have the butcher cut the veal cutlets into twelve thin slices, and pound them even thinner. Mix the salt and pepper with the flour. Dredge the veal slices with the seasoned flour, shaking off any excess. Melt the butter quickly in a large frying pan; when it is foaming hot, brown the floured veal slices on both sides, adding more butter if they should stick. Add the lemon juice, tarragon, and white wine, and simmer for 1 minute, deglazing the pan with a spoon. Add the bouillon and simmer briskly for 1 more minute. Correct the seasoning, sprinkle with freshly ground pepper, and transfer the meat to a heated platter. Pour the sauce over the meat and serve hot.

MENU 142   Baked Shrimp and Mushrooms *(for 6)*

2 pounds fresh shrimp
¾ pound mushrooms
¼ cup butter
1 cup light cream

½ cup Sherry
Salt and black pepper
Pinch of nutmeg
20 round salted crackers, crumbled

Poach the shrimp, cool, shell, and devein them. Slice the mushroom caps very thin, reserving the stems for some other use. Slowly cook the mushrooms with 2 tablespoons of the butter in a saucepan for about 10 minutes, or until they are dark and soft. Drain them thoroughly and put them into a 6-cup casserole. Stir in the cream and Sherry and add the prepared shrimp. Season lightly with salt and pepper and a pinch of nutmeg. Stir the mixture gently, just enough to be sure the ingredients are blended together. Cover the top of the mixture with the crumbled crackers and dot with the remaining 2 tablespoons butter. Put the casserole in a medium oven (350°) and bake for 30 minutes, or until the crackers are browned. Serve at once.

MENU 143   Chicken and Ham Paella *(for 6)*

½ cup olive oil
  3½-pound chicken, cut up
2 large Bermuda onions, chopped
2 garlic cloves, minced
  Salt and black pepper
  1-pound can tomatoes
1 cup raw white rice

4 cups clam juice
½ teaspoon saffron
1 package frozen artichoke hearts
  4-ounce can pimientos
½ pound cooked ham, diced
1 cup cooked green peas

Heat the olive oil in a paella, a large shallow earthenware casserole with a cover. Brown the chicken pieces on one side, turn them, and add the onions and garlic. Season with salt and pepper and continue to cook until the onions are browned. Add the tomatoes and cook for about 8 minutes, stirring to prevent scorching. Add the rice and stir to mix well. Bring the clam juice to a boil and stir in the saffron; add to the paella. Stir once and cover. Cook over low heat for 10 to 15 minutes; uncover, and continue to cook until the liquid has evaporated. Do not overcook. Correct the seasoning.

While the chicken and rice are cooking, cook the artichoke hearts until just tender in a separate saucepan. Drain the pimientos and cut into strips. Heat the diced ham, the peas, and the pimiento strips. Stir the ham, artichokes, and peas into the paella. Decorate the top with the heated pimiento strips and bring to the table hot in the casserole.

MENU 143   Crème de Marrons *(for 6)*

2 cups purée of *marrons glacés*
½ cup heavy cream

2 tablespoons sugar

Put the purée of *marrons glacés* into a bowl and stir vigorously with a silver fork. In a larger bowl beat the cream with the sugar until very stiff. Add the purée to the whipped cream and beat again rather gently. Transfer the mixture to a silver bowl (preferably!) and put it in the refrigerator for 2 hours or more. Serve very cold.

MENU 144   Broccoli with Prosciutto and
Almonds *(for 6)*

2 tablespoons butter
12 slices prosciutto
2 bunches of broccoli

3½ cups béchamel sauce (see
page 307)
½ cup slivered blanched almonds

Preheat the oven to very hot (450°). Butter an 8-cup casserole with the butter and put the prosciutto in it in layers; heat the prosciutto in the oven for 15 minutes. Separate the spears of broccoli from the main stems and simmer in salted water for about 10 minutes, or until the stems may be pierced easily with a fork. Remove the casserole from the oven. Take the prosciutto slices out singly and wrap each one around 2 or 3 spears of broccoli, leaving the broccoli flowerets free at one end. Arrange the prosciutto slices in the casserole, cover them with the béchamel sauce, and sprinkle thickly with the almonds. Return the casserole to the oven and heat until the sauce becomes bubbly and the almonds begin to brown. Serve at once.

MENU 145   Bombay Soup *(for 12)*

4 celery stalks
1 large onion
2 carrots
6 cups canned chicken broth
6 cups canned cream of chicken
  soup

½ cup cooked peas
2 brimming teaspoons curry
  powder
1½ cups light cream
1 cup heavy cream

Boil the celery, onion, and carrots in the chicken broth for 20 minutes. Remove the vegetables, discarding the celery and onion, and mix the broth into the cream of chicken soup, blending until smooth. Dice the carrots and add them to the soup. Add the peas and the curry powder; stir in well. Just before serving, stir in the light cream. Whip the heavy cream and season it with salt. Place a dollop of whipped cream on top of each bowl of soup.

MENU 145 Braised Leg of Lamb *(for 12 to 14)*

Two 5-pound legs of lamb
2 large garlic cloves
3 tablespoons olive oil
10 tablespoons butter
2 onions, chopped
Salt and black pepper
2 cups dry Vermouth
3 tablespoons tomato paste
6 cups beef bouillon, or more

Bouquet garni composed of 1 bay leaf, ½ teaspoon dried thyme, ½ teaspoon dried rosemary, 1 parsley sprig, tied in a cheesecloth bag
24 small white onions
8 carrots, quartered
2 teaspoons sugar
1 pound mushrooms, quartered

Have the butcher trim off the bones of the lamb to make a neat roast of each leg. Preheat the oven to medium (350°). Cut the garlic into slivers and push them into deep slits in the surface of the lamb. Heat the oil and 4 tablespoons of the butter in a large deep roasting pan with a cover, and brown the meat on all sides, on the top of the stove. Just before the lamb is completely brown, add the chopped onions for browning. Season with salt and pepper; add the Vermouth and tomato paste and enough bouillon to come half way up the meat. Stir the liquid around to mix well and add the *bouquet garni*. Cover the pan and put it in the oven to braise for 3 hours, turning the meat often. Add more bouillon as the liquids are absorbed.

Sauté the whole white onions and the quartered carrots in 4 tablespoons of the butter until slightly golden, sprinkling with the sugar to brown and caramelize the vegetables. Add these vegetables to the lamb. Deglaze the sauté pan with a little bouillon, add the liquid to the roasting pan, and continue to cook the lamb for 1 hour longer.

Sauté the mushrooms in the remaining butter and add them to the lamb. Roast for another 30 minutes. Serve the lamb sliced—it will be very tender and will almost fall apart. Arrange the onions, carrots, and mushrooms around the lamb. Remove and discard the *bouquet garni* and any fat from the surface of the sauce. Pour some sauce over the meat. Serve the remainder in a sauceboat.

MENU 145   *Frozen Rum Raisin Custard (for 12)*

1 cup seedless raisins	½ cup chopped pecans
1¼ cups dark rum	1 cup macaroon or cake crumbs
2 cups heavy cream	1½ quarts French vanilla ice cream

Soak the raisins in the rum for at least 1 hour. Whip the cream and fold in the chopped pecans, the raisins and rum, and the macaroon or cake crumbs. Gradually stir the mixture into the ice cream, which has been allowed to soften. Place the mixture in a 12-cup mould in the freezing compartment until serving time. Remove from the mould to a serving platter, slice, and serve.

MENU 146   Oyster Soufflé *(for 12)*

1 pint shucked oysters	6 tablespoons flour
1½ cups milk, approximately	10 eggs, separated
½ cup butter	

Put the oysters in a saucepan over low heat until the juice begins to simmer. Strain and reserve the juice. Add enough milk to make 2 cups liquid. Mince the oysters. Blend 6 tablespoons of the butter and the flour together in the saucepan with the mixture of milk and oyster juice. Cook over low heat, stirring constantly, until the sauce is thick and smooth. Remove from the heat, cool slightly, and add the lightly beaten egg yolks, mixing well. Add the oysters to the mixture and put it aside until ready to bake.

About 30 minutes before you plan to serve the soufflé, butter two 6-cup oven-proof glass baking dishes with the remaining 2 tablespoons butter. Now put the egg whites in a bowl and beat them until they stand in firm peaks. Fold the oyster mixture into the egg whites. Divide the soufflé between two prepared baking dishes and bake in a hot oven (400°) for 30 minutes, or until puffed and golden. Serve immediately.

MENU 146   Jellied Cold Duck with Black
Cherries *(for 12)*

Four 5-pound ducks
Salt and black pepper
2 oranges, cut in half
2 onions, cut in half
Four 6-inch pieces of celery
1 cup dry Port wine
1½ tablespoons unflavoured gelatine

⅓ cup cold water
2 cups strong beef bouillon
12 whole oranges
1-pound, 13-ounce can Bing
cherries

Preheat the oven to hot (400°). Wipe the ducks carefully and season the in-
sides with salt and pepper. Insert into each duck an unpeeled orange half, an
onion half, and a piece of celery. Prick the ducks well with a fork so the fat
will run out. Put the birds in a greased roasting pan and roast them for 30
minutes. Lower the heat to medium (350°). Pour off the fat in the pan and
pour the Port over the birds. Season the outsides of the ducks with salt and
pepper. Roast for 1 hour or longer, or until the ducks are tender, basting three
or four times with the Port. When the ducks are done, remove them to racks on
platters to cool. Soften the gelatine in the cold water. Pour off all the fat from
the roasting pan, deglaze with the bouillon, and simmer for a few minutes. Add
the softened gelatine and stir until it is dissolved; then strain the liquid into
a bowl and set it in the refrigerator to jell.

Scoop out the twelve whole oranges to make baskets with serrated edges.
Drain the cherries, reserving the syrup for another use. Fill the baskets with
cherries.

When the ducks are cold and the aspic on the point of setting, spoon aspic
jelly over the ducks several times until the birds are shiny. Put the ducks in the
refrigerator to set between each coating. Pour the remaining aspic, including any
that dripped into the platters beneath the ducks, into a shallow pan and chill
in the refrigerator to set. Keep the jellied ducks and the orange baskets
of cherries in the refrigerator until ready to serve. At serving time arrange the
ducks on platters and surround them with the orange baskets. Scramble the remaining aspic with a fork and arrange it in small mounds around the ducks.

MENU 146   Fruit Meringue *(for 12)*

1 quart fresh strawberries	8 egg whites
1 pint fresh raspberries	2 tablespoons sugar
1 dozen fresh peaches, peeled and sliced	1 teaspoon vanilla extract
	1½ quarts vanilla ice cream
1 cup Cointreau	Powdered sugar

Place the fruit in a deep 20-cup heatproof glass dish and pour the Cointreau over it. Put the dish in a large flat baking pan and surround it completely with ice cubes. Beat the egg whites with the sugar and vanilla extract until very stiff. Spread the ice cream over the top of the fruit, and spoon the meringue on top of the ice cream. Put the baking pan in a hot oven (400°) for 2 to 3 minutes, or until the meringue is light brown. Remove from the oven and serve the fruit meringue in the dish in which it was baked. Dust with powdered sugar.

This dessert is delicious either summer or winter. In winter substitute sliced brandied peaches or brandied cherries for fresh fruit.

MENU 147   Oxtail Soup Amontillado *(for 12)*

2 small oxtails, cut into 2-inch pieces	*Bouquet garni* composed of 1 bay leaf, 1 thyme sprig, 2 parsley sprigs, and 6 peppercorns, tied in a cheesecloth bag
½ cup flour	
2 teaspoons salt	
½ teaspoon black pepper	3 egg whites and shells
¼ cup olive oil	½ cup Amontillado, or more to taste
16 cups strong beef bouillon	
1 cup each of chopped onions, diced carrots, and diced celery	

This soup can be made 2 or 3 days ahead. Wash the oxtail pieces well. Put them in a large soup kettle with water to cover, and bring to a rolling boil. Lift out the oxtails and discard the water. Rinse and dry the oxtail pieces, then dredge with the flour mixed with the salt and pepper. Brown the pieces in the hot oil. Pour off all the fat possible, and add the beef bouillon, the vegetables, and *bouquet garni.* Simmer slowly, skimming carefully when the liquid first comes to a boil, and cook for 3½ to 4 hours, or until the meat falls off the bones. Strain the bouillon and discard the bones; dice the meat and reserve.

Cool the bouillon and remove the fat. Clarify the bouillon with the slightly beaten egg whites, and the crushed shells: add them to the cool broth and bring to a simmer, stirring constantly. Let the liquid simmer for 10 to 15 minutes, then strain through a fine strainer lined with a dampened cloth. At serving time, reheat by simmering for a few minutes. Add the Amontillado and salt and pepper to taste. The reserved diced meat may be added, too, or the consommé may be served without any further addition.

MENU 147   Pork à l'Orange *(for 12)*

5-pound boned fillet of pork	¼ teaspoon dried thyme
½ cup butter	1 bay leaf
6 carrots, sliced	1½ teaspoons salt
⅓ cup Cognac	½ teaspoon black pepper
2 cups dry white wine	6 oranges

Ask the butcher to trim all the fat from a boneless fillet of pork and tie it to keep its shape.

Melt the butter in a heavy saucepan and brown the pork and the carrot slices. When the meat is golden brown on all sides, pour the heated Cognac over it and ignite it. When the flame subsides, pour the heated wine over the meat. Add the thyme, bay leaf, salt, and pepper. Cover and cook over very low heat for 2 hours. Remove the pork from the pan and keep hot. Strain the pan juices through a sieve lined with a cloth wrung out in ice water. (This will remove excess grease.) Extract the juice of 2 of the oranges and cut the rind into thin strips; blanch the rind for 2 minutes in boiling water. Add the blanched rind to the sauce together with the orange juice and simmer, uncovered, for 10 minutes. Cut the pork into slices, arrange them on a serving platter, and pour the sauce over the meat. Peel the remaining 4 oranges, cut them into round slices, and seed them; cut the slices in half and arrange them around the meat. Serve very hot.

MENU 147   Baked Apple and Raisin Dumplings *(for 12)*

6 tablespoons raisins
½ cup Calvados
12 medium baking apples
¾ cup sugar
1 tablespoon cinnamon

½ cup butter
Dumpling pastry (see below)
1 egg yolk
1 teaspoon cream

Soak the raisins in the Calvados for 1 hour. Preheat the oven to hot (400°). Core the apples and sprinkle them with some of the sugar and cinnamon, inside and out. Fill the cavities with the soaked raisins and sprinkle sugar and cinnamon over them again. Dot the apples with 4 tablespoons of the butter, and butter a baking pan with 2 tablespoons of the butter. Bake the apples for 30 minutes. Cool; or refrigerate the apples if they are not to be used immediately.

Roll out dumpling pastry into a thin sheet. Use a saucer or a small plate as guide—the size of the rounds of pastry depends on the size of the apples—and cut out rounds of pastry. Put an apple in the centre of each, pulling the pastry up around the top, into a twist. Sprinkle the twist with the remaining cinnamon and sugar. Divide the remaining butter and put a small piece of butter on top of each twist. Prick the pastry on both sides of the apple. Beat the egg yolk with the heavy cream and paint the dumplings with this mixture, using a pastry brush. Bake the dumplings in a hot oven (400°) for about 15 minutes, until the pastry is crisp and golden. Serve warm, with hard sauce passed separately.

DUMPLING PASTRY

2½ cups sifted flour
5 teaspoons baking powder

6 tablespoons butter or vegetable
    shortening
¾ cup light cream, approximately

Resift the flour and baking powder together. Work in the butter or shortening and add just enough cream to make a soft but not sticky dough. The absorptiveness of flour varies and the amount of liquid needed is never quite the same, so it is impossible to say exactly how much cream will be needed. This dough may be made ahead and refrigerated. Take it from the refrigerator 1 hour before it is to be rolled and used.

MENU 148 *Roast Beef with Yorkshire Pudding (for 12)*

5-rib standing roast of beef
Salt and black pepper

Yorkshire pudding (see below)
2 cups beef bouillon

Preheat the oven to very hot (450°). Place the wiped and tied roast, fat side up, in a large roasting pan. Roast at 450° for 30 minutes; season with salt and pepper. Lower the heat to medium (350°) and continue roasting for 15 minutes per pound for rare; or roast in a low oven (325°) for 16 minutes per pound for medium. Remove the roast from the oven 30 minutes before it is done, as the meat will continue to cook from internal heat. When using a thermometer, it will register 130° when the meat is removed from the oven; the thermometer will continue to go up to 140° (for rare) even outside the oven. By following this method, the meat will be easier to slice. Cover the beef during this last 30 minutes outside the oven. Meanwhile, prepare and cook the Yorkshire pudding.

Make the gravy. Pour off any fat remaining in the roasting pan, add the beef bouillon, and deglaze over high heat, scraping up any brown particles with a spoon. Lower the heat and simmer for at least 5 minutes.

Slice the beef and cut the Yorkshire pudding into squares. Arrange the beef on a platter, put the squares of pudding around the meat, and serve the gravy in a heated sauceboat.

YORKSHIRE PUDDING

6 eggs
3 cups milk

3 cups sifted flour
1 scant teaspoon salt

Preheat the oven to very hot (450°). Beat the eggs and the milk in a large bowl. Sift the flour and salt and add to the egg and milk mixture. Beat together with a rotary beater for about 2 minutes. Prepare three 8-inch-square pans; pour several tablespoons of fat from the roast into each pan. The fat should be about 1/16 inch deep. If the roast does not render enough fat, add some extra beef fat to the roasting pan while the beef cooks. Pour the pudding batter into the greased pans and bake for 15 minutes. Lower the heat to medium (375°) and bake for 20 minutes longer, or until well puffed and brown.

MENU 148   Mousse Diplomate *(for 12)*

1 cup sugar	1 cup mixed candied fruits
12 egg yolks	3 tablespoons dark rum
3 cups heavy cream, whipped	

Beat the sugar with the egg yolks until thick and lemon-coloured. Fold the whipped cream gently and carefully into the egg and sugar mixture. Then gently fold in the cut-up candied fruits and the rum. Pour into a 10-cup melon mould and put in the freezer for at least 3 hours. At serving time, unmould and serve with an apricot or raspberry sauce poured around it.

This mousse can be prepared and frozen a day or so in advance, but if so, it should be put in lower part of refrigerator about 1 hour before serving, to prevent it from being too hard.

MENU 149   Braised Tongue (for 12)

1 smoked beef tongue, about 5 pounds	1½ cups dry white wine
4 tablespoons vegetable shortening	½ cup Madeira wine
2 large carrots, quartered	½ cup seedless white raisins
2 large onions, sliced	1 tablespoon cornstarch
1 large garlic clove, minced	1 tablespoon sugar
3 tablespoons tomato paste	
Bouquet garni composed of 1 bay leaf, 1 thyme sprig, and 1 parsley sprig	

Cover the tongue with cold water and bring it to a boil. Simmer for about an hour. Remove the tongue from the cooking liquid and reserve the liquid. As soon as the tongue is cool enough to handle, remove the skin.

Melt the vegetable shortening in a large heavy casserole with a cover. Brown the tongue, turning it over in the hot shortening to brown evenly. At the last turn, add the carrots and onions to brown. Add the garlic, tomato paste, the *bouquet garni*, white wine, and enough of the reserved cooking liquid to cover one eighth of the tongue. Cover the casserole and simmer for about 3½ hours over very low heat, so the liquid just shivers. Turn the tongue a few times and add a little of the reserved cooking liquid, if the liquid in the casserole cooks down too much. Meanwhile, heat the Madeira wine, and pour it over the raisins.

When the tongue is tender, remove it to a platter and keep it warm. Strain the sauce in the casserole into a saucepan. Mix the cornstarch with a little cold water, add a little hot sauce and stir until smooth, and return to the saucepan. Caramelize the sugar in a small iron skillet. When it has just coloured, add ¼ cup water, stir it into the sugar, and reduce it a little. Add the caramel to the sauce, and add the raisins and wine. There should be about 2 cups of sauce. Simmer very gently for about 3 minutes. Slice the tongue, pour the sauce over it, and serve very hot.

MENU 156   Risotto with Chicken Livers (for 16)

4 cups raw white rice
6 cups chicken broth
1 teaspoon salt
1 big pinch of saffron
  (optional)
4 white onions, sliced

½ cup butter, or more
2½ pounds chicken livers
Three 4-ounce cans button mushrooms
1 cup grated Parmesan cheese, or more

Measure the rice into a 16-cup pot and rinse it in three waters to remove all loose starch. Drain the rice and add the broth with the salt and the saffron and stir to mix well. Bring to a boil, cover, then lower the heat to simmering and simmer for 30 minutes, covered. At the end of this time, the rice should have absorbed all the broth and be ready to mix with the other ingredients of the *risotto*. Watch carefully that it does not stick.

Sauté the onions in half the butter in a large skillet. When the onions are transparent, add them with the butter in the pan to the cooked rice, turning with a fork until all the rice is buttered. Add the remaining butter to the same skillet and sauté the livers quickly. Drain the mushrooms, reserving the liquid. Add the mushrooms to the livers while they are still cooking. Stir to mix, then add the mushrooms and livers to the rice and onion mixture. Mix gently. Adjust the seasoning; add more butter if needed and some of the mushroom liquid if the mixture seems too dry. Transfer to serving casseroles. At serving time, heat the mixture through again and sprinkle with Parmesan cheese.

If risotto is being prepared in advance, it can be frozen, before the cheese is added, and stored in the freezer until 8 hours before serving time. When defrosted, reheat the mixture in a 400° oven for about 20 minutes to ½ hour, first sprinkling the top with the Parmesan cheese. Or, if preferred, the chicken livers only can be prepared ahead, frozen and defrosted in time to add to the rice mixture.

MENU 157   Sweet Ham Loaf *(for 16)*

2 cups fresh bread crumbs
¾ cup milk
4 eggs, beaten
5 pounds raw ham, ground
3 pounds fresh pork, ground

Salt and black pepper
Sweet and sour sauce (see below)
Two 12½-ounce jars preserved kumquats, drained

Soak the bread crumbs in the milk, beat in the eggs, then add the ham and pork and season with a very little salt and a generous amount of pepper. Form into two loaves. Place the loaves in a well-buttered roasting pan and bake in a preheated medium oven (375°) for 2 hours, basting with sweet and sour sauce. Serve surrounded with kumquats, with the sauce poured over all.

This ham loaf can be prepared ahead and frozen before baking, just after the loaves have been shaped. Thaw the frozen loaves for several hours before baking. Or bake the loaves without basting, freeze, and reheat just before serving, basting frequently with sweet and sour sauce during the reheating.

Sweet and Sour Sauce

1½ cups brown sugar
½ cup kumquat syrup
1 tablespoon prepared mustard

½ cup red-wine vinegar
½ cup water

Combine the ingredients in a saucepan and bring to a boil. Use to baste ham loaf during baking.

MENU 157   Délices du Jardin *(for 16)*

5 green peppers, cut into little sticks
2 very small green cabbages, shredded
2 very small red cabbages, shredded
2 medium cauliflowers, broken into flowerets
4 young cucumbers, sliced
12 young scallions, chopped
3 celery hearts, chopped
10 tomatoes, peeled, seeded, and cut into eighths
1 head escarole
1 head Boston lettuce
1 large head romaine
1 garlic clove
¼ cup chopped chives
2 tablespoons chopped fresh dill
3½ cups French dressing (see below)

Wash the vegetables and cut, shred, or chop them. Separate salad greens into leaves and wash them well. Put the greens and all the vegetables except the tomatoes in a bowl with lots of cracked ice until time to serve. Then drain and dry all the ingredients and place them in a large wooden bowl that has been well rubbed with the cut garlic clove. Add the tomatoes. Sprinkle the chives and dill over the salad. Pour the French dressing over all. Toss well and serve.

FRENCH DRESSING

3 teaspoons salt
¾ teaspoon freshly ground black pepper
2 tablespoons prepared mustard
¾ cup tarragon wine vinegar
3 cups olive oil, or corn oil

Mix all the ingredients together and shake well to blend the flavours.

MENU 158   Spaghetti with Red Clam Sauce *(for 16)*

4 large onions
3 garlic cloves
¾ cup olive oil
12 large ripe tomatoes
1 teaspoon salt
2 teaspoons black pepper
1 teaspoon basil
1 teaspoon orégano
1 bay leaf, crumbled
10 dozen littleneck clams, shucked
3 pounds spaghettini #2
1 cup butter
1 bunch fresh parsley, chopped

Chop the onions fine; force the garlic cloves through a garlic press, or chop them fine. Heat the olive oil, reserving 1 tablespoon, in a pan large enough to hold all the sauce. Sauté the onions and garlic without browning. Peel and slice the tomatoes and drop them into the pan, together with the salt, pepper, basil, orégano, and bay leaf. Simmer, uncovered, until the tomatoes are almost, but not entirely, cooked, approximately 45 minutes. (This sauce can be made up to this point days ahead, then frozen. Defrost for 1 hour before it is needed, then bring to a boil in a saucepan.)

Just before serving, put the clams into this hot tomato sauce, and simmer for about 5 minutes. Put the spaghetti into 24 cups boiling water with 1 teaspoon salt in a large kettle. Add the reserved 1 tablespoon olive oil to the water. After the water comes to a boil again, cook for 5 to 7 minutes. When the spaghetti is cooked to taste, drain. Put the butter in the serving dish, add the drained hot spaghetti, and stir to mix well. Pour the clams in their sauce over the spaghetti, sprinkle with parsley, and serve.

MENU 159   Curried Crab and Turtle Soup *(for 16)*

1 cup butter
1 cup flour
4 teaspoons curry powder
8 cups milk
3 cups canned turtle soup

3 pounds cooked crabmeat
Salt and black pepper
2 teaspoons Worcestershire sauce
1 cup Sherry
1½ cups light cream

Melt the butter in a double boiler and blend in the flour and the curry powder to make a smooth paste. Add the milk and the turtle soup, a little at a time, blending to keep smooth after each addition, until all the milk and soup have been added. Cook over boiling water, stirring constantly, until thickened to about the consistency of heavy cream. Then add the cooked crabmeat and salt and pepper to taste. Keep stirring this in the double boiler until the crabmeat is thoroughly blended with the soup mixture. Before serving, add the Worcestershire sauce, the Sherry, and the cream, and bring to top heat again, but do not boil. Serve in heated soup plates or cups, with toasted French bread.

MENU 160   Beef and Noodle Casserole *(for 16)*

Three 8-ounce packages medium-wide egg noodles

1¾ cups butter

3 large onions, chopped fine

6 pounds lean ground beef

Salt and pepper

2 large green peppers, seeded and diced fine

¾ cup chopped parsley

1 cup beef bouillon

¾ cup dry bread crumbs

Cook the noodles according to package directions, about 9 minutes, keeping them firm. Drain well and mix with ½ cup butter. Butter lavishly two 12-cup oven dishes and divide the noodles between them. In two large skillets, melt all but 3 tablespoons of the remaining butter; divide the chopped onion in half, and sauté half in each skillet until slightly golden. Divide the meat between the skillets and cook it until no red shows, stirring with a fork. Season with salt and pepper, add half the minced green pepper, half the chopped parsley, and ½ cup bouillon to each skillet. Now put the meat mixture on top of the noodles in the oven dishes. Sprinkle with the dry bread crumbs, and dot the top with butter. (The dish may be prepared ahead up to this point, and put in the refrigerator. Bring to room temperature an hour before reheating.) Preheat the oven to 400° (hot) and bake for 20 minutes.

CONCLUSION

Several times during the assembling of this book the question has been asked "Will all the recipes be complicated?" The answer is "Not all—but many." Many of them *are* complicated, and to a novice cook some of them may seem unnecessarily so. But the best of cooking is a more or less complicated affair, and these complex recipes are the result of minute and patient experiment as to the best way to reach a certain flavour, a certain texture in the particular dish. You may feel that it can be done more simply. In many cases a similar dish *can* be done more simply, but it will not be exactly the same. Through your own experimentation you may learn which parts of a given recipe you are able to simplify. But as believers in fine cooking, we urge you to try even the recipes that seem too complicated to you *once,* at least. Then you can decide whether or not they are worth the trouble.

This is not to say that every recipe in this book contains an involved number of steps; they are written out in explicit detail so that occasionally the reading makes them seem more complicated than they really are—certain processes, which fairly experienced cooks would do automatically, need to be pointed out and set down so that the recipes are mistake-proof even for a novice.

As knowledge about food and concern about cooking grow, especially among the intelligent, well-educated young, let us hope that Americans are pointed toward a general quickening of interest in the planning of delicious, well-composed menus. *Vogue*'s editors would like to hope, also, that this book will have a part in that stimulation.

MENU INDEX

In this index recipes have been arranged according to their menu categories. Some recipes appear in more than one place. With the exception of such basics as sauces and pastry, recipes are followed by the number (in parentheses) of persons to be served by that recipe.

APPETIZERS, COCKTAIL

bite-size tarts with ground ham, hot (16), 265
caviar tart (8), 266
cheese thimble biscuits (192), 262
cheese wafers with pecans (96), 260
chicken liver pâté (12), 273
cream cheese and nut balls (36 to 40), 260
curried shrimp tarts, miniature (16), 264
eggs stuffed with chopped olives (40), 259
eggs stuffed with red caviar (40), 259
hors-d'oeuvre puffs (36), 260
    with smoked salmon (36), 259
Parmesan greenery, hot (36), 264
Roquefort pecans (50), 259
Roquefort spread (36 to 40), 262
sesame shortbread, hot (50), 264
spicy pecans, 263
terrine of country pâté (20), 12
truffles, minced, in pastry (30), 262
turnovers filled with ground ham (30 to 36), 261
turnovers with ground chicken and chopped parsley (16), 265
    miniature (32 to 40), 265
turnovers with minced clams (30 to 36), 263
water chestnuts wrapped in bacon (30), 266

APPETIZERS, FIRST COURSE

blini with caviar (10), 194
caviar in aspic (12), 156
caviar tart (8), 266
chicken liver pâté (12), 273
clams southside (14), 216
coquilles St. Jacques (10), 35
egg and caviar mousse (24), 176
eggs en gelée with truffles and ham (16), 50
Francillon salad (10), 36
mushrooms, filled, with mushroom soufflé (8), 218
mushrooms, grilled, stuffed with minced clams (10), 139
onion and bacon tarts (20), 280
onion tart, hot (8), 217
oysters in Sherry (24), 179
oysters, low-country (12), 40

APPETIZERS, FIRST COURSE (*continued*)

oysters Rockefeller (24), 174
pizzas, individual (24), 73
quiche lorraine (16), 51
quiches lorraines, petites (12), 231
sausage in pastry (12), 232
shrimp in sauce piquante (20), 170
terrine of country pâté (20), 12

SOUPS, HOT

asparagus (8), 242
black bean, with diced ham and lemon (12), 196
Bombay (12), 310
borscht (20), 172
chicken gumbo (24), 71
clam stew (10), 133
consommé stracciatelle (16), 158
consommé with okra (18), 166
curried chicken (24), 67
curried crab (10), 140
curried crab and turtle (16), 322
lobster bisque (16), 159
onion (10), 303
oxtail, Amontillado (12), 314
petite marmite (12 to 14), 277
pot-au-feu (10), 306
purée Saint-Germain (20), 168
spinach (8), 128
tomato and dill (18), 164
tomato mushroom purée (10), 226
vegetable gumbo (14), 42
watercress (10), 224

SOUPS, COLD

billi-bi (20), 56
borscht (20), 172
cucumber (10 to 12), 33
curried chicken (24), 67
tomato and dill (18), 164

SOUPS, JELLIED

borscht (14), 43
tomato clam (24), 69

FISH

fish mélange (30), 25
fish pudding (8), 242
fish stew (12), 41
    as main course (8), 41

FISH (*continued*)

fish Tetrazzini (24), 101

salmon, mousse of, with green mayonnaise (10), 33

salmon, smoked, with hot boiled potatoes (12), 93

shad and roe normande (8), 222

shad roe with white wine (8), 126

sole, fillet of, in Chablis sauce (16), 161

sole, soufflé of (10), 137

striped bass in aspic (10), 141

SHELLFISH

clam(s)

southside (14), 216

stew (10), 133

crabmeat

creole, hot (12), 274

Mornay, hot (12), 157

mousse (10), 273

tomatoes stuffed with (24), 89

lobster

bordelaise (24), 177

in cucumber (20), 87

mussels, Francillon salad (10), 36

oyster(s)

chicken and, casserole of (12), 276

low-country (12), 40

Rockefeller (24), 174

in Sherry (24), 179

soufflé (12), 312

scallops, coquilles St. Jacques (10), 35

seafood risotto (10), 224

shrimp

curry (12), 12

jambalaya, quick (10), 306

and mushrooms, baked (6), 308

in sauce piquante (20), 170

supreme (20), 54

MEATS

beef

boeuf à la mode (24), 72

boeuf à la mode en gelée (20), 95

bourguignon (24), 66

carbonada criolla (10), 92

chinois (8), 243

cold boiled, en gelée (12), 229

corned beef hash, baked (14), 236

cous-cous (10), 19

kasha with meatballs (14), 236

and kidney pie (20), 87

meat loaf with pâté en croûte (12), 234

and noodle casserole (16), 323

paprika (30), 22

petite marmite (12 to 14), 277

poivrade (12), 38

pot-au-feu (10), 306

roast, with Yorkshire pudding (12), 317

roast fillet of, in aspic (10), 37

shepherd's pie (10), 305

tongue, braised (12), 318

MEATS (*continued*)

veal

roast, with carrots and onions (20), 53

roast, with mushrooms en croûte (16), 160

roast, with orange sauce (24), 69

roast loin of young, with tarragon sauce (24), 178

savoury roast (10), 140

scaloppini of, with tarragon (6), 308

spezzatino (20), 98

tendrons of (10), 15

vitello tonnato (10), 228

and water chestnut casserole (12), 13

lamb

braised stuffed shoulder of, with truffles (24), 180

crown roasts of, with barley pilaff (18), 165

cous-cous (10), 19

leg of, braised (12 to 14), 311

navarin of (30), 27

roast, en croûte (10), 138

saddle of, à l'orientale (10), 132

shepherd's pie (10), 305

pork

pork à l'orange (12), 315

sausage in pastry (12), 232

suckling pig, roast (10), 193

szekely goulash (12), 18

ham

boned, in pastry (10), 226

and chicken with noodles (10), 16

cornucopias filled with vegetables (20), 97

jellied parsleyed (24), 74

loaf, sweet (16), 320

mousse (8 to 10), 16

mousse ring filled with vegetables (10), 131

prosciutto and almonds with broccoli (6), 310

POULTRY

chicken

in aspic with ham cornucopias filled with vegetables (20), 97

breast of, in tarragon aspic (12), 92

breasts, sauté of, on cracked wheat pilaff (20), 170

breasts with wild rice and chestnuts (24), 100

Brunswick stew (12 to 14), 232

and celery hearts (24), 76

coq au vin (20), 169

cous-cous (10), 19

curried (24), 98

czarina (30), 24

gumbo (24), 71

and ham paella (6), 309

and ham with noodles (10), 16

liver pâté (12), 273

livers in Madeira sauce, chafing dish of (12), 17

POULTRY (*continued*)

livers, risotto with (16), 319
mousse, cold (10), 304
with noodles (12), 276
and oysters, casserole of (12), 276
petite marmite (12 to 14), 277
poulet chasseur (12), 41
with truffles (20), 58
turkey(s)
braised young, in Champagne (20), 172
hash, hot (8), 244
roast, with Port wine sauce and chestnut
stuffing (12), 197
smoked, gratin of (6), 307
Tetrazzini (20), 279
duck, duckling
jellied cold, with black cherries (12),
313
roast, with cherries (18), 166
goose
braised (12), 198
roast, with peaches (16), 162

GAME

guinea hen, breast of, Smitane (8), 125
guinea hen in casserole (8), 219
pheasant in casserole (24), 174
pheasants in cream (10), 135
quail, roast, on hominy (24), 99
rabbit négaunée (8 to 10), 130
venison, leg of, roast, with sauce poivrade
(10), 195
venison steaks, broiled (10), 143

PASTA

cannelloni Leonardo da Vinci (10), 20
gnocchi à la parisienne (8), 222
green noodles, hot, with cold pâté (10), 91
lasagne, hot casserole of, with beef sauce,
buffet (10), family dinner (6 to 8), 34
spaghetti with red clam sauce (16), 321

GRAINS

barley pilaff (18), 165
cracked wheat pilaff (20), 171
hominy grits, baked (18), 167
kasha with meatballs (14), 236
rice
green (10), 228
pilaff (10), 133
ring of brown, with baby Brussels sprouts
(24), 175
ring of red, filled with green peas (12),
40
semolina (10), 20
spoon bread (8), 217

VEGETABLES

asparagus casserole (20), 55
asparagus soufflé, crown of (10), 225
beans, baked brown (14), 43
beets, chopped, Smitane (10), 193
Brussels sprouts in brown rice ring (24),
175
cabbage, red, with apples (8), 129

VEGETABLES (*continued*)

carrot soufflé (8), 126
chestnuts, purée of (20), 173
corn pudding (12), 15
eggplant, corn, and tomato casserole (20),
59
green beans in mustard cream (10), 143
green peas, French style (10), 141
kidney beans, baked (10), 303
peas and lima beans au gratin (24), 89
potatoes Anna (10), 134
potatoes Dauphine (8), 220
potatoes, gratin of (12), 39
spinach rings with slivered parsley carrots
(30), 22
zucchini, baked (16), 163
zucchini casserole, baked (12), 235

VEGETABLES AS A SEPARATE COURSE

asparagus soufflé, crown of (10), 225
beans, baked brown (14), 43
broccoli with prosciutto and almonds (6),
310
carrot soufflé (8), 126
eggplant casserole (16), 94
kidney beans, baked (10), 303
mushrooms filled with mushroom soufflé
(8), 218
onion and bacon tarts (20), 280
onion tart, hot (8), 217
peas and lima beans au gratin (24), 89

LUNCHEON DISHES

black bean soup with diced ham and lemon
(12), 196
eggplant casserole (16), 94
eggs en gelée with truffles and ham (8), 50
green noodles, hot, with cold pâté (10), 91
lobster in cucumber (20), 87
smoked salmon with hot boiled potatoes
(12), 93
tomatoes stuffed with crabmeat (24), 89

SALADS

chicory and orange (24), 90
délices du jardin (16), 321
Francillon (10), 36
green bean (8), 244
lentil (20), 57
lobster in cucumber (20), 87
potato, hot (12), 230
rice, cold (24), 74
salade Schiaparelli (20), 96
tomato aspic ring (24), 71
tomatoes stuffed with crabmeat (24), 89

SALAD DRESSINGS

French, 321
herb, 90
lemon French, 75
mayonnaise (12), 233
green, 93
sauce gribiche, 142
Russian, 88
shallot and parsley, 57

CHEESE

Liederkranz mould (8 to 10), 130
quiche lorraine (16), 51
quiches lorraines, petites (12), 231
ramekins (10), 136
Roquefort cheese soufflé, cold (20), 88
soufflé (10 to 12), 234
soufflé, cold (14), 278

SAUCES

aspic for beef, 229
aspic, white-wine, 227
béchamel, 307
court bouillon, 26
curry, 13
fish stock, 160
gribiche, 142
Madeira cream, 76
marinade, juniper berry, 143
    red wine, 73
mushroom, 235
mustard, 52
poivrade, for beef, 39
    for venison, 195
shrimp and mushroom, 137
sweet and sour, 320
white, 20
    thick, 34

BREADS

blini (10), 194
brioche dough, 227
cheese biscuit dough, 261
pancakes, dessert (30), 26; (24), 176
pizzas, individual (24), 73
spoon bread (8), 217
Yorkshire pudding, 317

PASTRY

almond tart pastry, 220
dumpling pastry, 316
flaky pastry, 161
flaky pastry shells, 52
graham-cracker piecrust shells, 56
hors-d'oeuvre puffs, 260
puff pastry, 138
sweet tart pastry, 275
sweet tart pastry shells, 91
tart pastry, 136

DESSERTS, COLD

apple tart (8), 219
apple turnovers (12), 275
apricot meringue (20), 57
apricot trifle (12), 231
baba ring (12), 21
burnt almond chiffon pie (16), 158
chocolate-hazelnut cream (12), 156
chocolate mousse (14), 278
chocolate mousse cake (12), 18
coeurs à la crème (24), 67
coffee cream (8), 129
coffee walnut roll (16), 163
Cognac cream on toasted spongecake (20), 171

DESSERTS, COLD (continued)

crème brûlée (14), 44
crème de marrons (6), 309
English custard (8), 128
English trifle (8), 127
fruit compote brûlée (24), 99
fruit pudding with vanilla sauce (12), 42
fruit soufflé (8), 243
Lady Baltimore cake (12), 70
lemon mousse (10), 139
lemon soufflé, cold (16), 50
macaroon and pear tart (24), 90
marrons café bombe (12), 230
Mont Blanc (20), 280
mousse diplomate (12), 318
orange cream tarts (20), 55
oranges Dulcinea (8), 243
peaches cardinal on pineapple ice mould (10), 196
praline Bavarian cream with strawberries (18), 167
raspberries frangipane (24), 179
raspberry charlotte (10), 23
rum raisin custard, frozen (12), 312
Sherry macaroons (10), 36

DESSERTS, HOT OR WARM

apple(s)
    porcupine (8 to 10), 131
    and raisin dumplings, baked (12), 316
    tart (8), 219
    turnovers (12), 275
applesauce cake (20), 54
apricot(s)
    Colbert (10), 134
    meringue (20), 57
    "omelette" (12), 94
Austrian Nockerln (12), 157
beignets soufflés (20), 59
chocolate mint soufflé (8), 125
eggs à la neige (10 to 12), 38
flaming ginger pancakes (24), 176
fruit
    compote, baked (12), 274
    compote brûlée (24), 99
    compote with marrons glacés (14), 216
    meringue (12), 314
    pudding with vanilla sauce (12), 42
gâteau basque (24), 67
Indian pudding, hot, with ice cream sauce (20), 52
lemon pudding (8), 221
macaroon and pear tart (24), 90
marrons croquettes (24), 75
oranges Dulcinea (8), 243
pancakes, filled, with strawberry preserves (30), 26
pots de crème, assorted (12), 14
prune soufflé with lemon custard sauce (8), 223
rice pudding, hot (20), 60
tarte à l'orange (24), 181
tarte Tatin (18), 165
vanilla soufflé with rum sauce (8), 217

DESSERT SAUCES
  apricot, 135
  apricot marmalade, 51
  brandy, 75
  cherry, 68
  English custard, 128
  ginger pastry cream, 177
  Lady Baltimore frosting, 70
  lemon custard, 223
  lemon, hot, 54
  liqueur syrup, 22
  praline powder, 168
  rum, 218
  Sherry, 221
  vanilla (cold), 42
  vanilla (hot), 158
  vanilla sugar, 27
  zabaglione, 60
BEVERAGES
  bishop (12), 186

BEVERAGES (*continued*)
  blue blazer (1), 186
  buttered rum, hot (1), 188
  carol punch (42), 187
  celery cup (15), 187
  Clover Club (1), 187
  Fish House punch (30), 187
  glögg (12), 188
  le brulo (4), 188
  milk punch (8), 189
  mulled cider (15), 189
  mulled wine (4), 189
  posset (2), 190
  punch, 190
  rumfustian (12), 190
  Sazarac (1), 192
  syllabub (6), 191
  Tom & Jerry (1), 191
  wassail bowl (18), 191
  white Christmas punch, 192

GENERAL INDEX

Almond tart pastry, 220
Appetizers
  bite-size tarts, hot, with ground ham, 265
  blini with caviar, 194
  caviar in aspic, 156
  caviar tart, 266
  cheese thimble biscuits, 262
  cheese wafers with pecans, 260
  chicken liver pâté, 273
  clam southside, 216
  cream cheese and nut balls, 260
  curried crab tarts, miniature, 265
  curried shrimp tarts, miniature, 264
  egg and caviar mousse, 176
  eggs en gelée with truffles and ham, 50
  eggs stuffed with chopped olives, 259
  eggs stuffed with red caviar, 259
  Francillon salad, 36
  hors-d'oeuvre puffs, 260
    with smoked salmon, 259
  low-country oysters, 40
  mushrooms, filled, with mushroom soufflé, 218
    grilled, stuffed with minced clams, 139
  onion tart, hot, 217
  oysters in Sherry, 179
  oysters Rockefeller, 174
  Parmesan greenery, hot, 264
  pizzas, individual, 73
  quiche lorraine, 51
  quiches lorraines, petites, 231
  Roquefort pecans, 259
  Roquefort spread, 262
  sesame shortbread, hot, 264
  shrimp in sauce piquante, 170
  spicy pecans, 263
  terrine of country pâté, 12
  truffles, minced, in pastry, 262
  turnovers
    hot, with ground chicken and chopped parsley, 265
    hot, miniature, with ground chicken and chopped parsley, 265
    small hot, filled with ground ham, 261
    small hot, with minced clams, 263
  water chestnuts wrapped in bacon, 266
Apple(s)
  porcupine, 131
  and raisin dumplings, baked, 316
  tart, 219
  turnovers, hot, 275
Applesauce cake, 54
Apricot(s)
  Colbert, 134

Apricot(s) (continued)
  marmalade sauce, 51
  meringue, 57
  "omelette," 94
  sauce, 135
  trifle, 231
Asparagus
  casserole, 55
  crown of, soufflé, 225
  soup, 242
Aspic
  aspic for beef, 229
  aspic mayonnaise, 97
  tarragon aspic, 92
  white-wine aspic, 227
Aspic dishes
  boeuf à la mode en gelée, 95
  boned ham in pastry, 226
  breast of chicken in tarragon aspic, 92
  caviar in aspic, 156
  chicken in aspic with ham cornucopias filled with vegetables, 97
  cold boiled beef en gelée, 229
  eggs en gelée with truffles and ham, 50
  jellied cold duck with black cherries, 313
  jellied parsleyed ham, 74
  roast fillet of beef in aspic, 37
  striped bass in aspic, 141
  tomato aspic ring, 71
Austrian Nockerln, 157

Baba ring, 21
Barley pilaff, 165
Bean(s)
  baked brown beans, 43
  baked kidney beans, 303
  black bean soup with diced ham and lemon, 196
  green bean salad, 244
  green beans in mustard cream, 143
  lima beans au gratin, peas and, 89
Béchamel sauce, 307
Beef
  aspic, 229
  boeuf à la mode, 72
  boeuf à la mode en gelée, 95
  bourguignon, 66
  carbonada criolla, 92
  chinois, 243
  cold boiled, en gelée, 229
  corned beef hash, baked, 236
  cous-cous, 19
  eggplant casserole, 94
  kasha with meatballs, 236

330

Beef (continued)
  and kidney pie, 87
  meat loaf with pâté en croûte, 234
  and noodle casserole, 323
  paprika, 22
  petite marmite, 277
  poivrade, 38
  pot-au-feu, 306
  roast, with Yorkshire pudding, 317
  roast fillet of, in aspic, 37
  sauce for lasagne, 34
  shepherd's pie, 305
  tongue, braised, 318
Beets, chopped, Smitane, 193
Beignets soufflés, 59
Beurre manié, 169
Beverages
  bishop, 186
  blue blazer, 186
  buttered rum, hot, 188
  carol punch, 187
  celery cup, 187
  Clover Club, 187
  Fish House punch, 187
  glögg, 188
  le brulo, 188
  milk punch, 189
  mulled cider, 189
  mulled wine, 189
  posset, 190
  punch, 190
  rumfustian, 190
  Sazarac, 192
  syllabub, 191
  Tom & Jerry, 191
  wassail bowl, 191
  white Christmas punch, 192
Billi-bi soup, 56
Bishop, 186
Black bean soup with diced ham and lemon, 196
Blini with caviar, 194
Blue blazer, 186
Boeuf à la mode, 72
Boeuf à la mode en gelée, 95
Bombay soup, 310
Borscht, cold, 172
Borscht, jellied, 43
Brandy sauce, 75
Breads
  blini, 194
  brioche dough, 227
  cheese biscuit dough, 261
  cheese thimble biscuits, 262
  cheese wafers with pecans, 260
  pancakes, dessert, 26, 176
  pizzas, individual, 73
  sesame shortbread, hot, 264
  spoon bread, 217
Brillat-Savarin, x, 118
Brioche dough, 227
Broccoli with prosciutto and almonds, 310
Brunswick stew, 232

Brussels sprouts, baby, in brown rice ring, 175
Buckwheat, 24
  kasha with meatballs, 236
Buffet, after-cocktail (20 to 24), 253
Buffet breakfast, outdoor (200), 113
Buffet de gare (50 to 60), 106
Buffet dinners
  choose any table—serve yourself (16 to 20), 45
  elegant little tables (24), 61
  with place cards (10 to 14), 28
  very informal—more food than service (30), 5
    à la carte, 6
    one big dish, 9
Buffet luncheons (10 to 24), 78
  at one long table (10 to 12), 81
  find your own place (20 to 24), 79
  small tables, casual seating (16 to 20), 83
  small tables with place cards (24), 85
Buffet meals, history, 3
Buffet parties, 2
  on the grand scale, 102
Burnt almond chiffon pie, 158
Butter
  beurre manié, 169
  clarified, 24, 194
Buttered rum, hot, 188

Cabbage, red, with apples, 129
Cakes
  applesauce, 54
  chocolate mousse, 18
  coffee walnut roll, 163
  gâteau basque, 67
  Lady Baltimore, 70
Cannelloni Leonardo da Vinci, 20
Caramel, 99, 307
Carbonada criolla, 92
Carol punch, 187
Carrot soufflé, 126
Carrots, slivered parsleyed, in spinach rings, 22
Caviar
  in aspic, 156
  mousse, egg and, 176
  tart, 266
Celery cup, 187
Cheese
  biscuit dough, 261
  coeurs à la crème, 67
  cream cheese and nut balls, 260
  Liederkranz mould, 130
  Parmesan greenery, hot, 264
  ramekins, 136
  Roquefort pecans, 259
  Roquefort soufflé, 88
  Roquefort spread, 262
  soufflé, 234
  soufflé, cold, 278
  thimble biscuits, 262
  wafers with pecans, 260

Cherry sauce, 68
Chestnuts
    crème de marrons, 309
    fruit compote, hot, with marrons glacés,
        216
    marrons café bombe, 230
    marrons croquettes, 75
    Mont Blanc, 280
    purée of, 173
    stuffing (for turkey), 197
Chicken
    in aspic with ham cornucopias filled with
        vegetables, 97
    Bombay soup, 310
    breast of, in tarragon aspic, 92
    breasts, sauté of, on cracked wheat pilaff,
        170
    breasts with wild rice and chestnuts, 100
    Brunswick stew, 232
    and celery hearts, 76
    coq au vin, 169
    cous-cous, 19
    curried, 98
    czarina, 24
    gumbo, 71
    and ham with noodles, 16
    and ham paella, 309
    mousse, cold, 304
    with noodles, 276
    and oysters, casserole of, 276
    petite marmite, 277
    poulet chasseur, 41
    soup, curried, 67
    with truffles, 58
Chicken liver(s)
    chafing dish of, in Madeira sauce, 17
    pâté, 273
    risotto with, 319
Chicory and orange salad, 90
Chocolate
    -hazelnut cream, 156
    mint soufflé, 125
    mousse, 278
    mousse cake, 18
    pots de crème, 14
Christmas Day feast in Provence, 183
Christmas Eve supper, 272
Clam(s)
    minced, in small hot turnovers, 263
    sauce, red, 321
    southside, 216
    stew, 133
Clover Club, 187
Cocktail parties
    after-cocktail buffet (20 to 24), 253
    large (50 or more), 246
    small (6 to 8), 255
Coeurs à la crème, 67
Coffee
    cream, 129
    maroons café bombe, 230
    pots de crème, 14
    walnut roll, 163

Cognac cream on toasted spongecake, 171
Committee food: luncheons and teas, 238
Consommé with okra, 166
Consommé stracciatelle, 158
Coq au vin, 169
Coquilles St. Jacques, 35
Corn casserole, eggplant, tomato, and, 59
Corn pudding, 15
Corned beef hash, baked, 236
Court bouillon, 26
    for salmon, 33
Cous-cous, 19
Crab, crabmeat
    creole, hot, 274
    Mornay, hot, 157
    mousse, 273
    soup, curried, 140
    tarts, curried, miniature, 265
    tomatoes stuffed with, 89
    and turtle soup, curried, 322
Cracked wheat
    pilaff, 171
    stuffing for goose, 162
Cream cheese and nut balls, 260
Cream desserts, see also custard desserts
    chocolate-hazelnut cream, 156
    Cognac cream, 171
    crème de marrons, 309
    Mont Blanc, 280
    praline Bavarian cream with strawberries,
        167
    Sherry macaroons, 36
Crème brûlée, 44
Crème de marrons, 309
Crowninshield, Frank, 78
Cucumber soup, cold, 33
Curry, curried
    Bombay soup, 310
    chicken, 98
    chicken soup, 67
    crab soup, 140
    crab tarts, miniature, 265
    crab and turtle soup, 322
    sauce, 13
    shrimp curry, 12
    shrimp tarts, miniature, 264
Custard desserts, see also cream desserts
    apricot trifle, 231
    Austrian Nockerln, 157
    coffee cream, 129
    crème brûlée, 44
    eggs à la neige, 38
    English custard, 128
    English trifle, 127
    macaroon and pear tart, 90
    orange cream tarts, 55
    pots de crème, 14
    raspberries frangipane, 179
    raspberry charlotte, 23

Deep-fried desserts
    beignets soufflés, 59
    marrons croquettes, 75

Délices du jardin, 321
Derby Day, Kentucky, 113
Dessert sauces
    apricot, 135
    apricot marmalade, 51
    brandy, 75
    cherry, 68
    custard, for meringues, 38
    Lady Baltimore frosting, 70
    lemon custard, 223
    lemon, hot, 54
    liqueur syrup, 22
    rum, 218
    Sherry, 221
    vanilla (cold), 42
    vanilla (hot), 158
    zabaglione, 60
Dinner parties
    circumstantial dinner (12 to 24), 145
        elegant black-tie dinner, 145
        formal dinner party, 153
    holiday dinners (10 to 12), 182
    little dinners (8 to 10), 118
    seated, 115
Duck, duckling
    jellied cold, with black cherries, 313
    roast, with cherries, 166
Dumpling pastry, 316
Dumplings, apple and raisin, baked, 316

Egg(s)
    à la neige, 38
    and caviar mousse, 176
    en gelée with truffles and ham, 50
    stuffed with chopped olives, 259
    stuffed with red caviar, 259
    yolks, how to use, 223
Eggplant
    casserole, 94
    casserole, corn, tomato, and, 59
    sautéed, 132
English custard, 128
English trifle, 127

Fish
    mélange, 25
    pudding, 242
    stew, 41
    stock, 160
    Tetrazzini, 101
Fish House punch, 187
Flaky pastry, 161
    flaky pastry shells, 52
Food, amount to serve, xiii
    choice of, x
Francillon salad, 36
French dressing, 321
Friday night supper (10), 286
Frozen desserts
    frozen rum raisin custard, 312
    marrons café bombe, 230
    mousse diplomate, 318

Frozen desserts (continued)
    peaches cardinal on pineapple ice mould,
        196
Fruit
    compote, baked, 274
    compote brûlée, 99
    compote, hot, with marrons glacés, 216
    meringue, 314
    pudding with vanilla sauce, 42
    soufflé, 243
Fruit desserts
    apples porcupine, 131
    apricots Colbert, 134
    fruit compote, baked, 274
    fruit compote, hot, with marrons glacés,
        216
    fruit meringue, 314
    fruit soufflé, 243
    oranges Dulcinea, 243
    peaches cardinal on pineapple ice mould,
        196
    raspberries frangipane, 179

Gâteau basque, 67
Ginger pancakes, flaming, 176
Ginger pastry cream, 177
Glögg, 188
Gnocchi à la parisienne, 222
Goose
    braised, 198
    roast, with peaches, 162
Goulash, szekely, 18
Graham-cracker piecrust shells, 56
Gratin of potatoes, 39
Gratin of smoked turkey, 307
Green mayonnaise, 93
Green noodles, hot, with cold pâté, 91
Green rice, 228
Gribiche sauce, 142
Guests, choice of, vii
Guinea hen
    breast of, Smitane, 125
    in casserole, 219

Ham
    boned, in pastry, 226
    chicken and, with noodles, 16
    cornucopias filled with vegetables, 97
    ground, in hot bite-size tarts, 265
    ground, in small hot turnovers, 261
    jellied parsleyed, 74
    loaf, sweet, 320
    mousse, 16
    mousse ring filled with vegetables, 131
    prosciutto with broccoli and almonds, 310
Herb dressing, 90
Holiday dinners, 182
Holiday drinks, 186
Holiday suppers, 272
Hominy, 99
    grits, baked, 167
Hors-d'oeuvre puffs, 260
    with smoked salmon, 259

Impresario's holiday party, buffet (70), 110
Indian pudding, hot, with ice cream, 52

Jullian, Philippe (*Maison et Jardin*), 3
Juniper berry marinade, 143

Kasha, 24
  with meatballs, 236
Kidney pie, beef and, 87

Lady Baltimore cake, 70
Lady Baltimore frosting, 70
Lamb
  braised stuffed shoulder of, with truffles, 180
  cous-cous, 19
  crown roasts of, with barley pilaff, 164
  leg of, braised, 311
  navarin of, 27
  roast, en croûte, 138
  saddle of, à l'orientale, 132
  shepherd's pie, 305
Lasagne with beef sauce, hot casserole of, 34
Le brulo, 188
Lemon
  custard sauce, 223
  French dressing, 75
  mousse, 139
  pudding, 221
  sauce, hot, 54
  soufflé, cold, 50
Le Nôtre, 3
Lentil salad, 57
Liederkranz mould, 130
Liqueur syrup, 22
Liver(s), chicken
  chafing dish of, in Madeira sauce, 17
  pâté, 273
  risotto with, 319
Lobster
  bisque, 159
  bordelaise, 177
  in cucumber, 87
  seafood risotto, 224
Louis XIV, 3
Louis XV, 3
Low-country oysters, 40
Luncheons
  in the country (12 to 14), 214
  in town (8 to 14), 202
  Saturday (6), 289
  Sunday, weekend (16), 299
  with the committee (8), 239
Luncheons, cocktails, eleven-thirty suppers, 199

McAllister, Ward, 78
Macaroon and pear tart, 90
Madeira cream sauce, 76
Maison et Jardin (Phillipe Jullian), 3
Marinade
  juniper berry, 143
  red wine, 73

Marinade (*continued*)
  for beef, 38
  for venison, 195
Marrons café bombe, 230
Marrons croquettes, 75
Mayonnaise, 233
  blender, 233
  green, 93
  green, blender, 233
  sauce gribiche, 142
Meat loaf with pâté en croûte, 234
Meats, *see* names of meats
Meringue desserts
  apples porcupine, 131
  apricot meringue, 57
  eggs à la neige, 38
  fruit meringue, 314
Milk punch, 189
Mont Blanc, 280
Morgan, J. P., 153
Mousses
  chicken, cold, 304
  crabmeat, 273
  egg and caviar, 176
  ham, 16
  ham ring filled with vegetables, 131
  salmon, 33
Mousses, dessert
  chocolate, 278
  diplomate, 318
  lemon, 139
Mulled cider, 189
Mulled wine, 189
Mushroom(s)
  baked, shrimp and, 308
  filled with mushroom soufflé, 218
  grilled, stuffed with minced clams, 139
  sauce, 235
  sauce, shrimp and, 137
  tomato purée, 226
Mussels
  billi-bi soup, 56
  Francillon salad, 36
Mustard cream, 143
Mustard sauce, 52

Navarin of lamb, 27
New Year's Eve supper, 272
Nockerln, Austrian, 157

Onion
  and bacon tarts, 280
  soup, 303
  tart, hot, 217
Orange(s)
  cream tarts, 55
  Dulcinea, 243
  salad, chicory and, 90
Outdoor breakfast, buffet (200), 113
Oyster(s)
  chicken and, casserole of, 276
  low-country, 40
  Rockefeller, 174

Oyster(s) (continued)
  in Sherry, 179
  soufflé, 312
Oxtail soup Amontillado, 314

Paella, chicken and ham, 309
Pancakes
  blini with caviar, 194
  filled with strawberry preserves, 26
  flaming ginger, 176
Parmesan greenery, hot, 264
Pasta
  cannelloni Leonardo da Vinci, 20
  gnocchi à la parisienne, 222
  green noodles, hot, with cold pâté, 91
  lasagna with beef sauce, 34
  noodle casserole, beef and, 323
  spaghetti with red clam sauce, 321
Pastry
  almond tart pastry, 220
  dumpling pastry, 316
  flaky pastry, 161
  flaky pastry shells, 52
  graham-cracker piecrust shells, 56
  hors-d'oeuvre puffs, 260
  puff pastry, 138
  sweet tart pastry, 275
  sweet tart pastry shells, 91
  tart pastry, 136
Pâtés
  chicken liver, 273
  terrine of country pâté, 12
Peaches cardinal on pineapple ice mould, 196
Pear tart, macaroon and, 90
Peas
  green, French style, 141
  and lima beans au gratin, 89
  purée Saint-Germain, 168
Pecans, Roquefort, 259
Pecans, spicy, 263
Pepys, Samuel, xi
Petite marmite, 277
Petites quiches lorraines, 231
Pheasant(s)
  en casserole, 174
  in cream, 135
Pies and tarts
  beef and kidney pie, 87
  caviar tart, 266
  cheese ramekins, 136
  curried crab tarts, miniature, 265
  curried shrimp tarts, miniature, 264
  onion and bacon tarts, 280
  onion tart, hot, 217
  quiche lorraine, 51
  quiches lorraines, petites, 231
  tarts, hot bite-size, with ground ham, 265
Pies and tarts, dessert
  apple tart, 219
  burnt almond chiffon pie, 158
  macaroon and pear tart, 90
  orange cream tarts, 55
  tarte à l'orange, 181
  tarte Tatin, 165

Pizza filling, 73
Pizzas, individual, 73
Poivrade sauce for beef, 39
Poivrade sauce for venison, 195
Porc à l'orange, 315
Pork
  porc à l'orange, 315
  sausage in pastry, 232
  suckling pig, roast, 193
  szekely goulash, 18
Posset, 190
Potato(es)
  Anna, 134
  boiled, hot, with smoked salmon, 93
  Dauphine, 220
  Francillon salad, 36
  gratin of, 39
  salad, hot, 230
  shepherd's pie, 305
Pot-au-feu, 306
Pots de Crème
  assorted, 14
  chocolate, 14
  chocolate-hazelnut cream, 156
  coffee, 14
  strawberry, 14
Poulet chasseur, 41
Poultry, see names of poultry
Praline Bavarian cream with strawberries, 167
Praline powder, 168
Prune soufflé with lemon custard sauce, 223
Puddings
  corn, 15
  fish, 242
  Yorkshire, 317
Puddings, dessert
  fruit, with vanilla sauce, 42
  Indian, hot, with ice cream, 52
  lemon, 221
  rice, 134
  rice, hot, 60
Puff pastry, 138
Punch, 190
Purée Saint-Germain, 168

Quail, roast, on hominy, 99
Quiche lorraine, 51
Quiches lorraines, petites, 231

Rabbit négaunée, 130
Raspberries frangipane, 179
Raspberry charlotte, 23
Red wine marinade, 73
Rice
  boiled, 25
  green, 228
  pilaff, 133
  pudding, 134
  pudding, hot, 60
  ring of brown rice with baby Brussels sprouts, 175
  ring of red rice filled with green peas, 40
  risotto with chicken livers, 319

Rice (*continued*)
  salad, cold, 74
  seafood risotto, 224
Rice, wild, and chestnuts, 100
Risotto with chicken livers, 319
Roasts
  beef, with Yorkshire pudding, 317
  chicken with truffles, 58
  duckling with cherries, 166
  goose, with peaches, 162
  lamb, crown roasts, of, 164
  lamb en croûte, 138
  lamb, saddle of, à l'orientale, 132
  quail on hominy, 99
  suckling pig, 193
  turkey with Port wine sauce and chestnut stuffing, 197
  veal, with carrots and onions, 53
  veal, loin of young, with tarragon sauce, 178
  veal with mushrooms en croûte, 160
  veal, with orange sauce, 69
  veal, savoury, 140
  venison, leg of, with sauce poivrade, 195
Roquefort cheese soufflé, 88
Roquefort pecans, 259
Roquefort spread, 262
Rumfustian, 190
Rum raisin custard, frozen, 312
Rum sauce, 218
Russian dressing, 88

Salad dressings
  anchovy, for salade Schiaparelli, 96
  French, 321
  herb, 90
  lemon French, 75
  mayonnaise, 233
    blender, 233
    green, 93
    green, blender, 233
    sauce gribiche, 142
  Russian, 88
  shallot and parsley, 57
Salade Schiaparelli, 96
Salads
  chicory and orange, 90
  délices du jardin, 321
  Francillon (mussels and potatoes), 36
  green bean, 244
  lentil, 57
  lobster in cucumber, 87
  potato, hot, 230
  rice, cold, 74
  salade Schiaparelli, 96
  tomato aspic ring, 71
  tomatoes stuffed with crabmeat, 89
  Salmon mousse, 33
Salmon, smoked
  in hors-d'oeuvre puffs, 259
  with hot boiled potatoes, 93
Saturday breakfast, 289
Saturday lunch (6), 289

Saturday night dinner party (12), 293
Sauces
  béchamel, 307
  beef, for lasagne, 34
  clam, red, 321
  curry, 13
  gribiche, 142
  Madeira cream, 76
  mushroom, 235
  mustard, 52
  mustard cream, 143
  poivrade, for beef, 39
  poivrade, for venison, 195
  shrimp and mushroom, 137
  sweet and sour, 320
  white, 20
  white, thick, 34
Sauces for desserts, *see* dessert sauces
Sausage in pastry, 232
Savoury roast veal, 140
Sazarac, 192
Scaloppini of veal with tarragon, 308
Scallops
  coquilles St. Jacques, 35
  fish mélange, 25
  seafood risotto, 224
Seafood risotto, 224
Semolina, 20
Service at parties, xii
Sesame shortbread, hot, 264
Shad and roe normande, 222
Shad roe with white wine, 126
Shallot and parsley dressing, 57
Shepherd's pie, 305
Sherry macaroons, 36
Sherry sauce, 221
Shrimp
  curry, 12
  fish mélange, 25
  jambalaya, quick, 306
  and mushroom sauce, 137
  and mushrooms, baked, 308
  in sauce piquante, 170
  supreme, 54
  tarts, curried, miniature, 264
Smorgasbord supper, buffet (200 to 300), 103
Sole
  fillet of, in Chablis sauce, 161
  fish mélange, 25
  soufflé of, 137
Soufflés
  asparagus, crown of, 225
  carrot, 126
  cheese, 234
  cheese, cold, 278
  oyster, 312
  Roquefort cheese, 88
  sole, 137
Soufflés, dessert
  chocolate mint, 125
  fruit, 243
  lemon, 50

Soufflés, dessert (*continued*)
  prune, with lemon custard sauce, 223
  vanilla, with rum sauce, 217
Soups
  asparagus, 242
  billi-bi (mussels), 56
  black bean, with diced ham and lemon,
      196
  Bombay, 310
  borscht, cold, 172
  borscht, jellied, 16
  clam stew, 133
  consommé with okra, 166
  consommé stracciatelle, 158
  cucumber, cold, 33
  curried chicken, 67
  curried crab, 140
  curried crab and turtle, 322
  lobster bisque, 159
  onion, 303
  oxtail, Amontillado, 314
  petite marmite, 277
  pot-au-feu, 306
  purée Saint-Germain, 168
  spinach, 128
  tomato clam, jellied, 69
  tomato and dill, 164
  tomato mushroom purée, 226
  vegetable gumbo, hot, 42
  watercress, hot, 224
Spaghetti with red clam sauce, 321
Spicy pecans, 263
Spinach rings with slivered parsleyed car-
      rots, 22
Spinach soup, 128
Spoon bread, 217
Stews
  beef bourguignon, 66
  beef paprika, 22
  Brunswick, 232
  carbonada criolla, 92
  chicken gumbo, 71
  clam, 133
  cous-cous, 19
  fish, 41
  navarin of lamb, 27
  petite marmite, 277
  pot-au-feu, 306
  szekely goulash, 18
  veal spezzatino, 98
Strawberry pots de crème, 14
Striped bass in aspic, 141
Stuffings
  chestnut (for turkey), 197
  cracked-wheat (for goose), 162
Suckling pig, roast, 193
Sunday breakfast, 297
Sunday luncheons (8 to 14), 202
  in the country (12 to 14), 214
  in town (8 to 14), 202
  weekend (16), 299
Supper dance, buffet (250), 108
Suppers at eleven-thirty (12 to 20), 267

Suppers, holiday (20), 272
Sweet and sour sauce, 320
Syllabub, 191
Szekely goulash, 18

Tarragon aspic, 92
Tarte à l'orange, 181
Tarte Tatin, 165
Tarts, *see* pies and tarts
Tea with the committee, 240
Tendrons of veal, 15
Terrine of country pâté, 12
Tevis, Mrs. William, 116
Tom & Jerry, 191
Tomato(es)
  aspic ring, 71
  baked, 132
  casserole, eggplant, corn, and, 59
  clam soup, jellied, 69
  and dill soup, 164
  mushroom purée, 226
  stuffed with crabmeat, 89
Tongue, beef, braised, 318
Trifle, apricot, 231
Trifle, English, 127
Truffles, minced, in pastry, 262
Turkey(s)
  hash, hot, 244
  roast, with Port wine sauce and chestnut
      stuffing, 197
  smoked, gratin of, 140
  Tetrazzini, 279
  young, braised, in Champagne, 172
Turnovers
  hot, with ground chicken and chopped
      parsley, 265
  hot, miniature, with ground chicken and
      chopped parsley, 265
  minced truffles in pastry, 262
  small hot, filled with ground ham, 261
  small hot, with minced clams, 263
Turnovers, dessert, hot apple, 275
Turtle soup, curried crab and, 322

Vanilla
  pots de crème, 14
  sauce (cold), 42; (hot), 158
  soufflé with rum sauce, 217
  sugar, 27
Veal
  roast, with carrots and onions, 53
  roast, with mushrooms en croûte, 160
  roast, with orange sauce, 69
  roast, savoury, 140
  scaloppini of, with tarragon, 308
  spezzatino, 98
  tendrons of, 15
  vitello tonnato, 228
  and water chestnut casserole, 13
  young, roast loin of, with tarragon sauce,
      178
Vegetable gumbo, hot, 42
Vegetables, *see* names of vegetables

Venison
  leg of, roast, with sauce poivrade, 195
  steaks, broiled, 143
Versailles, 3
Vitello tonnato, 228

Wassail bowl, 191
Water chestnuts wrapped in bacon, 266
Watercress soup, hot, 224
Weekend, Friday-to-Sunday guests, 284
White Christmas punch, 192

White sauce, 20
White sauce, thick, 34
White-wine aspic, 227
Wines, choice of, xi
Wright, Frank Lloyd, 249

Yorkshire pudding, 317

Zabaglione sauce, 60
Zucchini, baked, 163
Zucchini casserole, baked, 235

Oyster Rockefeller page 174 (24)
carbonada criolla, 92 (10)
(spanish beef w. peaches)

| page 291 Scallopini